RAISED AT RUTGERS

RIVERGATE REGIONALS

Rivergate Regionals is a collection of books published by Rutgers University Press focusing on New Jersey and the surrounding area. Since its founding in 1936, Rutgers University Press has been devoted to serving the people of New Jersey and this collection solidifies that tradition. The books in the Rivergate Regionals Collection explore history, politics, nature and the environment, recreation, sports, health and medicine, and the arts. By incorporating the collection within the larger Rutgers University Press editorial program, the Rivergate Regionals Collection enhances our commitment to publishing the best books about our great state and the surrounding region.

RAISED AT RUTGERS

A PRESIDENT'S STORY

Richard L. McCormick

RUTGERS UNIVERSITY PRESS

New Brunswick, New Jersey and London

Library of Congress Cataloging-in-Publication Data
McCormick, Richard L.
Raised at Rutgers : a president's story / Richard L. McCormick.
Pages   cm. — (Rivergate regionals)
Includes bibliographical references and index.
ISBN 978-0-8135-6474-6 (hardcover : alk. paper)
ISBN 978-0-8135-6475-3 (e-book)
1. McCormick, Richard L. 2. Rutgers University—Presidents—
Biography. 3. Rutgers University—History. 4. College
presidents—New Jersey—Biography.   I. Title.
LD4752.7.M44A3 2014
378.749'41—dc23   2014000066

A British Cataloging-in-Publication record for this book is available
from the British Library.

Visit our website: http://rutgerspress.rutgers.edu

Manufactured in the United States of America

For Joan Barry McCormick

CONTENTS

PREFACE AND ACKNOWLEDGMENTS

This book is my story about Rutgers, the university where I have spent most of my life—as a child of a faculty member, a faculty member, a dean, a president, and now, once again, a professor. Most of the narrative covers my presidency from 2002 to 2012, although one chapter sets the stage by recalling fondly my earlier days at Rutgers. Occasionally my personal life intrudes, but this is mainly a chronicle of my professional experiences and of the University itself. I recount with pride Rutgers's notable accomplishments, both before and during my time as president, but I have tried to be truthful, as well, about its shortcomings and, especially, about my own. This is the story of earnest but imperfect men and women, the author among them, energetically pursuing honorable goals on behalf of, and through the instrument of, a high-achieving but also highly unusual state university. That institution, moreover, is situated in New Jersey, a place rich in human and material resources, proud of its diverse people and ambitious for them, but rough-and-tumble in its manners and mores. Rutgers is like that, too.

In almost every respect, Rutgers looks like a large and very good American state university, similar to others in the top ranks of such institutions. It has over 65,000 students, two-thirds of them undergraduates; three main campuses well distributed around the state; more than 900 buildings; a full array of highly regarded professional schools; distinguished faculty who garner over $700 million annually to support their research; membership in the prestigious Association of American Universities; and a big football stadium. The governor of New Jersey appoints a majority of the members of the University's principal governing board, and the state provides about 20 percent of the institution's total annual budget, now more than $3 billion. An informed and attentive observer would readily compare Rutgers to its counterparts in, say, Pennsylvania, Minnesota, or Arizona. And that comparison would be accurate. But Rutgers is also different from its peers. Alone among them it was founded before the American Revolution (as a private institution called Queen's College), and alone among them it was almost 180 years old before finally being designated as the state university, an obligation it is still learning fully to discharge. That history helps explain why large swaths of what is now Rutgers—including its recently acquired health science schools—originated as something else, outside the bounds of the University, and had to be cobbled together within it, usually through difficulties of one kind or another. That job of cobbling has confronted virtually every Rutgers president, including me and my successor, and is still a work in progress. By and large, the results have been highly positive; indeed, Rutgers would not look nearly as much like a highly ranked state university without these accretions. But they have made for a tumultuous history.

Rutgers is unique in other ways, too. Growing up as a mainly private institution in the northeastern United States, its immediate "neighborhood" included such outstanding schools as Princeton, Penn, Columbia, NYU, and Yale—and, a bit farther afield, Johns Hopkins, Cornell, Brown, and Harvard. These universities became somewhat more distinguished than Rutgers—in part, because we were struggling to become a state university, while they were not, and to win support from the government of New Jersey, which was unaccustomed to funding higher education. But Rutgers benefited immeasurably by comparing itself to its nearest neighbors, unlike us as they increasingly became, and by striving for academic achievements equal to theirs. Now Rutgers is in a new "neighborhood" called the Big Ten, whose inhabitants, the great midwestern state universities, are not quite as geographically proximate as the old neighbors, but whose missions and characteristics are far more similar to our own. In the years ahead, Rutgers will benefit—athletically, to be sure, but even more academically—from its new neighbors, just as much as it has from its historic ones.

While the Princetons and Columbias attracted elite students from around the nation and the world, and while America's most renowned public universities increasingly became destinations for affluent and well-prepared young men and women from within their respective states, Rutgers took a third pathway in composing its student body. Beginning early on, Rutgers offered an avenue of upward mobility for economically disadvantaged students, for those whose parents never attended college, for the children of immigrants, and for those who could study only part time because they were already supporting their families. These are somewhat unusual characteristics for the student body of a flagship state university, but Rutgers retains them today on all three of its campuses, in Newark, Camden, and New Brunswick. Eighty percent of the University's undergraduates depend upon some form of financial aid, more than a third qualify for federal Pell grants (which means they come from families that are truly disadvantaged economically), 30 percent are the first in their families to attend college, and fully half identify themselves as racial or ethnic minorities. In light of its diverse student body and its location at the center of the innovative, enterprising, and progressive northeastern corridor of the United States, it is not surprising that Rutgers forged a culture that is instinctively open to new ideas, highly tolerant of difference and disagreement, and well accustomed to learning from adversity. These characteristics have served Rutgers, and New Jersey, very well.

Proudly distinctive though it is, Rutgers has never been immune from the most powerful forces affecting and transforming American higher education. That was true when it was a fledgling private college in the early nineteenth century, when it became New Jersey's Land Grant institution decades later, and again when it grew and changed dramatically in the years after World War II. During my time as president, too, Rutgers was in the throes of the same change-bearing circumstances as the rest of the nation's public colleges and universities: the ongoing decline of state support and the consequent inevitability of raising tuition; the endeavor to provide access and opportunity for students unable to pay the increased costs; the growing demand for public accountability, especially in undergraduate education; the imperative of advancing interdisciplinary research in a world that is hungry for knowledge-based solutions to practical human problems; the development of new information technologies, both expanding the universities' reach and disrupting their existing educational practices; the internationalization of the higher education enterprise; and, finally, even more conspicuous than the other contemporary trends, the continued ascent of intercollegiate athletics, especially football, as a cultural and economic behemoth. The chapters that follow recognize all of these forces and developments, some more extensively than others, because they acutely and inescapably affected Rutgers and because we responded to them both consciously and effectively. But this book does not attempt to provide definitive analyses of these nationwide issues; nor, with maybe one or two exceptions, does it claim for Rutgers extraordinary or unparalleled success in meeting them.

Indeed, this book is focused tightly upon Rutgers and New Jersey and upon events and developments in which I actively participated or that I witnessed. The opening chapter recounts six scenes from my presidency, some quite dramatic, others less so, each of which opens up one or more subjects that are explored in the chapters that follow. Virtually all of the book's most important themes are introduced through these six episodes, including Rutgers's relationship to New Jersey and its politics, undergraduate education, intercollegiate athletics, student diversity and opportunity, and, perhaps biggest of all, returning Robert Wood Johnson Medical School to Rutgers. The second chapter, as promised, tells the story of my own beginnings as a child in the Rutgers community, my improbable return to the University as a young faculty member in 1976, and my later service as dean of arts and sciences. Chapter 3 recounts my second return to Rutgers in 2002, following a decade in leadership roles at the University of North Carolina and the University of Washington. This time I came back as president, a homecoming that was exhilarating and perhaps less improbable than the first but, at the same time, as I will explain, privately very difficult. A challenging first year as president followed. The next chapter goes to the heart of the academic goals we pursued, with particular emphasis on reorganizing the New Brunswick campus for the benefit of undergraduates and on faculty research, for which Rutgers obtained significant increases in coveted federal funding. Chapter 5 treats intercollegiate athletics, including both the elation and the upheaval wrought by the success of our football program. Chapter 6 relates Rutgers's continuing efforts to become the state university of New Jersey and a decade of strenuous encounters with legislators, governors, and state agencies. The seventh chapter tells a characteristic New Jersey tale of how Rutgers reclaimed the medical school (and much more). In the final chapter, I reflect on my presidency and look ahead for Rutgers. Many other subjects have also found their way into this book, but that's probably enough of a road map to give readers an idea of what to expect.

✻

Many friends, colleagues, and family members gave generously of their time to assist me while I was writing this book. I thank them all warmly for their help and support and especially for their personal encouragement. At the beginning, as I imagined and planned the project, several individuals played particularly critical roles. Shaun Illingsworth, director of the Rutgers Oral History Archives, shared with me his considerable knowledge of how historical memoirs are organized and constructed. As we talked, I began to imagine the contents and contours of this book. Paul G. E. Clemens, a friend for decades and a colleague in the history department, also participated in those conversations; even more important, Paul shared with me the early chapters of his own work in progress on the history of Rutgers from 1945 to the present, a volume whose publication by the Rutgers University Press will help commemorate the University's 250th anniversary in 2016. As Paul and I swapped chapters and ideas throughout the course of my project, his knowledge of Rutgers's history and his shrewd insights proved invaluable. Michael Meagher, my former colleague and speechwriter in the president's office, agreed at the outset to assist me in research and to provide a careful reading of my draft manuscript.

With permission from his current boss, President Robert L. Barchi (to whom I am very appreciative), Mike expertly accomplished both of those tasks, with good humor and an unerring eye for sentences that truly needed to be rewritten. Finally, at the earliest stages of this work, it was Marlie Wasserman, director of Rutgers University Press and, like Paul, a longtime friend, who encouraged me to write the book and, after reading a single chapter, offered to publish it (as I had hoped she would). As further chapters emerged, Marlie read them cheerfully and critically and, like any good editor, repeatedly prodded me to get the book done.

Along the way, a large number of accomplished men and women, most but not all of whom are my Rutgers colleagues, took time to share their recollections and observations about our work together and to provide essential information. Practically every section of the book benefited from the assistance of these friends: Stephen G. Abel, Jonathan R. Alger, Gregory S. Blimling, Lavinia M. Boxill, Kenneth J. Breslauer, Antonio Calcado, Robert E. Campbell, Arthur D. Casciato, Jesse Clemens, Susan A. Cole, Richard L. Edwards, Gail Faber, John J. Farmer Jr., Leslie A. Fehrenbach, David L. Finegold, Thomas J. Frusciano, Philip Furmanski, Lloyd C. Gardner, Peter J. Gillies, Gerald C. Harvey, Robert J. Heffernan, Kathleen P. Hickey, Paul Johnson, Roger A. Jones, Ralph Izzo, Carol J. Koncsol, Jeannine F. LaRue, Susan E. Lawrence, Kim Manning, Courtney O. McAnuff, Elizabeth Minott, Christopher J. Molloy, Richard J. Novak, Dean J. Paranicas, Michael J. Pazzani, Wendell E. Pritchett, Tim Pernetti, Barry V. Qualls, Robert P. Roesener, Eve R. Sachs, Jorge Reina Schement, Joann L. Segarra, Linda L. Stamato, George B. Stauffer, Karen R. Stubaus, Maryann Szymanski, Donna Thornton, Scott Walker, Jianfeng (Jeff) Wang, Nancy S. Winterbauer, John Wolf, and Philip L. Yeagle. Jane Hart, the media archivist in the Rutgers Office of Creative Services, carefully reviewed thousands of photographs from which she and Marlie Wasserman and I selected the images that appear in this book. Several other talented women and men graciously provided essential support for my work: Cheryl A. Wisnack and Shakirat B. Ibraheem in the Office of the Executive Vice President for Academic

Affairs, and Jon L. Oliver and Matthew Sarte in the School of Communication and Information. I am deeply grateful to all of them.

Six very special individuals unselfishly read my entire draft manuscript and offered immensely valuable comments on it. I have cited them already, but I want to thank them again for giving so much of their time and for their observations, large and small, about how to make this a better book: Jon Alger, Paul Clemens, Phil Furmanski, Mike Meagher, Elizabeth Minott, and Marlie Wasserman. Willa Speiser, my talented editor at Rutgers University Press, proved to be an outstanding collaborator as the manuscript neared completion. None of the individuals named here is responsible for any errors of fact or judgment that remain in this book; they are all my own.

Finally I want to thank the members of my family. My older children, Elizabeth Wells McCormick and Michael Patrick McCormick, helped from afar by patiently and affectionately responding to my reminiscences of events through which we lived together. My younger daughter, Katheryne Joan McCormick, is too little to have helped, or even hindered, this project, but she contributes immeasurably to the spirit and happiness of an old dad. My father-in-law, William E. Barry Sr., picked up the manuscript on Thanksgiving Day and wouldn't put it down until he finished; his encouraging comments brightened the holiday. My sister, Dorothy Boulia, read the entire manuscript with a keen but kindly eye, and her good questions distinctly improved it. Lastly my wife, Joan Barry McCormick, gave this book a wise and helpful final reading, but, far more important, she lovingly supported me and it every day. I have placed Joan's name at the beginning, confident she will know why.

NEW BRUNSWICK, NEW JERSEY

JANUARY 2014

RAISED AT RUTGERS

SIX SCENES FROM
A UNIVERSITY
PRESIDENCY

A HELICOPTER CONVERSATION WITH
GOVERNOR McGREEVEY

On a late October afternoon in 2002, Governor Jim McGreevey was yelling at me on the telephone—he in a helicopter somewhere over New Jersey and I at my home in Seattle. He knew that the Rutgers Board of Governors was intending to appoint me as the University's nineteenth president within the next several days, and he was not happy about that. The leaders of the state legislature, he said, specifically naming the copresidents of the senate and the speaker of the assembly, shared his opposition to my appointment. The governor wanted me to withdraw as a candidate for the position because I could not, he shouted, succeed as the leader of Rutgers without political support. Our conversation became even more ragged when his cell phone dropped the call from the helicopter several times, and eventually our connection was irretrievably lost. The governor's angry words left me shaken, but I had no intention of walking away from the opportunity to become president of Rutgers.

The phone conversation differed greatly from my first encounter with Governor McGreevey. A month earlier, when I was the leading candidate for the job at Rutgers but had not yet decided whether to accept it, he and I met for an hour or more, seated on a sun porch at the back of Drumthwacket, the governor's official residence in Princeton. But the presidency of Rutgers was not the only subject on his mind that day. First-term United States Senator Robert Torricelli, running for reelection that fall but beset by ethics allegations, was being hounded by political opponents and by the press to drop out of the race. So while the governor was talking with me, he was also thrashing out with his political advisors how to deal with the Torricelli problem and specifically whom to select as a senate candidate in his place. To my amazement, the governor carried on both conversations—his interview of me and his brainstorming about the election of a senator—at the same time, on the sun porch, and with complete control of both topics. He had a Bill Clinton–like ability to keep you in his gaze, and he proved to be remarkably well informed about Rutgers in particular and higher education in general. Simultaneously, he was having his urgent political powwow, and he was thoroughly wrapped up in that, too. I was flattered to be allowed to overhear such a thing and was dazzled by the governor's ability to focus, at the same moment, on two such different subjects.

I don't really know what kind of an impression I made on Governor McGreevey during the Drumthwacket conversation, nor do I know what caused the feelings he later expressed from the helicopter. Almost certainly his views were shaped, in part, by a looming battle over a controversial plan to reorganize the public research universities of New Jersey, a plan authored by Dr. P. Roy Vagelos, the retired CEO of Merck, and strongly supported by the governor. That controversy will receive the attention it deserves at the appropriate points in the chapters that follow. But of this much I am sure: my encounters with the governor marked an alarming introduction to the hard-edged world of New Jersey politics and the beginning of an exceedingly difficult first year as president of Rutgers. A big chunk of that early trouble was of my own making, and that, too, will be explained later.

Not just in New Jersey but throughout America, the politics of public higher education has been extremely challenging since the late 1980s. State funding for colleges and universities has steadily declined, and, more generally, higher education has lost the golden aura of support it had enjoyed at every level of government in the decades just after World War II. When the GIs came home from the war, the federal government was there to help them go to college, and in the years that followed the nation adopted successive and ever more generous programs of student support. That investment in higher educational opportunities for young American men and women transformed the United States into a more egalitarian, more democratic, and, of course, better-educated society than it had ever been before. These were the same years when the federal government began spending billions of dollars annually in support of university-based scientific research—with historic results for the nation's prosperity, the health of its people, and the alleviation of social and economic problems of practically every kind. Not to be outdone by the federal government, the states made dramatically farsighted, and expensive, investments in their existing public colleges and universities and, in partnership with local governments everywhere, invented and supported a whole new kind of educational enterprise: community colleges. Together, these governmental choices, which were truly popular American choices, greatly improved life in the United States and bolstered our nation's leadership of the world.

Then the tide turned, not on a dime, but it turned nonetheless, most visibly at the level of state politics and government. By the 1990s, state funding for the colleges and universities was stagnating, fewer new institutions were being established, and the enrollment growth of the preceding decades was leveling off. A new generation of higher education leaders, of whom I was one, began to encounter far more difficulty than our predecessors in making the case for public investments in our institutions. We told the story, each in our own state, of the economic and social benefits that had flowed from the post–World War II growth of the colleges and universities, but now the politicians seemed far more interested in K–12 schools, services for senior citizens, and transportation, to name just three worthy public purposes with which the colleges were competing for funding. According to one argument that was commonly used against us, higher education was now a mature industry that no longer needed the same level of subsidization it had required before. Even more commonly, we heard that those who directly benefited from a college education, namely the individuals who graduated with the degrees our institutions conferred, should bear most of the costs themselves. Now withering as a political force was the belief held by my parents' generation that the whole society prospered when more men and women received a college education and that it was in the best interest of the whole society to pay for that education. Perhaps the newer leaders like me were simply less able and less inspiring than those who came before us, but the pervasiveness of these trends across the country argues against that explanation. In every state, college and university presidents struggled to find convincing words, to identify the examples of economic growth, and to tell heartwarming stories of their students' personal triumphs that would rekindle the golden glow around our enterprise—and almost everywhere we seemed to be failing.

New Jersey illustrated all these trends, and, just as in practically everything else, New Jersey was also a special case. State funding for higher education peaked in the late 1980s during the governorship of Thomas H. Kean (of whom more will be told later), and thereafter it began a slow but steady decline, in real dollars and in funding per student. Despite the voters' resounding passage of a bond issue for college and university facilities construction in 1988, state support for that purpose all but disappeared in the years that followed. Even prior to the 1990s loss of funding, the government of New Jersey had never been particularly supportive of the state's public colleges and universities. In its relative stinginess toward higher education, New Jersey had much in common with other northeastern states whose private colleges and universities are so numerous and so outstanding. There just wasn't the same level of demand for public higher education as in the Midwest or the South. In this arena, as in so many others, New Jersey's experiences and political choices were also shaped by the state's small

size and by its proximity to the great cities of New York and Philadelphia. Very large numbers of New Jersey young men and women traditionally wanted to attend college out of state, which meant crossing the
Hudson River or the Delaware River to find places in the classrooms
of New York, Pennsylvania, Delaware, or Maryland. Many attended
schools still farther away, and, indeed, New Jersey has led the nation
for decades in the number of high school graduates who choose to continue their education beyond the boundaries of their home state and,
in many cases, never return. The pressures faced by politicians in other
states to provide ever more opportunity within their public colleges
and universities were thus always much reduced in New Jersey. When
the national tide turned against funding for higher education in the
1990s, New Jersey's leaders had really been there all along. They readily
took up the new arguments justifying their decisions not to fund the
state's colleges very well.

So that was, and to a great extent still is, the political environment
in which I became president of Rutgers in 2002: a national trend that
was running against support for public higher education, some special
New Jersey circumstances that worsened the trend, and, ever present,
the harsh political behavior that is characteristic of our state, behavior
that sometimes serves useful purposes but that also brings a lot of pain
to many of the participants and widens differences of opinion that
might otherwise be narrowed.

Thanks, however, to good fortune and, even more, to the hard work
of many people, the story that follows has two remarkable outcomes
that could not have been predicted on the basis of the political situation I have described. First, like the very best public universities across
the country, Rutgers developed and expanded sources of monetary
support that did not depend upon the government of New Jersey.
Every year the percentage of the University's budget that came from
the state went down—not only because the state was insufficiently
generous but also because other revenue streams went up. Rutgers
probably would not have chosen to pursue this business plan, which is
not without its drawbacks, if state funding had been nearly adequate to
the attainment of the University's goals for itself, for its students, and

for the wider communities of which it is a part. But state funding was not adequate, and there was no choice. It's a good story, not unique to Rutgers, and it suggests that the argument about a "mature industry" requiring less subsidization than it formerly did may have some merit.

The second remarkable outcome, unlike the first, owes a great deal to the political leaders of New Jersey, perhaps above all to Tom Kean and Chris Christie: the fulfillment of Rutgers's long quest to regain Robert Wood Johnson Medical School (originally the Rutgers Medical School), while, as it turned out, also absorbing most of the rest of New Jersey's health sciences university, the University of Medicine and Dentistry of New Jersey (UMDNJ). Returning the medical school to Rutgers was a central goal of my presidency. It succeeded in 2012 through an almost unbelievable sequence of "only in New Jersey" twists and turns, but at the end of the day it would not have happened without the politicians.

THREE HOURS OF QUESTIONS FROM THE WOMEN OF DOUGLASS COLLEGE

It was September 16, 2005. Carrying banners and singing and chanting, they marched from their beloved Douglass College campus down George Street, the main thoroughfare of New Brunswick, to the College Avenue campus. There were a hundred or more of them, mainly students but also some alumnae of Rutgers's historic women's college, all of them determined to protect and defend it. Their destination was the hall in which I would deliver my annual address to the university community. I knew they were coming and knew they represented values and traditions that mattered deeply at Rutgers. I also knew the University had to face up to some serious problems that were imperiling the quality of education that they and all Rutgers–New Brunswick undergraduates were receiving.

Just as I did every September, I had taken seriously my presidential obligation to provide a compelling, even inspiring, account of the University's most pressing issues and to summon the community to meet its challenges and seize its opportunities. As always, too, the event was attended by six or seven hundred faculty, staff, students, and board members, all crowded into the multipurpose room in the College Avenue student center. I would speak for perhaps forty minutes and then take questions until there were no more. On this particular day, the inflamed and articulate contingent from Douglass stood with their banners, many rows deep at the back of the hall throughout the afternoon. They interrupted my speech a bit at the beginning, but when I said "I'll listen to you if you'll listen to me," the audience applauded and the Douglass students grew quiet and waited their turn. When it came, they had three hours of questions for me. Some were angry, some merely anguished. Why did I want to hurt their college? Didn't I know that only Douglass College offered Rutgers women opportunities for leadership in student organizations? Why did I want to damage the institution that historically had been New Jersey's avenue for women in higher education? The questions were worthy, and I did my best to give thoughtful, respectful replies to each. It was the beginning of a momentous campus conversation that lasted throughout the academic year.

The media, of course, widely reported the Douglass protest, and the students and especially the alumnae of Douglass succeeded in keeping their point of view in the headlines for many months. A casual observer of New Jersey news that year might easily have concluded that the state university was bent on destroying its venerable women's college. Founded in 1918 as the New Jersey College for Women and later renamed for its founding dean, Mabel Smith Douglass, it had provided opportunities for women to get a college education in the state at a time when there were virtually none. Even when those opportunities became more plentiful, Douglass had remained in the vanguard of educating women, preparing women for leadership, and, in more recent years, advancing feminist teaching and scholarship. Douglass had been and still was a vitally important part of Rutgers and New Jersey. If there was any doubt about the devotion that students and alumnae had for Douglass, the events of that day and the subsequent months dispelled it.

But Douglass was not the cause of the problem to which I devoted my annual address and which I exhorted the university community to join me in solving. Douglass was a special case of the problem, and Douglass gained most of the headlines throughout the year because its supporters wanted it to. There was a *Rutgers* problem, far bigger than Douglass, and, upon the advice of a task force composed of faculty and students, which had made its report two months earlier, I was determined to see it fixed. The University's New Brunswick campus included four liberal arts colleges—Rutgers, Livingston, Douglass, and University College, none with its own faculty, but each with its own admissions process, core educational requirements, honors programs, academic advising, graduation standards, and much more. Each college also provided nonacademic services like psychological counseling and recreational opportunities for its students alone. The colleges competed with each other for students, established divergent educational requirements that constrained students from transferring among the colleges, and promulgated regulations that were difficult to understand or explain. "If you live here you can't study that; if you are enrolled in that college you can't do this." Meanwhile the Faculty of Arts and Sciences, whose eight hundred members taught students in all the colleges, had no obligation or authority as a body in regard to admissions standards, the general education curriculum, or graduation requirements. "So we have," I said in my address, "degree-granting colleges without faculties and an arts and sciences faculty without students. This has got to be the weirdest academic setup in America." It denied students the full range of educational opportunities offered by the University's outstanding departments and faculty, and it absolved faculty of comprehensive responsibility for their students' education.

The setup was also excruciatingly difficult to explain to prospective students and their parents, high school guidance counselors, or the citizens of New Jersey. A state senator once said to me, "Dick, my son has been admitted to Livingston College but not to Rutgers College. Can you tell me what that means?" I did my best to answer his question—but the system had to be repaired, above all for the benefit of our students. That was the most important single challenge for Rutgers for the year ahead and, indeed, for the next several years.

The confusing and constraining character of undergraduate education on the New Brunswick campus illustrated an even larger Rutgers
problem: the University was disorganized and difficult to understand.
It was unwieldy and confounding to practically every observer and, as
a result, was achieving far less than it could have in many areas. To be
sure, criticisms like these apply in some measure to most large organizations, including many universities, but those who knew Rutgers well
agreed that our institution had a bigger than average case of disorganization and confusion. These conditions owed a great deal, as most
conditions do, to history. Rutgers had grown over the centuries and
decades by accreting, one might even say cobbling together, disparate
elements whose origins lay in a multitude of places and purposes. Its
Newark and Camden campuses, which were joined to Rutgers in the
middle of the twentieth century, had beginnings that were entirely separate from the rest of the University. The School of Pharmacy, born in
Newark, was something else altogether before it became part of Rutgers and relocated to Piscataway. These characteristics of accreting and
cobbling were especially pronounced on the largest Rutgers campus, in
New Brunswick, where each of the undergraduate colleges had come
into existence at a particular historical moment in response to the educational and social challenges of the time. Despite decades of efforts, the
colleges had never really been integrated into a single university. There
had been previous attempts to transform undergraduate education in
New Brunswick, but they had failed, in part because of opposition
from entrenched interests like those at Douglass and in part because
historic-structural problems are intrinsically so difficult to understand
or explain, not to mention boring. The defenders of Douglass had a
story that was easy to grasp—Rutgers was out to destroy New Jersey's main instrument of educational opportunity for women—while
the university administration had a more difficult public relations challenge. Little wonder Douglass dominated the headlines.

In the months that followed, the New Brunswick campus community set to discussing the problems of undergraduate education
and evaluating the recommendations of the task force: establishment of a single set of admissions standards for all arts and sciences

undergraduates; creation of a school of arts and sciences with faculty *and* students whose faculty would take responsibility for the educational curriculum; and equal access to every academic program for all undergraduates. These were not wild-eyed, radical proposals; practically every university in America, as well as Rutgers's campuses in Newark and Camden, already had them. But they were new to Rutgers–New Brunswick, and it took a monumental effort, indeed, a model process of shared governance involving students, faculty, staff, alumni, and board members to get it done. I was fond of saying that year that practically every university president in America had a report on his or her desk about how to improve undergraduate education at a time when the greatest prestige and the highest kudos went to graduate education and research. But while most of those reports gathered dust, we at Rutgers actually enacted the recommendations of ours. We also saved and improved Douglass—a subject to which I will return at a later point.

As a coda to this scene, I should observe that practically every Rutgers president, in his time, has faced the task of integrating, within one university, disparate elements that had wholly separate origins, many of which resisted true inclusion in a single institution. My successor as Rutgers president, Dr. Robert L. Barchi, is dealing with such a challenge, but far greater in magnitude than the one I faced—bringing within Rutgers most of the schools and colleges of UMDNJ. The challenge of integrating divergent elements, and thus expanding educational opportunities for everyone, is ever-present at Rutgers. It was, and is, well worth unceasing efforts to achieve.

RUTGERS 28, LOUISVILLE 25

The 44,000 fans who attended the football game in Piscataway, and the many more thousands who followed it on television or radio, will talk about it for the rest of their lives. On the clear, mild evening of Thursday, November 9, 2006, Rutgers (ranked fifteenth in the nation) beat Louisville (third) by the score of 28 to 25. Down by 25 to 7 after only seventeen minutes and by 25 to 14 at halftime, Rutgers roared back on the strength of tailback Ray Rice's running (131 rushing yards and two touchdowns) and a 67-yard pass play from quarterback Mike Teel to wide receiver Kenny Britt. With the score tied 25 to 25 and just seventeen seconds to play, Rutgers kicker Jeremy Ito missed a 33-yard field goal. When an offside penalty against Louisville gave Ito another shot at the field goal, now from 28 yards, he made it. A frantic Louisville comeback attempt fell short—and Rutgers Stadium exploded with joy. There was "Pandemonium in Piscataway," proclaimed Chris Carlin, the play-by-play radio voice of Rutgers football. The Scarlet Knights' charismatic coach, Gregory E. Schiano, ran onto the field, already swarmed by thousands of students, pointing his finger skyward as if to indicate the source of the victory. The celestial moment, like the game itself, was indelibly captured on national TV.

As everyone who follows Rutgers football knows, the joy in the victory over Louisville reflected the memory of years of futility, even humiliation. Rutgers went 1 and 10 and then 3 and 8 in 1999 and 2000, the seasons just before Schiano's arrival at the University. His first four years at Rutgers saw a combined record of 12 and 34. Those who knew the football program best, however, knew that Greg was laying the groundwork for success. The year 2005 brought a 7 and 5 breakout season and an invitation to the Insight Bowl in Phoenix. And then the next year, not really from heaven but from hard work by players and coaches, came the Louisville game, an 11 and 2 record, a decisive victory in the Texas Bowl over perennial football power Kansas State, and a final ranking of twelfth in the nation. On November 10, 2006, Lee Jenkins wrote in the *New York Times*, "Once a laughingstock, then an upstart, the Rutgers Scarlet Knights are suddenly and unbelievably in the national championship conversation."

Even before the Louisville game on that Thursday evening, New Jersey was ablaze with Rutgers football. Winning eight games in a row to start the season, the Scarlet Knights were brightening practically every occasion and every conversation that was in any way connected with Rutgers. Nowhere was this truer than on campus, where students arrived at the stadium many hours before the game, hoping for tickets. But the excitement was not confined to New Brunswick and

Piscataway. I was in Trenton on the morning of the Louisville game, there to testify before a legislative committee and to meet individually with several key members of the assembly and senate. The football game was all they wanted to talk about! Little though I had contributed to the team's success, like everyone from Rutgers that fall I basked in their glory. It was the friendliest legislative hearing during my years as Rutgers president, and the individual meetings with the members were equally convivial. A few legislators asked if tickets were still available to the game that evening, and with a phone call back home I was able to help.

The game still lives on in Rutgers's collective memory. Just as 85 percent of Americans who were of voting age in 1960 now recall that they cast their ballots for John F. Kennedy (who actually received 49 percent of the vote), nearly everyone you encounter from Rutgers was at the Louisville game. (I *really was* at the game, of course, and was on the sidelines when Jeremy Ito made his historic field goal.) That was the moment when caps with the big red Rutgers R began showing up on the heads of men and women and boys and girls across the state and around the country, and when Rutgers bumper magnets became practically ubiquitous. And although there has been nothing since quite like the Louisville game or the 2006 season, the winning ways of Rutgers football have continued—more successful seasons, more bowl games and victories, and more red Rutgers Rs everywhere you look. The Rutgers football program had made a dramatic turnaround, with visible benefits for the whole University.

The credit for this achievement belongs, above all, to Greg Schiano, who was selected as national coach of the year in 2006; to the director of intercollegiate athletics, Robert E. Mulcahy III, who appointed the then-very-young Schiano before the 2001 season and stuck with him during the early lean years; and to Rutgers alumni and board members like Ron Giaconia and Mark Hershhorn, who prophesied that elevating Rutgers football to respectability, and beyond, would be a huge asset for the University. Under Schiano, moreover, the football program was built in the right way. There were no major NCAA violations; no significant embarrassments by players, coaches, or fans; and, above all, there was academic as well as athletic success. Year after year, the Rutgers football program has ranked at or near the top nationally in graduation rates and other indices of educational achievement. Critics, at Rutgers and elsewhere, who believe that winning football is at odds with academic achievement, cannot find in our program any valid evidence for their conviction. Football's success also played an important role in starting the quiet conversations, beginning in late 2009, that led eventually to Rutgers's invitation to join the Big Ten Conference. That conference is composed of the very best public research universities in the East and Midwest, exactly the club that Rutgers wanted to be in. Getting into the Big Ten involved much more than football and depended on a number of factors beyond Rutgers's control, but it would not have happened without the rise of the football program.

As the saying goes, however, "At Rutgers nothing is ever easy." The football program's hard and honestly gained successes contributed to several challenges for the University in the years following the landmark victory over Louisville. The first involved expanding Rutgers Stadium. Constructed in 1994 with help from the state of New Jersey on the site of an older facility that had been a 1930s WPA project, the stadium was now enlarged in two phases. Nearly 1,000 club seats on the mezzanine level of the east side of the stadium (to be sold at premium prices) opened in time for the 2008 season, and more than 11,000 new seats at the south end of the stadium were completed in the summer of 2009. Together these additional seats brought the stadium's overall capacity to 52,454. Although the project was essential if Rutgers football was going to be competitive at the new, higher level to which Coach Schiano had taken the program, the expansion of the stadium was troubled from the start. Some faculty and students loudly asserted that the money pegged for the project would be better spent on academic buildings. Then inevitably, as construction went forward, the original cost estimates proved to be inadequate. In order to keep within the $102 million budget approved by the Board of Governors, the University had to scale back the project by eliminating a number of components that were unrelated to seating capacity. Finally, and most troubling, promises of financial assistance made by Governor Jon S.

Corzine and State Senator Raymond J. Lesniak proved unreliable. The University ended up borrowing the full cost of stadium expansion.

Worse than the controversy over expanding Rutgers Stadium was a crisis fomented by a newspaper investigation of athletics finances. Beginning in July of 2008 and continuing throughout the rest of the year, the (Newark) *Star-Ledger*, the paper with the largest circulation and the greatest influence in New Jersey, ran a series of very critical articles exposing what it called "the cost of big-time college football at Rutgers." Although no actual wrongdoing by anyone was ever alleged, the *Star-Ledger* disclosed a lack of transparency in athletics spending, inadequate oversight of the department's budget, and the existence of "secret" clauses in the contract extension that had been negotiated with Coach Schiano following the successful 2006 season. In early August, I appointed an independent Athletics Review Committee to study the criticisms, and in November the committee issued its report and recommendations. The report was scathingly critical of me for failing to exercise my presidential authority over athletics, and it was critical, as well, of Bob Mulcahy, the director of intercollegiate athletics, and the Board of Governors. I quickly pledged to implement all the recommendations in the report, but the crisis was not yet over. In the weeks that followed, I dismissed Mulcahy, and numerous legislators then assailed me—both for the alleged financial mismanagement and for removing Mulcahy. One powerful state senator called for my ouster as president and threatened to withhold state funding for Rutgers if I did not go. The Office of the State Comptroller, which earlier had begun an investigation of athletics finances at Rutgers, now expanded its inquiry into a comprehensive audit of the University's processes for procurement and contracting. This was the most stressful episode of my presidency, not least because the criticism of me for paying too little attention to the management of athletics was valid. The crisis did not end until the Board of Governors and I appointed a new director of intercollegiate athletics in February 2009.

With the appointment of new leadership in athletics and completion of the stadium's expansion, the worst was over. But criticism of the high cost of intercollegiate athletics persisted, both on campus and in the media. The annual budget for Rutgers athletics was now close to $60 million. Almost one-third of that amount came as a direct subsidy from the University; the rest was generated by athletics. Although the subsidy amounted to a little less than 1 percent of the University's overall annual expenditures, critics continued to assert that the millions spent on athletics should have gone instead to academics. Strange as it may seem to say, these critics both exaggerate the problem and fail to appreciate its full seriousness. The subsidy represented, after all, *less than 1 percent* of the University's then-$2 billion annual budget. On the other hand, national trends and competitive pressures will inexorably drive up spending on intercollegiate athletics. While the crisis of 2008 probably inoculated Rutgers against tolerating any lapses in the management of athletics finances for many years to come, the cost of athletics is going to go up and up.

AN INFURIATING, INSIGHTFUL OBSERVATION ABOUT RUTGERS'S RELATIONSHIP TO NEW JERSEY

Three days before Christmas 2008, when the furor over dismissing Bob Mulcahy was swirling around my head, the venerable *Star-Ledger* columnist Bob Braun leapt from the athletics crisis to a profoundly insulting and infuriatingly insightful observation about why Rutgers, he said, would never really be the state university of New Jersey. "The real problem," Braun wrote, "is that, while New Jersey has big-time state university football, what it doesn't have is a traditional, big-time state university. . . . That's no knock on Rutgers. Just history. New Jersey and Rutgers did not grow up together, one dependent on the other, each loyal to the other, creating the sort of bond seen in the Midwest and other states. A bond personified in, symbolized by, football. There is no University of New Jersey. Never was, never will be." Later in the column he observed, "New Jersey loves RU football, but it doesn't love RU." By contrast, Braun named two midwestern schools, Michigan and Nebraska, that were "valued partners in the historic development of the state" and whose leaders "historically aided their states."

Braun's column hurt so much because it was largely true. Unlike virtually all of the other state universities in America, Rutgers was established as a private, sectarian institution, before the Revolution. The state of New Jersey didn't yet exist and, when the state appeared—in 1776, ten years after the founding of Rutgers (then called Queen's College)—it had no responsibility for the college, or vice versa. Even after Rutgers became New Jersey's Land Grant institution in 1864, it was still private and still essentially unconnected to the state government. This was the era when, as Braun observed, state universities like Michigan and Nebraska were becoming "valued partners" in the economic and social development of their states. Rutgers and New Jersey had some of that relationship, mainly in the field of agriculture, but far less than universities in other regions of the country. Rutgers was still governed, moreover, by its private Board of Trustees, who appointed themselves and had no formal obligations to the state. During the first decades of the twentieth century, Rutgers's relationship to New Jersey began to change. The University gained modest financial support from Trenton beginning in the 1900s, but its connection to New Jersey remained ambiguous and peculiar. A 1945 act of the legislature designated Rutgers as New Jersey's state university, but its governance continued to rest in private hands and even its own press releases failed to describe Rutgers as the state university of New Jersey. Finally in 1956, by virtue of what was in essence a compact between the state of New Jersey and the Board of Trustees, Rutgers's status as the state university of New Jersey was confirmed, and the University acquired a new governing body, the Board of Governors. Six of the eleven members of the new board would be appointed by the governor of the state, and five would be named by the historic Board of Trustees. Even afterward, the trustees continued to be very present in the governance of Rutgers.

So of all the institutions in America that are now state universities, Rutgers was the first founded (1766) but the very last to become a state university (1945/1956). As Braun's insightful column suggested, that history still matters. The habits of routinely responding to the state's needs and regularly receiving love and loyalty from the state were far scarcer at Rutgers and in New Jersey than almost anywhere else in the

United States (except perhaps in New York and New England). The University's College of Agriculture, under various names, has always fulfilled the obligations of state service that it acquired at birth in the nineteenth century, and several newer elements of Rutgers, which were established after it became the state university, also intrinsically respond to that mission. These include, for example, in New Brunswick the Edward J. Bloustein School of Planning and Public Policy (1992) and the Institute of Marine and Coastal Sciences (1989); in Newark the School of Public Affairs and Administration (2006); and in Camden the Center for Urban Research and Education (2011). But much of the University still shows its private origins and still lacks a full complement of state university DNA. Correspondingly, and perhaps understandably, Rutgers has not received from the state the same levels of attention and support that characterize state universities elsewhere. Members of the legislature in whose districts Rutgers campuses are located support the University loyally, but legislators elsewhere around New Jersey are more likely to support *their* local colleges or universities and not to perceive Rutgers as having significant value to their communities or their constituents. Where there are social and economic problems to be solved, some legislators and state agencies turn for advice to experts at Rutgers, but many others do not.

Becoming president of Rutgers in late 2002, I was well aware of this historical condition, and the following April I devoted much of my inaugural address to the subject. My title expressed it: "Affirming Our Values—Serving Our State." Mentioning briefly the global and economic difficulties of the early twenty-first century, I said, "It may be a troubled time [ahead], and New Jersey is going to need a fully developed state university to meet the requirements and expectations of its citizens. Rutgers accepts the challenge to be that university. . . . The relationship between Rutgers and New Jersey must become far deeper and more extensive than it is today, and we at Rutgers must bear the largest share of responsibility for making it so." I had no illusions that this would be easy or that the relationship would be completely transformed on my watch. But we tried very hard. Looking back, the situation was even more vexing than I had imagined. My administration should have devoted more time and thought to identifying the goals we wanted to achieve in binding Rutgers closer to New Jersey, determining how to attain those goals, and deciding how to measure progress toward them.

Early on, through the services of an expert consultant, interviews were conducted with thousands of New Jerseyans representing every constituency that was relevant to Rutgers: state residents, business executives, political leaders, alumni, prospective students and their parents, high school teachers, and Rutgers students, faculty, and staff. Some of the findings were satisfying: awareness of Rutgers was high and opinions of the university were generally favorable. But other results were worrisome. In the minds of many, Rutgers was not much different from other universities in the state; it was not associated with clear and consistent images or messages; and "top of mind" ideas about Rutgers were alarmingly scattered and imprecise. Few of those who were surveyed (outside of the University's own faculty and staff) had any idea that Rutgers was a research university. I regretted, in particular, the finding that few of New Jersey's business leaders saw the value of Rutgers research.

So we set out to connect the University more deeply with the people of New Jersey and to sharpen the images that they associated with Rutgers. Here are just two examples of what we did. For five years running, following the end of the spring semester, I led a week-long bus tour of New Jersey for about thirty-five new members of the faculty. The idea was that Rutgers faculty, most of whom had not grown up in New Jersey, should become familiar with the state and with the communities from which their students came. Ideally the bus tour would influence their teaching and research, and in many cases it did. Each year a different group of faculty and I visited every region of New Jersey and saw farms, factories, high tech, low tech, cities, shore, and highlands. Each year the tour took us to different sites, but the first stop was always Trenton. When our bus pulled into a town, local leaders were there to greet us and to share with us the issues and challenges they were facing in their corner of New Jersey. Our visits usually were covered in the local media. Toward the end of my presidency, we started Rutgers

Day. It was the reverse of the bus tour: we invited everyone in the state to come to the New Brunswick campus on the last Saturday in April, when four hundred or more departments and programs showed their stuff by putting on demonstrations, making presentations, and offering opportunities for hands-on participation—all designed to entertain and educate the seventy-five thousand men, women, and children who attended. The day concluded with the football program's annual intra-squad game in the stadium. With the huge Rutgers Day audience to draw from, the game now attracted more fans than it ever had before. Imagine that: the lure of academic programs actually brought increased attendance at a football game!

These initiatives, along with others to be recounted later, no doubt helped to close the gap between Rutgers and the people of New Jersey. But we don't really know by how much. The success of the football team almost certainly mattered more than the faculty bus tour or Rutgers Day. Bringing the health science schools into Rutgers will probably make a bigger difference, too. According to columnist Braun, "There is no University of New Jersey. Never was, never will be." I believe that time will prove him wrong about the second part of that stark declaration, but it hasn't yet.

WELCOMING THE FIRST CLASS OF RUTGERS FUTURE SCHOLARS

On our Piscataway campus on the morning of June 26, 2008, I welcomed almost two hundred seventh-grade boys and girls, together with many of their parents, to Rutgers and to membership in the first class of the Rutgers Future Scholars Program. All of the youngsters lived in one of Rutgers's hometowns—Newark, New Brunswick, Piscataway, or Camden; all were academically promising and had been recommended to us by their teachers, but most came from backgrounds that were challenged by poverty and social disorder. Few of them had a parent who had gone to college, let alone graduated, and almost all of the scholars from Newark, New Brunswick, and Camden were African American or Hispanic/Latino. Both nervousness and excitement pervaded the room. Even though all of the boys and girls and their parents lived in one of the communities where Rutgers was located, most had never before been to the campus, and they must have found it intimidating; certainly none of them had ever before felt the burden of university expectations placed upon them. Now Rutgers was making promises to them, but also was challenging them to prepare to attend college, hopefully *this* college.

The promise was this: We would provide tutoring and mentoring as they continued their education in grades eight through twelve and would guide them in selecting their courses and monitor their progress so they stayed on track for college. We would bring them to programs on a Rutgers campus, probably the campus nearest where they lived, during the academic year and also every summer for a college preparatory experience. And—the big promise—if as high school seniors they were admitted to Rutgers and chose to attend, they would pay nothing in tuition and fees. They clapped and cheered as we welcomed them and set forth the deal that morning. Each of them was wearing a red Rutgers T-shirt that said Rutgers Future Scholar on the front and Class of 2017 on the back. To their amazement and their parents' amazement, they were headed for Rutgers. At the conclusion of that very first day of welcome and orientation, one girl from Camden was asked what she had liked best about the experience. Was it the academic program, was it meeting the president, was it the lunch? No, she said, it was the bus. When the big red Rutgers bus pulled up on her block, everyone in the neighborhood came out to see it and asked what that bus was doing there and why it came. "It came for me," she explained.

Inspiration for this program had come a couple of years earlier from the Reverend M. William Howard Jr., a member of the Rutgers Board of Governors and pastor of Bethany Baptist Church in Newark. Bill had observed that he could foresee the day when not a single child who was educated in the public schools of Newark would even be qualified to attend Rutgers. He was reflecting, of course, upon the quality of the schools and of life in Newark, but he could have made the same observation with almost equal accuracy about New Brunswick and Camden, the other two older industrial cities where Rutgers has its campuses. Bill's remark got our attention, and it helped inspire Courtney O. McAnuff, the University's vice president for enrollment management, to develop the outlines of the Rutgers Future Scholars Program and present them to me. Courtney suggested launching the program in 2009, but I wanted to begin immediately. So during the winter and spring of 2008, he and his staff worked with the four school districts where Rutgers is located (the three cities plus suburban Piscataway) to identify close to fifty students from each community who would make up the first class of Future Scholars. These were the boys and girls I welcomed that morning—and I did the same again in June of 2009, 2010, 2011, and 2012. By the time I left the presidency of Rutgers, there were nearly one thousand Rutgers Future Scholars.

Two core commitments lay behind Rutgers's creation and embrace of this program: the University's obligations to the people of New Jersey, especially those who lived in our four hometowns, and its commitment to the diversity of the student body. No one would claim that throughout its long history Rutgers had always lived up to those two responsibilities. The University came late, as we have seen, to an acceptance of its duty to the state, and, like virtually all American colleges and universities, it placed far too little value upon the racial and ethnic diversity of the student body until forced to do so by the demands of its own students beginning in the late 1960s. Over the course of the following four decades, however, through hard work by several generations of men and women, Rutgers had achieved an enviable record of student diversity. Beginning in the 1990s, the Newark campus was ranked year after year as the most diverse in America, and the campuses in New Brunswick and Camden were not far behind. The percentages of African American, Hispanic/Latino, and Asian students at Rutgers now nearly approximate the representation of these groups in the population of New Jersey, and, to judge from surveys, the vast majority of Rutgers students appreciate getting an education in such a diverse environment. Diversity is highly prized at Rutgers for reasons of social justice, to be sure, but also because it contributes to the quality of everyone's education by readying graduates for life and work in the heterogeneous, global twenty-first century.

For all that, however, Rutgers's diversity is mostly suburban. The towns of Edison, West Windsor, and Cherry Hill send many students of color to the University, but the cities of Newark, New Brunswick, Camden, Paterson, Jersey City, Elizabeth, Trenton, and Atlantic City send far fewer compared to their populations. That was Bill Howard's point. To date, neither New Jersey nor Rutgers has come close to meeting the challenge of providing college opportunities for the children, mostly children of color, who are growing up in our state's older cities.

The struggle to maintain, and even increase, the racial and ethnic diversity of the Rutgers student body arose in another compelling way during my presidency. As explained earlier, the changes we made in undergraduate education on the New Brunswick campus involved eliminating the historically separate admissions programs of the several colleges and establishing a campus-wide admissions process. One of the colleges, Livingston, was widely perceived as an avenue through which students of color had gained admission to Rutgers over the years because of that college's less demanding admissions standards. So the reorganization of undergraduate education brought with it a major worry that the representation of minorities in the student body would decline. Just the opposite happened. Courtney McAnuff and his colleagues undertook such a wide range of successful multicultural recruitment initiatives that the numbers of minority students actually increased following the demise of Livingston College. Through nationwide mailings to targeted student populations, visits to high schools with large numbers of disadvantaged students, on-campus recruiting events, open houses, summer programs, phone calls to admitted students, and dozens of specialized programs, Rutgers's already-large minority student population grew larger still. The University continued its practice of affirmative action, that is, using race as a plus factor in admissions decisions, but the availability for admission of so many outstanding minority students was the result of massive outreach and recruitment.

This story matters because some day the United States Supreme Court may declare the consideration of race in college and university admissions decisions to be unconstitutional. In a nation where economic and social circumstances are so often much more limited for children of color than for white boys and girls, the tool of affirmative action has opened up the doors of higher education—and all of its lifelong benefits—for millions of people. No one wants to return to an America in which college opportunities are as unequally distributed as they were a couple of generations ago. In 2003 and again in 2013, the Supreme Court upheld affirmative action, in significant part because of research documenting the value to students of living and learning in a diverse environment. But if the court decides the issue afresh and differently, on the grounds that using race in admissions decisions is unconstitutional, then Rutgers's experiences can be instructive and valuable. The nation's colleges and universities will need to dramatically expand their recruitment and outreach to disadvantaged populations. And while it is beyond the power of universities unilaterally to solve the problems of urban America's K–12 schools (although our colleges of education are helping), the proliferation of programs like Rutgers Future Scholars could make a real difference for those who are able to participate. All of this will be labor-intensive, strenuous, costly—and absolutely essential. The quality of American higher education, and so much of what it contributes to American life, will depend upon it.

In the spring of 2013, 170 out of 183 members of that first class of Rutgers Future Scholars graduated from their high schools in Newark, New Brunswick, Piscataway, and Camden. Their graduation rate was far above the predicted levels based on their social and economic backgrounds. Even more gratifying is that 163 were admitted to college, including 99 who enrolled at Rutgers and 64 who entered other four-year institutions or community colleges. As promised, the Rutgers students are paying no tuition or fees. In spite of these successes and the enormous needs that are being met through this program, it will be challenging to keep it up, much less to expand it. Although most of these students are eligible for financial aid from the federal and state governments, the undocumented among them are not, and the full cost of their education will have to be borne by Rutgers or whatever other college they attend. The most expensive part of the program, however, is not the Future Scholars' college education, but rather all the nurturing support they received during their high school years to get them ready for college. That's the biggest miracle of the Rutgers Future Scholars Program—and it will be worth whatever it takes to maintain and emulate it.

A MEETING WITH FORMER
GOVERNOR TOM KEAN

On a propitiously sunny July day in 2010, Phil Furmanski, Rutgers's executive vice president for academic affairs, and I met with former governor Tom Kean at his office in Far Hills. Several months earlier, Governor Chris Christie had appointed Kean to chair the New Jersey Higher Education Task Force, and Phil and I were there to share with the former governor the issues we hoped his task force would consider in writing its report. The meeting was long and substantive and cordial. (*All* meetings with Tom Kean are cordial; he's just a remarkably classy guy.) Our topics included state funding for higher education, regulatory relief for the colleges and universities, and higher education governance. But our main message was that New Jersey needed Rutgers to become a truly outstanding public research university and that the single most important step that could be taken to achieve that goal was to bring Robert Wood Johnson Medical School (RWJMS) back into Rutgers. Kean didn't tip his hand about what the task force would recommend, but he certainly heard us, especially regarding the medical school. Later in the summer, Phil and I would have similar meetings with the other four members of the task force, but the conversation with Kean heartened us the most. We left his office with soaring hopes for a report that would lead to significant outcomes for higher education and for New Jersey—maybe even a historic turnaround in the state's relationship with its public colleges and universities. As events developed over the next two years, the final years of my presidency, we were not disappointed.

Our hopes were boosted not only by the tenor of the meeting with Kean but also by Governor Christie's charge to the task force and, above all, by Kean's unmatched record in New Jersey public life. Governor

Christie had placed all the big issues before the task force: keeping pace with higher education in other states; freeing New Jersey's colleges and universities from onerous regulations; increasing state funding for the institutions, especially their capital needs; and stemming the brain drain of many of the top students who leave New Jersey to attend college elsewhere. Observing that the state's long-term economic prosperity was tied to its colleges and universities, the governor gave the task force wide latitude to develop recommendations for improving "the overall quality and effectiveness of the State's higher education system." Although gubernatorial task forces are frequently appointed and frequently ignored, we had confidence in this one because it was headed by Tom Kean. As governor in the 1980s he had made higher education a statewide priority. He worked closely with the college and university presidents, especially with Rutgers President Ed Bloustein; made strategic investments in the appointment of world-class faculty and in research; and championed the successful higher education bond issue of 1988. Following two terms as governor, Kean had served for fifteen years as president of Drew University. The most respected person in New Jersey public life, and Governor Christie's own mentor, Kean had the political clout and the higher education knowledge to produce an outstanding report and then see to the adoption of many of its recommendations. Media stories on the establishment of the New Jersey Higher Education Task Force did not fail to mention that Kean had chaired the National Commission on Terrorist Attacks Upon the United States, commonly known as the 9/11 Commission. Following the issuance of that commission's highly regarded report, Kean did not close up shop but lobbied persistently for the enactment of its proposals. In the summer of 2010, we had plenty of good reasons to be hopeful about his newest undertaking.

Although Governor Christie's charge to the task force did not mention medical education, it was widely assumed that the report would address the subject of New Jersey's troubled health sciences university, UMDNJ, which had been revealed in recent years to be badly, even corruptly, managed. As federal prosecutor for the district of New Jersey, a position he held from 2002 to 2008, Christie had been directly involved in the efforts to clean up UMDNJ. He was known to be highly familiar with its problems and was even thought to be dubious about its continued existence. In our meeting with Governor Kean, Phil Furmanski and I felt no need to mention UMDNJ's troubles; they were widely known. We concentrated on the benefits of bringing into Rutgers what we regarded as the best part of UMDNJ and the missing piece of our New Brunswick campus, RWJMS. The medical school was located adjacent to Rutgers facilities in both New Brunswick and Piscataway, and some of it was actually *on* our property. For decades, its faculty and ours had collaborated in education and research. Phil's background in biology, and especially in cancer research, fit him well to join with me in making the case. The two of us tag-teamed it with Kean, just as we did in so many situations and on so many subjects during our eight years together. New Jersey needed a first class, university-based health science center, we said. Practically every top medical school in the country was part of a major comprehensive university, and, although Rutgers and RWJMS already had a long and successful record of collaboration, independently the two were unable to fully exploit their combined strengths. If joined together, however, they could enable New Jersey to take a leadership role in the biomedical sciences, with major benefits for education, health care, and the state's economy. We gave Governor Kean plenty of examples of these opportunities. In the months ahead, Phil and I would return again and again to the themes we articulated that day. Kean agreed with us about the benefits of attaching Robert Wood Johnson Medical School to Rutgers, but he wondered aloud what do to with the rest of UMDNJ, especially the parts of it that were located in Newark and were so important to that city. Kean's prescient concern, to which Phil and I did not then offer a solution, reverberated continuously throughout the next two years—until the question was given a surprising and definitive answer in June of 2012.

Later in the summer of 2010, following the meeting with Governor Kean, a small incident occurred in regard to Rutgers and the task force that disturbed me, probably well out of proportion to its actual importance. To assist them in their work, the members of the task force sent nine questions to higher education leaders throughout the state and requested written replies. The Rutgers recipients of the questions were Ralph Izzo, chair of the Board of Governors; Bob Stevenson, chair of the Board of Trustees; and me. The three of us agreed that it would be desirable for the task force to receive a single set of answers from Rutgers and that I, working with my administrative team, would draft a document for review by Ralph and Bob. Not surprisingly, the answers that my colleagues and I drafted included a call for "reuniting" RWJMS with Rutgers and offered a rationale that was very similar to the one Phil and I had given orally to Governor Kean. Although Bob Stevenson signed off on the answers, Ralph Izzo did not, on the grounds that the proposal to combine the medical school with Rutgers had not been sufficiently discussed by the Board of Governors and that as the new chair he needed more conversation with the members of the board. His point may sound reasonable, but it stunned me. In fact, there had been many recent discussions of this subject among board members, and although there had been no occasion for a formal vote on bringing the medical school into Rutgers, none of them had objected and, indeed, all of them expressed strong support. Many vital issues remained to be resolved, including the terms of the merger and the fate of the rest of UMDNJ, but the basic idea of reuniting RWJMS with Rutgers was not controversial within the Board of Governors. I am certain that Governor Kean would have been very surprised if Rutgers had failed to advocate for this outcome in responding to the task force questionnaire. Ralph surely had reasons for not endorsing our answers, but I didn't know what they were. This was the beginning of a challenging two years for Ralph and me. Much later, as I will recount, he would play an essential role in bringing this project to a successful conclusion, but it worried me that we were not together on it in the summer of 2010.

When Governor Christie released the task force report in early January 2011, it was everything we had hoped it would be. The report included an emphatic call for significantly improved state funding of the colleges and universities, both their operating budgets and their capital needs. The section on Rutgers began with thirteen resounding words that directly recalled the conversation Phil and I had had with

Governor Kean: *"For a state to be great, it must have a great state university."* And, above all, the report firmly recommended merging Robert Wood Johnson Medical School and the UMDNJ School of Public Health (also located in New Brunswick/Piscataway) into Rutgers "to establish a first-class comprehensive university-based health science center." Even beyond its specific recommendations—and there were many of them, including several recommendations that took Rutgers to task—the report was pitch-perfect in its respect for public higher education and its recognition of everything that New Jersey's colleges and universities, if properly supported, could mean for the people of the state. It was the report that New Jersey's higher education leaders had been waiting for . . . all our lives.

We had confidence that this report was the real deal, that it would not gather dust on a shelf but, owing to Governor Kean's reputation and Governor Christie's determination, would lead to actual results. We were right. But the pathway from the report's recommendation concerning the medical school to implementation was anything but straight. Almost all the varieties of craziness that are possible in New Jersey were visited upon the drama that unfolded over the year and a half that followed. Not just craziness, however, but also enormous amounts of hard work by men and women of good faith went into getting this done. Two days before the end of my presidency, the legislature enacted a law giving Rutgers Robert Wood Johnson Medical School, and much, much more. It was a satisfying way to go.

COMING OF AGE
AT RUTGERS

SOMETIMES ON SATURDAY mornings in the early 1950s, my father would visit Dr. William H. S. Demarest, who lived in the brown stone house that still stands at the corner of George Street and Seminary Place in New Brunswick. Dr. Demarest had served with distinction as president of Rutgers from 1906 to 1924 and had written a weighty volume on its history. Now in his nineties, he loved to talk about that subject. My father, a young faculty member trying to learn about the history of Rutgers, valued these opportunities to spend time with the genial, gentlemanly Dr. Demarest. Occasionally I accompanied my dad on these visits, although as a young child I had no interest in what they were saying. I did, however, grow attached to a small cast-iron replica of the Liberty Bell that sat on Dr. Demarest's desk. He had purchased the bell, I learned later, as a schoolboy when he and his classmates made a trip to Independence Hall in 1876, the centennial of the Declaration of Independence. One Saturday, Dr. Demarest, seeing how much I liked that bell, gave it to me, and I have cherished it ever since. From 2002 to 2012, it rested on my desk in historic Old Queens, the stately Federal-style building where his presidential desk also had been.

A bit later in the 1950s, but again on Saturday mornings, I would finish swimming lessons in the College Avenue gym and walk across the street to Bishop House, where my father was teaching his graduate seminar in American political history. A stucco mansion in the Italianate style, Bishop House had been the nineteenth-century home of the industrialist and Republican politician James Bishop. Rutgers purchased it in 1925, and now it housed faculty offices of the departments of history and political science, as well as several classrooms. When my father's seminar was over and he had finished talking with his students and I had finished playing with the old-fashioned revolving wooden bookshelf in his office, my dad and I would get into his car and drive home for lunch. We didn't have far to go, just a couple of miles across the Raritan River to our house on River Road in Piscataway. When I was a child, Rutgers was seldom far away.

Many occasions brought me to the campus, including football games. The old Rutgers Stadium was about a mile from our house. For home games the gates would be flung open at halftime and anyone could come in for free. I would ride my bicycle to the stadium, lean it unlocked against the chain link fence on the west side of the grandstands, and go in to find my parents. They would be sitting near the top of section W2, together with Rutgers friends. The football player I liked best was the All-American tailback Billy Austin, who led the Scarlet Knights to an 8–1 record in 1958. The teams they beat that season included Princeton, Colgate, Lehigh, Lafayette, and Columbia. I was ten years old. Holidays, too, found the McCormick family on the Rutgers campus. As members of the University Outing Club, which sponsored hikes and canoe trips for faculty families, my parents and sister and I attended the club's Christmas parties at the log cabin on the College of Agriculture campus (now Cook). Seated on a chair in front of one of the great stone hearths, Santa Claus handed presents to the children. Somewhat later, in high school, I took a Rutgers summer school course in intensive German and another in speed reading. The swimming lessons were more effective than the German or the reading.

I grew up at Rutgers because that's where my parents had their careers. Newly married, they settled in New Brunswick in 1945 when my father, who was still completing his Ph.D. at the University of Pennsylvania, was appointed to a position in the history department. Seven years earlier he had graduated from Rutgers, the first person in his family to attend college, and now he was back as a faculty member. My mother, with her master's degree in chemistry from the University of Delaware, obtained a part-time teaching position across town at Douglass College. I was born in 1947 and my sister Dorothy arrived in 1950. That was the year when our family moved from an apartment on Hamilton Street in New Brunswick to the ranch house on River Road where my parents would live for the next fifty-three years.

A short bicycle ride from our house was the wide-open Rutgers campus called University Heights (now Busch). When I was a child, many of the buildings there were barracks-like structures that had been built cheaply and hastily to accommodate the housing needs of married faculty and students and their young families. The old nine-hole golf course was there, too, as were a growing number of the University's newer buildings for science and, soon, engineering. The most imposing of these was the Waksman Institute of Microbiology, a 1954 Georgian-style structure that was financed with income from the discovery at Rutgers of the then-miraculous antibiotic streptomycin. One summer I went into business selling lemonade at the sixth tee of the old golf course, right across the road from the institute. Before long the University's single police officer shut down my business on the grounds that I was competing with the Coca-Cola machine at the golf house. The golf house consisted of a few folding chairs and a table, a counter where greens fees could be paid, a Popsicle machine, and my competitor, the Coke machine. Outside there was a telephone booth.

When my father left home in the mornings to drive to work, he always said he was going over to "the college." He knew, of course, that Rutgers was fast becoming a large, multi-campus university, and he soon became a well-known citizen of that growing institution, but his own corner of it on the College Avenue campus was always just "the college." Our family's dinner table talk often turned to Rutgers, and, although as a youngster I absorbed relatively little of that, I saw clearly my parents' enormous pride in the University—its growing numbers of students, its new buildings, and its importance to New Jersey. Their social life revolved around Rutgers friends, including couples like themselves with young children but also older members of the community who remembered Rutgers as it had been in the decades before World War II. As a child, although I followed scarcely a fraction of the Rutgers events that were so important to my parents, I remember their joy in 1959 when a bond issue for the support of higher education was overwhelmingly approved by the state's voters. Later, writing about that successful referendum in his 1966 history of the University, my father chose his words with optimism: "Not only did it promise the achievement of long-deferred hopes for adequate physical facilities, it meant also that Rutgers had at last gained public acceptance as New Jersey's State University—an acceptance that it fully reciprocated." As he came to appreciate, probably better than anyone, the reality of Rutgers's relationship to New Jersey would prove to be more complicated than that.

Especially as I grew older, I grasped not only my parents' great affection for Rutgers but also their concerns for the University's needs— to ensure its academic quality, to improve its financial resources, and, yes, to become more fully New Jersey's state university. In my father's long and prolific academic career, three of his books and many, many of his articles concerned the history of Rutgers, and for decades he had the title university historian. Occasionally a critic of Rutgers, he was always a loving critic. He was also the most accomplished scholar of New Jersey history, with three books, countless articles, and a lifetime of speeches around the state. And, for all that, Richard P. McCormick was actually best known at Rutgers as a charismatic, caring teacher and, beyond the campus, as the author of influential works on the history of American politics and especially on party formation in the Jacksonian period. My father and I were very close, and I admired him tremendously. When he was in the room, I had trouble paying attention to anyone else. As a teenager, however, I hadn't the remotest plan to follow in his professional footsteps. And yet that's what I did, up to a point.

Graduating from Piscataway High School in 1965, I made a choice that so many New Jersey boys and girls made then and still do: I went out of state to college, to Amherst College in western Massachusetts. With my departure for Amherst, I left the Rutgers community where I had spent my childhood and gave little thought to whether or when I would be back. Over the course of the next eleven years, first as a college student, then briefly as a sixth-grade teacher in Philadelphia, and then as a graduate student at Yale University, I visited Piscataway frequently because it was the home of my parents and many friends, but I wasn't there to stay, only to visit. Then, to my amazement, in 1976, I returned to Rutgers as a faculty member in United States political history, practically the same academic field as my father's. That happened because of the fine education I received at Amherst and Yale and the directions in which it led me.

This book isn't *The Education of Henry Adams*, and there are only a few things about mine that are worth telling. There are three to be exact. One is that at Amherst I got really excited about studying the history of the United States. More than half of my college classmates had graduated from elite private high schools, but my public school education in Piscataway had prepared me at least as well as theirs. As a seventeen-year-old freshman, I wanted to become a Presbyterian minister. But that ambition received little nourishment at Amherst in the 1960s, and it soon perished altogether before my growing fascination with what I was learning in the still-new interdisciplinary field of American studies. Small as it was, Amherst College was a center of American studies scholarship, and its faculty included such luminaries as Leo Marx and John William Ward, both of whom became my revered teachers. Though soon to be dominated by concepts of social conflict and ethnic diversity, the field of American studies in the mid-1960s was still lodged in what is sometimes unkindly called its "myth and symbol" phase. Distinctive beliefs and enduring themes comprised an identifiable American culture that could be understood through its literature and history. Marx and Ward and their faculty colleagues were masterly in bringing alive that literature and history, and I was swept up in trying, as best a sophomore or junior could, to understand America. I did not pursue the American studies approach beyond college, but I was permanently influenced by a fascination with American history.

It is next worth mentioning that this *was* the 1960s and, like most people of my generation, I paid a lot of attention to the riveting, divisive issues of civil rights and the war in Vietnam. But my engagement with those issues was mainly intellectual, rather than activist, and found its most satisfying expression in the study and teaching of African American history. As a college sophomore I took a bus to Cambridge one day and interviewed the thirty-eight-year-old Daniel Patrick Moynihan, then a faculty member at Harvard, about his controversial study of *The Negro Family*, popularly known as the Moynihan Report. I then wrote a paper analyzing the report and the outraged responses it evoked as expressions of the cry for "Black Power" that had recently emerged from the splintering civil rights movement. After taking a number of relevant Amherst courses and having secured Bill Ward as my adviser, I researched and wrote a senior thesis quaintly titled "Ideas about Africa in American Negro Social Thought." These intellectual exercises were remote, to say the least, from the actual struggle for racial equality, but from them I gained understandings and sympathies that always remained with me. Most immediately, this learning led to several teaching opportunities. In the summer of 1968, following the assassination of Dr. Martin Luther King Jr., I joined with two other (white) instructors teaching African American history to a small group of black and white high school students at the Mount Hermon School (now Northfield Mount Hermon) in western Massachusetts. The next summer, following my graduation from Amherst, I was back home at Rutgers teaching the same subject to "high-risk" students in a newly established program designed to take them from their presumably inadequate high school educations into Rutgers. Then, for the single academic year of 1969–70, I taught a class of sixth-graders in an all-black elementary school in Philadelphia. The latter two teaching assignments were extremely challenging, and I was not really ready for them. Following the year in Philadelphia, I retreated to graduate school in New Haven.

The last thing to say about my education is that at Yale I became an American political historian. Just as in college, I was strongly influenced by several outstanding professors, including my adviser, C. Vann Woodward, the most respected scholar of the post–Civil War South; John Morton Blum, author of many well-regarded works on twentieth-century politics; and Michael F. Holt, a brilliant younger historian of politics in the nineteenth century. From these men, particularly from Holt, I developed a passion for the historical study of political parties and elections, government policy making, and corruption and reform. The late nineteenth and early twentieth centuries became my particular stomping ground, and I wrote a doctoral dissertation, which later became a book, on New York State politics in the 1890s and early 1900s. In the years that followed, I published articles analyzing and interpreting political change in America from the nineteenth century to the twentieth.

I have often been asked whether the study of United States political history was helpful to my work in university administration and especially to my dealings with state legislators and governors. To this I have answered yes and no. On the "yes" side of things: my habit of thinking like a historian has been intrinsic and valuable. Every problem or condition has a history, so understanding the origins of whatever challenge you are facing is helpful to finding pathways forward. University presidents who were trained in mathematics or law or anything else would probably say with equal conviction that their educational background shaped their approach to leadership, and I am sure they would have a point. *My* approach was benefited by the study of history. On the "no" side: my experience in analyzing and interpreting large-scale political changes as they evolved over time was not really useful in conducting relationships with real live politicians who were dealing, in the moment, with tricky political calculations. I found that I had no more insight into their thinking than anyone else.

As I neared completion of my doctoral dissertation in 1976, I now wanted very much to follow my mentors Leo Marx, Bill Ward, Vann Woodward, John Blum, Mike Holt—and my father—into the profession of teaching and writing American history. In a tough job market for historians, I was fortunate that four outstanding universities were seeking to appoint American political historians that year, including Washington University in St. Louis, the University of Minnesota, Purdue University, and Rutgers. Receiving an offer as an assistant professor at any one of them would have been highly satisfying, but I remember hoping especially for the position at Minnesota. As things turned out, I was lucky enough to have a choice between Purdue and Rutgers—and I chose Rutgers. My father, with whom I had remained very close and who had read and commented upon successive chapters of my dissertation, was not enthusiastic about my joining the faculty at Rutgers. But that's what I did, and in the late summer I moved my books and papers into an office on the third floor of Bishop House. The third floor must have been the servants' quarters when the Bishop family lived there. My office was long but quite narrow, and the ceiling sloped so sharply toward the exterior wall that even a person of my short stature could not stand fully upright at the side of the room. My mother, who by this time held the position of director of space and scheduling at Rutgers, rigorously tracked the utilization of academic spaces throughout the University and was widely believed to keep a tape measure handy in her purse when traveling around campus. One day the phone rang in my office, and it was my mother. "Dickie," she said, "your office has more square feet than is allowed for an assistant professor." I answered, "Mother, in the case of *this* office you've got to come and measure the cubic feet." She dropped the subject. Unexpectedly, I was back home at Rutgers.

⁂

The Rutgers whose faculty I joined in 1976 was large and geographically dispersed. Of its 46,500 students, nearly 32,000 were enrolled on the New Brunswick campus; the others were in Newark (9,600) and Camden (5,000). About 70 percent of the students were undergraduates; the rest were engaged in graduate and professional studies. Ninety-five percent of Rutgers undergraduates had grown up in New Jersey; more than three-quarters were white, and just over 10 percent were black. Full-time faculty members numbered a little more than 2,500, and they were joined by hundreds of part-time lecturers. The

University's total annual budget came to a little under $200 million. Just as it does today, the New Brunswick campus had the geographic challenge of five separate campus locations, including three in the city of New Brunswick itself (College Avenue, Douglass, and Cook) and two across the Raritan River in the township of Piscataway (Busch and Kilmer, later called Livingston). And just as they do today, Rutgers students spent a lot of time traveling from campus to campus on the University's buses. As if all this weren't complicated enough, Rutgers–New Brunswick included four separate undergraduate liberal arts colleges: Rutgers, Douglass, Livingston, and University College. In 1976, each of the colleges still had its own faculty as well as students.

My home base in all of this, the Rutgers College history department in Bishop House on the College Avenue campus, was a memorably spirited academic community. The department chairman, Warren Susman, was brilliant, large, and loud. Everything about Warren was, to use one of own his favorite words, extraordinary. A hugely popular teacher and a widely recognized (although little published) guru of American cultural history, Warren was the mayor of Bishop House. Day after day students and faculty gathered around this man as he prowled the building's halls and paced its ornately tiled lobby, imprinting his remarkable personality on our department. Not everyone in the department was equally close to Warren, but there was a coterie of us, including some of the most senior members as well as some of the more junior faculty like me, who were Warren's special followers. We conspired with him and with each other on departmental business, and it was great fun. Several of my coconspirators, including Paul Clemens and Rudy Bell, are today still in the history department at Rutgers. Sadly, Warren was not yet sixty when in 1985 he died just as dramatically as he had lived—felled by a heart attack in mid-sentence while presenting a paper at the annual meeting of the Organization of American Historians in Minneapolis. I was there. The University's most prestigious teaching award now bears Warren's name, as does an annual graduate student history conference. My own book of essays titled *The Party Period and Public Policy* is dedicated to Warren's memory.

Warren dominated every activity in the department, but his particular sphere of influence was undergraduate education. A masterly teacher himself, he demanded a significant commitment to teaching from each of us. In an era when expectations were rising swiftly that faculty members would do research, write, and publish, the devotion within Bishop House to students and teaching remained unusually high. Returning to our offices after teaching our classes, faculty members would gather in the lobby and share observations about their courses and about students they had in common. As a first-year assistant professor, I felt pleased and proud that older members of the department knew what courses I was teaching and asked me about how they were going. One day a few years later, my much-admired senior colleague Lloyd Gardner, an outstanding, globally minded diplomatic historian, asked me what I had taught my students that day in my course on the Progressive era. I said that we had covered the federal meat inspection act of 1906, a signature regulatory measure championed by President Theodore Roosevelt after he and millions of other Americans had learned from Upton Sinclair's novel *The Jungle* about the disgusting conditions in which meat was processed and packed. "The meat inspection act," exclaimed Professor Gardner. "I'm teaching *my* students about global war and peace and the fate of humankind, and you're teaching yours about *meat inspection!*" Lloyd and I and everyone within earshot roared with laughter. It was a truly wonderful time to be a young history teacher at Rutgers.

In those days, each of us taught five courses a year, three in one semester and two in the other. Most members of the history faculty had a wide range of courses in their repertoire; over these early years mine included both semesters of the introduction to U.S. history, the history of American politics, populism and progressivism, the Civil War and Reconstruction, and several mini-courses on presidential elections and political corruption. During my first years as a faculty member, I had serious stage fright before teaching my large lecture courses, especially if they met early in the morning. To judge from student evaluations, I was a successful teacher, but I couldn't shake my nervousness. One early morning, in front of three or four hundred students in the introductory course, I had a panic attack and actually sat down on the stage for a couple of minutes while I calmed down. After a few years, my stage fright went away, which is a good thing because speaking before large audiences became a regular part of my life.

My most memorable teaching occurred in the late 1970s and early 1980s when my father and I jointly taught the history of American politics. This had been his course long before I came to Rutgers, then it became mine, and then for two glorious years it was ours. We loved teaching it together, and the students, knowing of our relationship, would look and listen intently for any signs of a father-son disagreement over some historical interpretation. We may even have exploited that a little bit to keep their attention. My father was the better teacher, but I will never forget those joint courses, and to this day I still encounter former students who fondly remember having my dad and me as teachers together. By this time my father, although still active in both teaching and research, was no longer a member of the history department and no longer had his office in Bishop House. As a "university professor" he was freed from the obligation to participate regularly in departmental affairs and was not party to the political shenanigans recounted below.

Back then there were *four* history departments within Rutgers–New Brunswick because each of the colleges had its own faculty. Not surprisingly, there were rivalries between the four, and each nurtured unfavorable caricatures of the others. We at Rutgers College believed that the historians at Douglass College were traditional and conservative; they regarded us as arrogant and elitist. The historians at Livingston College prided themselves on their singular sensitivity to the challenges of a multicultural society, sensitivity that the rest of us evidently lacked. Warren Susman fanned the flames of rivalry, and most of us in Bishop House enjoyed the sport. While each of the four history departments had its own chairperson, Warren being ours, there was also a chair of the overall New Brunswick history department and, of course, endless quarrelling over the respective authority of the New Brunswick chair and that of the collegiate chairs. We in Bishop House regarded the New Brunswick chair as the tool of the Douglass history department. Sometimes the language of rivalry got a little rough. One morning we found in our departmental mailboxes mimeographed copies of a letter from one of our colleagues to the New Brunswick chairperson, a letter in which, owing to whatever was in dispute between them on that particular day, our colleague called the chair a "fucker." Then, returning to Bishop House after lunch, we found mimeographed copies of the New Brunswick chairperson's reply to our colleague, a reply expressing disagreement, as he put it, over who was the "fucker" and who was the "fuckee." History at Rutgers was a lively place.

It was also, for all the spirited jibes, a generally collegial and democratic place. History was unusual, maybe even unique, among Rutgers academic departments in permitting untenured assistant professors to attend the meetings at which their senior colleagues discussed the qualifications for tenure of the assistant professors who were being considered for promotion. Those of us who were untenured listened silently at these meetings, and, of course, we were not permitted to vote. But we had the invaluable opportunity of observing as our senior colleagues fulfilled one of their most important faculty responsibilities, that of deciding whom to recommend for permanent tenure. What we heard on those occasions was eye-opening and sobering: the expectations for tenure were high and getting higher, and the most important consideration was the quality of the candidate's scholarly publications. A book published by a respected press might get you tenure, but only if your senior colleagues considered it a very good book and generally only if you also had published some articles in highly regarded scholarly journals. No form of mentoring could possibly have been as valuable as sitting through these meetings. Some of us assistant professors were going to be recommended for tenure, but others were not. Fortunately I was, and on July 1, 1981, I became a tenured associate professor.

That was the same day on which a comprehensive, long-planned reorganization of the Rutgers–New Brunswick campus became effective. Led by President Edward Bloustein and engineered by Provost Kenneth Wheeler, the reorganization abolished the separate college faculties and created a single Faculty of Arts and Sciences. Four history departments now became one, and the same was true for every other arts and sciences discipline. It was a wrenching change, even for history, which for years had had a New Brunswick chairperson and had operated in many respects as a single department, factionalized though it was. Each of the four history departments now left behind its ancestral home, ours being Bishop House, and moved into Van Dyck Hall on the Voorhees Mall of the College Avenue campus.

With the demise of the separate collegiate departments of history, the choice of the New Brunswick chairperson became more important than ever, and inevitably some of the old rivalry resurfaced in the run-up to the election of the chair. As in any election, the first question to be answered is who would be allowed to vote, and on this issue some of us in the Rutgers College department believed that our Douglass colleagues were inflating the list of eligible voters by insisting on the inclusion of faculty who, by our lights, possessed only remote connection to the department. At this juncture and in this crisis, I was dispatched by my fellow Bishop House partisans to seek an audience with the newly appointed dean of the Faculty of Arts and Sciences, the distinguished social scientist David Mechanic, and to ask him to intervene by declaring ineligible those faculty members who were being spuriously added to the departmental voting roster. When the appointed hour came, I climbed the stairs to the third floor of the stucco house on Bishop Place where Dean Mechanic had his temporary offices. Seated in shirtsleeves on a sofa, he was surrounded by papers and swamped by the unprecedented challenge of forming a single arts and sciences faculty. After I nervously explained my mission, he responded that he had no intention whatsoever of involving himself in deciding who could vote in a history department election. He said he had far, far weightier matters to decide—and, indeed, he did. Disappointed though I was, I recognized that Dean Mechanic had made the right decision. So the bogus voters cast their ballots, our candidate for chair lost the election, and we all became members of a single history department.

For Rutgers and for history, Ed Bloustein's reorganization proved to be a giant step toward academic distinction. Now the arts and sciences departments, formerly scattered and small, acquired critical masses of faculty. Many of them, including history with its fifty tenured and tenure-track faculty members, gained national recognition for the first time. Some individual Rutgers scholars had previously enjoyed such reputations, but with a few exceptions their departments had not. In 1989, eight years after the reorganization, Rutgers was invited to join the Association of American Universities (AAU), the prestigious and exclusive organization of the top fifty-eight public and private research universities in the United States and Canada. (Today the AAU has sixty-two members.) At the risk of getting ahead of my story and perhaps of attributing too much significance to the reorganization, I believe that the changes of 1981 were essential to the University's attainment of that honor. Fortunately, the reorganization was followed not by resting upon laurels but by the exercise of remarkable academic leadership by President Bloustein and his new top partner in Old Queens, the mysterious and inscrutable but brilliant T. Alexander (Alec) Pond, who became the University's executive vice president and chief academic officer in 1982. Ed and Alec, helped by strong support from Governor Tom Kean and from key deans and faculty members, lifted Rutgers to heights in research and reputation that it had never enjoyed before. There was only one flaw in the new arrangements: the undergraduate students had been left behind in the now faculty-less colleges, a problem to which I will return.

Unified and physically consolidated in Van Dyck Hall, the history department proved highly capable of meeting, and even exceeding, the demands and expectations placed upon it. Undergraduate and graduate teaching programs had to be revised, new faculty appointed, existing faculty reviewed for promotion, and much more. Naturally there were sometimes disagreements about these things. One faculty member was fond of declaring that we couldn't possibly devise a new history curriculum for the undergraduates until we all agreed on the meaning of history. That proved difficult to achieve. Notwithstanding such hindrances, our well-led department accomplished a great deal and enjoyed the high regard of students, University administrators, and our peers in the field of history around the country and the world. Within a few years following the 1981 reorganization, almost every faculty member would have agreed that the changes had been highly beneficial. It was satisfying to belong to a large and outstanding history department.

Soon enough, however, Rutgers's ongoing transition from its collegiate past to a research-intensive university brought challenges to history. In their general outlines, the same issues also affected other Rutgers departments, as well as research universities across the country. One concern was equality and fairness among faculty, values to which academics in general and historians in particular traditionally expressed allegiance. Now the University's push toward research excellence potentially threatened these values. Faculty with significant scholarly publications, especially if their fields were hot or trendy, often received job offers from other universities. Some of our colleagues accepted these outside offers and left the University, but most remained at Rutgers in exchange for increased compensation or, in some cases, reduced teaching responsibilities. Sometimes research-active faculty who had little or no intention of leaving Rutgers sought outside offers just for the purpose of raising their salaries. It was hard to blame them, but hard feelings developed within the department over the resulting inequalities. During these same years, the University and the department, with help from the state of New Jersey, sought to attract outstanding faculty from elsewhere, new colleagues who would be highly compensated because of the premium the academic market placed upon their scholarly achievements. In the Rutgers lingo of the day, a distinguished senior faculty member recruited to the University was a World Class Scholarly Leader, a WCSL (pronounced "wicksul," with the accent on the first syllable). A highly promising junior faculty recruit was a Henry Rutgers Research Fellow, a HRRF (pronounced "herf"). WCSLs and HRRFs arrived in the department with higher salaries and more generous perks than faculty of approximately the same age who had been here for a while. One day a longtime history colleague who deeply resented the new state of affairs drew and circulated within the department a cartoon of a WCSL festooned as a monarch wearing an ermine gown that was forbidden to those of lesser rank. Given history's high ambitions, such distress could not be completely eliminated, but the department acknowledged it and tried to alleviate it by spending a lot of time in meetings discussing these prospective new hires and chewing over the rules that would govern responses to outside offers when our colleagues received them.

Another challenge that emerged from the University's growing emphasis upon scholarly publication was this: How should faculty members balance the demands of teaching and research? There was nearly unanimous agreement that these two core faculty responsibilities were complementary and mutually supportive. Teaching is enhanced when faculty bring to the classroom the latest information obtained through their research and, perhaps even more important, the excitement of discovery and the enthusiasm that comes from being at the forefront of new knowledge. Seeing a faculty member's enthusiasm, students soon share it. The reverse is also true: a faculty member's research is benefited by the questions that students ask and by the transmission of their own curiosity to their teachers. There are, to be sure, exceptions to these generalizations: the brilliant scholar who fails to communicate effectively with students and the non-scholar who proves to be a caring and successful teacher. But the principle that teaching and research are mutually beneficial was, and still is, widely accepted.

Complementary though they may be, both teaching and research are labor intensive and time consuming, and it is almost impossible to be doing both of them at once. A historian who is in the library archives carrying on research cannot simultaneously be lecturing in the classroom or holding office hours for her students. Younger faculty members who hear their tenure clocks ticking or who face daunting scholarly expectations for promotion to full professor feel the countervailing pressures acutely. And so questions emerge: How many courses should a faculty member teach each year? How often may a faculty member take a leave of absence from teaching in order to have a semester or a year in which to concentrate exclusively upon research and writing? These specific questions intensely occupied the Rutgers history department in the mid-1980s, and I took a leadership role in persuading the department to change its policies so that faculty could spend more time on research. By contacting friends and professional acquaintances in thirty top history departments across the country,

I accumulated data showing that virtually all of those departments expected faculty to teach four rather than five courses a year, two each semester. With help from my colleagues, I then analyzed our course offerings and showed how history could move to a four-course teaching load without sacrificing the essential characteristics of our curriculum or curtailing our students' educational opportunities. After a year of advance planning, the change became effective in the fall of 1987. I similarly succeeded in persuading the department to adopt a more generous policy regarding leaves of absence for research.

With the passage of a quarter century since adoption of these policies benefiting research at the possible expense of teaching, they may appear to have been less than noble, even misguided. But my colleagues and I who urged the department in these directions were committed and successful teachers as well as researchers; none of us had any intention of shortchanging our students. We were, moreover, ambitious not just for ourselves but also for Rutgers and for history at Rutgers. Our department and the University were on the cusp of academic distinction (more on that shortly), and research was the means through which such distinction was attained. The balance we now struck between teaching and research was consistent with the national norm for departments like ours, no more and no less. It accurately reflected the direction in which the finest American universities were going, and we were determined that history at Rutgers should be in that company. As I would discover within the next few years, fierce ambitions like ours burned in many, many departments at Rutgers. But for the moment I was totally focused on history.

In February 1987, as the three-year term of our department chairperson, John Gillis, was nearing an end, I asked my colleagues to give me the opportunity to serve in that role. Although department chairs were formally appointed by the dean of the Faculty of Arts and Sciences, the vote taken within the discipline was normally the decisive factor. Unlike previous chair elections in history, this one was uncontested. Despite having no competition for the job, I wrote and circulated to my faculty colleagues a campaign letter of six single-spaced pages covering every issue before the department: faculty recruitment, student enrollment, evaluations of teaching effectiveness, graduate education, incentives for research, departmental democracy, and more. I even devoted a paragraph to the value of social occasions within history, and, just like a candidate for president of his sixth-grade class, I promised "more parties." The final paragraph of my letter was personal. "I do want to be chairman of the history department," I wrote. "If I am chair you need never have a moment's doubt about where my loyalty lies or whom I am working for." My focus was on history. The rest of the University didn't matter. I won the election, such as it was, and became chair on July 1.

The very next month, my colleagues and I received the long-awaited report of an external review committee charged with evaluating history at Rutgers. It was then the University's practice to have every department reviewed on a regular basis, normally by three distinguished scholars in the field who would make a site visit and then prepare a comprehensive report and recommendations. This report was everything we had hoped it would be. "Our first and foremost observation," it said, "is that the department of history at Rutgers has reached a level of excellence which places it among the very best history departments in the nation." These were magical words that I knew would gain the attention of the University's leadership. The report praised the department as "a leader nationally in innovative scholarship" and cited especially its strengths in the burgeoning fields of American social and cultural history. The Rutgers "program of study in women's history is the best in the country," the report observed. It went on and on about our fine undergraduate and graduate programs ("the department has an enviable reputation for good teaching") and declared that "departmental governance is robustly democratic and collegial." After reading the report, Executive Vice President Alec Pond wrote to me in his inimitable style: "In full many a moon of reading external reviews, I have not had before anything approaching the academic satisfaction and institutional delight that the report of Professors Geyer, Ranum, and Griffith [the three reviewers] gives." I was a lucky guy: having done nothing as chair to deserve this wondrous report (which likely was drafted by its authors before I was even in office), I now would have the pleasure of leading a department that was sure to be rewarded for its excellence by the University administration. That much proved to be true. In another respect, however, the years of my chairmanship took me in completely unanticipated directions.

As chair I happily threw myself into leadership of the department's activities, including the recruitment of new faculty (a WCSL and a HRRF among them), evaluation of existing faculty for tenure and promotion, curriculum development, and much more. But by far the most rewarding initiative of my term as chair was proposing and establishing an interdisciplinary research institute called the Rutgers Center for Historical Analysis (RCHA). As my colleagues, chiefly Rudy Bell and Judy Walkowitz, and I developed the concept, the RCHA would identify a succession of historical themes on which the center would focus for two years at a time and would invite applications from prospective visiting scholars at all stages of their careers from across the humanities and social sciences. The chosen fellows would spend a semester or a year at Rutgers, during which they would carry on their research, present papers for discussion, and engage with each other and with faculty and students in history and in every other discipline that was relevant to that year's theme. A steady stream of top scholars applying innovative approaches to important historical subjects was sure to elevate further the intellectual life of our students and faculty and to enhance the department's growing reputation.

With this vision in mind, we moved quickly during the fall of 1987 and the winter of 1988, and, with approval from the department, placed a full-blown proposal and a budget for the RCHA before the dean, the provost, and the executive vice president. This was my first experience trying to do something that required support at the highest reaches of Rutgers, and it brought lots of stress but lots of satisfaction, too. My colleagues and I were optimistic from the beginning because so many of the University's ambitious initiatives in the 1980s had targeted the sciences; string theory and molecular biology were two of the most prominent of these. Knowing that faculty in the humanities and social sciences were uneasy about the privileging of the sciences, the University's top leaders were looking for a worthy project somewhere in our corner of Rutgers. The RCHA proposal, coming right on the heels of history's glowing external review, gave them just what they needed.

One evening that spring I was invited, along with a dozen other faculty members, to a dinner at President Bloustein's home. Alec Pond was there, too. Before we sat down to dinner, Alec whispered to me that at some point during the evening he would say, "Dick, please tell the president about your history center," and at that moment I would have one or two minutes to share with President Bloustein (and everyone else) our plans for the RCHA. Everything happened just as Alec said it would, and the end of the evening found me floating on air. Later in the year, the University administration approved the $300,000 annual budget we had requested for the RCHA and gave us the keys to a handsome Victorian building at 88 College Avenue, which has now been the center's home for more than twenty-five years. The required resources having been secured, planning and preparation proceeded throughout the 1988–89 academic year. Acting upon a proposal by our former chair John Gillis, the department chose "The Historical Construction of Identities" as the center's initial two-year theme and recruited the first class of distinguished visiting fellows. They arrived at Rutgers in the early fall of 1989, and successive cohorts of fellows have been coming ever since.

In the final years of the 1980s, not just the history department but also the whole University was experiencing significant change. By now, the effort to move Rutgers into "the front ranks of American research universities" (a phrase we overworked) was bringing notable achievements in many disciplines, but, just as in history, there were also sore feelings, rough edges, and plenty of areas where the University's policies and practices had not fully kept pace with its aspirations. The University's leaders, including Ed Bloustein, Alec Pond, Kenneth Wheeler (now senior vice president for academic affairs), and Paul L. Leath (the New Brunswick provost), knew this, and in the space of just a few years they undertook impressive steps to bring Rutgers's realities into line with its soaring ambitions. These efforts included a major reform of the faculty promotion process, a serious endeavor to strengthen faculty governance on the New Brunswick campus, and an unprecedented review of the composition of the University's student body. As the chair of a large and well-regarded academic department, I was invited to become involved in these initiatives and, in fact, was asked to provide leadership for several of them.

This was the moment at which I broke the campaign promise I had made to the history faculty to be loyal exclusively to our department and to work only for them. Although I do not remember my colleagues complaining, and there's no evidence that my activities hurt history, probably the reverse, my new assignments took me beyond history, beyond arts and sciences, and beyond New Brunswick. I now discovered that there was a whole big state university out there, exceptional faculty and students in dozens of fields, and many missions that transcended the ones I had come to love in Bishop House and Van Dyck Hall. For the first time in my own career, I began to encounter the full range of goals and dreams for Rutgers that I dimly remembered hearing my parents share with each other and with their friends when I was a child. Four Rutgers projects in which I became involved from 1988 to 1990 brought a turning point in my life.

In 1988, the state legislature and Governor Tom Kean placed before the voters a $350 million bond issue for the support of higher education facilities and a network of high technology centers throughout New Jersey. Colleges and universities desperately needed the funds. Approving the requisite legislation, Kean called it "the most important bill I'll ever sign as governor." Together Rutgers and the New Jersey Agricultural Experiment Station, located on our Cook campus and around the state, were slated for almost $107 million of the bond revenues. Libraries on all three campuses would be the biggest beneficiaries, but more than a dozen other projects for teaching and research in New Brunswick, Newark, and Camden would also gain funding if voters approved the measure. Newspapers, politicians, corporations, trade organizations, and chambers of commerce across the state endorsed its passage, and almost everyone regarded the bond issue's prospects as very good. In April 1988, even before the legislation was approved, President Bloustein asked me to chair the faculty and staff committee to promote support for the bond issue; I suppose he felt there had to be such a committee at Rutgers. I was pleased to accept. In no way, however, was my work or that of the committee essential to the bond issue's approval. Tom Kean and Ed Bloustein, together with political and business leaders around New Jersey, did the heavy lifting by convincingly linking the bonds to job creation and economic development. I chaired faculty and staff meetings on all three campuses, organized phonathons, distributed flyers, and helped develop three- and seven-minute speeches that faculty and staff could deliver in their hometowns and community organizations whenever they had an opportunity to do so. On November 8, the bond issue passed by a wide margin, and, despite the limits of my role, I enjoyed the taste of involvement with a result that was very important for New Jersey and for Rutgers. Not until 2012 would the state enact another higher education bond issue.

Back on campus while the bond issue was pending, the Bloustein administration undertook a major effort to improve the faculty promotion process, which was then commonly regarded as contentious, secretive, and overly complex—"byzantine" we called it. The previous year, the president had received the report of an external review committee from which he had requested recommendations for bringing the promotion process into alignment with the University's now-elevated academic ambitions. The committee, chaired by Dale R. Corson, the former president of Cornell University, issued a compelling critique of a system in which many departments and deans shirked their responsibility for difficult personnel decisions and shifted the burden of making tough calls to the highest level of review, the Promotion Review Committee, unpopularly called the Summit Committee. Faculty, the report said, "must take responsibility for making the critical judgments about appointments and promotions in their own field." The report also faulted the Rutgers promotion process for its excessive convolution and for the paucity of communication up and down the promotion approval chain. In March 1988, President Bloustein appointed a Special Committee on Promotions to consider the external report and make recommendations for changing and simplifying the process. The committee was chaired by David Mechanic, whose shirt-sleeved refusal to prevent ballot-box stuffing in a history department election I still admired, and included fifteen of the University's most distinguished faculty members from all three campuses and a wide range of academic disciplines. I was amazed to find myself among them. As the committee deliberated throughout the spring and early summer of 1988, I played a modest role appropriate to my relatively junior status, but I relished the opportunity to learn from the likes of Elihu Abrahams, Daniel Gorenstein, and G. Terence Wilson, all named professors in top departments. Like the other members of the committee, I was proud of our final recommendations to the president, but mainly I was appreciative just for the opportunity to be there.

Next came a committee to which I made significant contributions, the New Brunswick Committee on Faculty Governance, which I chaired from October 1988 to March 1989 and whose report I wrote. An accrediting team from the Middle States Association of Colleges and Schools had recently faulted the University for having "no effective, credible, and clearly-defined structure for faculty governance at Rutgers–New Brunswick, comparable to what one would find at most major research universities." Provost Paul Leath appointed a group of twenty-four professors to study the problem and make recommendations for strengthening faculty governance on academic issues where the faculty's voice ought to be authoritative, such as curriculum, faculty personnel, and graduation requirements, as well as in other areas where faculty opinion should be heard and respected, if not necessarily decisive. After holding hearings, surveying deans, institute directors, and faculty, and accumulating a vast amount of information about the existing state of faculty governance, the committee identified structural problems deriving from "the unusual complexity of Rutgers–New Brunswick" and from a "culture in which many faculty regard administrators as adversaries and in which some administrators appear to have disdain for faculty opinion." Throughout the committee's work, my father, who had a great deal of experience in this area, provided wonderful, confidential advice to me. I still have a file of the memos he wrote. One of his missives began: "The responses to the faculty questionnaires present a picture of alienation, mistrust, and cynicism.

Only at the department level do faculty feel involved and efficacious."
He was right about that, and he was also enormously helpful in suggesting remedies for the problems we were identifying. The committee
recognized that there would be no "quick fix," and indeed there was not,
but we made a compelling case for establishing an elected New Brunswick Faculty Council, a body that still exists today and provides a regular means for expressing faculty views on the most important issues
at Rutgers.

Last among the four projects that drew me from history into the
larger University was the Committee on the Character and Composition of the Future Undergraduate Student Body, which I chaired
during its overly long life from October 1988 to September 1990. Up
until now, the University had given little systematic thought to the
goals and values of an undergraduate admissions process that was
appropriate for the kind of institution Rutgers was becoming: a distinguished, multi-mission state university. Senior Vice President Kenneth
Wheeler had long been interested in this subject, and he charged our
committee with exploring it and making recommendations. This we
did. Today, a quarter century later, the committee's recommendations
appear unremarkable and, indeed, the issues we grappled with have
become entirely familiar: how to communicate Rutgers's strengths to
the very best high school students and enroll more of them, how to
attract more out-of-state students to the University, and how to maintain and enhance the diversity of the student body. For me, however,
the committee's work was exciting and revealing: I grasped an essential component of the University's mission that I had scarcely encountered before.

By the end of the 1980s, I was married—to a highly regarded faculty
member in the history department—and together we had two young
children. Both my wife and I were trying to balance the demands of
family and profession, and I was about to make our balancing acts
even more difficult. I had not planned to change careers at this point,
but that's what happened. Although I had been promoted to full professor in 1985, my research and scholarship were stalled. Working on
what I hoped would be a big and important book on the history of

political corruption in America, I had done a good deal of the research and given some conference papers, but none of the book was written, and, truthfully, I was having trouble deciding what its focus really was going to be. My growing activity, first in the history department and then in the University, took time away from the book or, perhaps more accurately, gave me an excuse not to write it. Without fully realizing it, I had gotten myself onto a pathway leading from a professor's career to an administrator's. And the transition came quickly and unexpectedly. In March 1989, when the dean of the Faculty of Arts and Sciences (FAS), Tilden Edelstein, accepted a senior position in academic leadership at the State University of New York at Stony Brook, Provost Leath asked me to become the acting dean of the FAS, and I agreed. Our understanding was that a national search would be conducted to fill the position on a permanent basis, and I could be a candidate for it if I wanted. I had been chair of the history department for less than two years. My father said to me that the position of dean of arts and sciences was the lousiest (he actually used a stronger word) job in a university, and that the only reason to take it was if you wanted to become a president. Ambitious though I was, my ambition was in history, not administration—or at least it had been up until this point. So I became acting dean and, a year later, dean, and I had made my career transition. As always, my father's words remained in my head.

The year in which my deanship began, 1989, was momentous for Rutgers. In February, President Bloustein proudly announced that we had been invited to join the Association of American Universities. "With membership in this organization," he said, "Rutgers . . . now stand[s] with the finest company in American higher education." The president's untiring efforts to transform the University had been validated in exactly the way he hoped they would. Our invitation to join the AAU provoked excitement within the Rutgers community, even giddiness. A decade of remarkable academic progress and of growing distinction in many disciplines had brought greater recognition to the University than it had ever before received. But the joy was short-lived. Within just a few months, scarcity, conflict, and sorrow darkened the Rutgers scene. After years of adequate funding by the government of

New Jersey, the beginnings of an economic recession now led to significant budget cuts for the state's colleges and universities (as well as for most other public services). Although we did not know it at the time, these reductions launched an era of declining state support for higher education that has continued to the present day. To counter the impact of the budget cuts, Rutgers raised student tuition by 13 percent in 1989, almost double the increase of the previous year. That action, together with subsequent tuition hikes, gave a nascent group of activist students the galvanizing issue they needed to become a significant and divisive factor in the University's life. Then on December 9, Ed Bloustein, the most accomplished president in Rutgers's history, died of a heart attack at age sixty-four. The University was thrust into mourning and into an unwelcome and uncertain leadership transition.

These were the circumstances in which I became dean of the largest faculty at Rutgers. Inevitably the FAS was deeply affected by budget cuts, student protests, and the passage of leadership. But the arts and sciences faculty existed to some degree in a world of its own, a world that for all its difficulties offered greater satisfaction and fulfillment than outward conditions would appear to justify. At least that's how I experienced it.

The budget cuts were unrelenting and excruciating. Even before I was formally in the post of acting dean, I was conferring and conspiring with the dean's office staff and with the FAS department chairs to find ways of coping with the loss of millions of dollars and dozens of faculty and staff positions, while minimizing the damage to the departments and their students. Despite our efforts, the budget cuts were felt everywhere: in the abandonment of many searches for new faculty, in the cancellation of hundreds of courses, and in the postponement of equipment purchases and facility renovations. Every year I was dean, more cuts followed, and the FAS struggled just to offer the courses our students required and, through the recruitment of at least a few new faculty members, to maintain the academic progress to which we had become accustomed at Rutgers in the 1980s. Most of the burden fell upon the department chairs, who formed close bonds with each other and with me. I made some early decisions: that I myself would understand the FAS budget thoroughly and that I would share complete budgetary information with the department chairs. At first, to take one example, French was shocked to discover how much money physics had, with its multiple revenue streams, but, after the shock wore off, it became clear that French and physics, and all the rest of us, were really together in the same predicament. Yes, physics had more money, but it needed more for its expensive laboratories. Each discipline was struggling in its own way to teach students and carry on research.

The budgetary sunshine, the camaraderie born of shared pain, and even the gallows humor that punctuated our meetings—all these things contributed to my discovery of the unity of the arts and sciences and the genuineness of the community of disciplines that comprise the fundamental store of human knowledge. Geologists and philosophers may go about their work in different ways and within unique settings, but both are seeking to acquire new knowledge and to share that knowledge with their students, some of whom will ultimately repay the debt by rejecting what they were taught and imparting new truths to students of their own. This is an ideal, of course, but great endeavors rest upon ideals. In 1989, I became an arts and sciences believer, and I have been one ever since.

Within the FAS dean's office, we tried to learn everything we could about where the money was and how to stretch it. Rutgers had strict rules distinguishing the permanent salary dollars that were associated with faculty and staff positions from the one-time dollars that were available for the purchase of equipment, supplies, travel, or whatever. In principle, the two kinds of dollars could not be mixed or mingled, but in a budget crisis it just seemed sensible to put every dollar to its best possible use, no matter where that dollar had originated. This required considerable ingenuity within the thicket of Rutgers rules and regulations. If we had been engaged in organized crime, our transactions might have been called money laundering, but we weren't, so we gave it other names. One morning we learned that a senior faculty member in the mathematics department had passed away. Within the dean's office, we did not know him well, but he had a good reputation, and we spoke for a few moments about Rutgers's loss of a fine man. That done, four of us exclaimed in unison, "How much money is on his line?"

The two projects on which we worked hardest with the available money were recruiting and retaining faculty and protecting the quality of our students' education. As dean I learned that practically every department chair had the same passion that I did. Those who led sociology and chemistry were just as committed to their disciplines as I had been to history. Since the most important way to strengthen any department was by appointing outstanding new faculty members, department chairs were continually seeking authorization from the dean's office to launch faculty searches. Many considerations went into the decision to approve a search, including the extent of student demand for courses in that area, the availability of dollars, and the likelihood of making an appointment that would truly advance the distinction of Rutgers. Such likelihood was always increased if the department was prepared to exploit any comparative advantages it possessed, and, indeed, the FAS departments were eager to do so. Some examples will clarify the point. The progressive downsizing of nearby Bell Labs and the consequent availability of excellent Bell researchers who were seeking new employment gave our science departments the opportunity to recruit faculty colleagues who could accept positions at Rutgers without having to uproot their families. The University's proximity to New York gave many departments a chance to attract faculty who wanted to live in or near the great city; within arts and sciences, this was especially helpful for the language and literature disciplines, which benefited from New York's prominence as a literary center. (Outside the FAS, this same comparative advantage proved fortunate for the musical, theatrical, and fine arts departments at Rutgers, which have always drawn talented faculty from the arts communities of New York.) Newer academic areas such as women's studies and cultural studies found their comparative advantage in the University's reputation for daring scholarship at the cutting edge; subjects of research that had not yet reached the mainstream were often welcome at Rutgers. By employing strategies like these, the FAS made many outstanding faculty appointments. In a difficult budgetary environment, the exploitation of comparative advantages proved to be even more valuable than money laundering.

One FAS department was an outlier, not because it rejected making new appointments but because the members of its faculty were at war with each other. In 1987, the University's central administration had made a decision to invest in the growing field of molecular biology by transforming the small biochemistry department into a research powerhouse. Renamed the department of molecular biology and biochemistry (MBB), it was slated to have a star scientist recruited to Rutgers as its chairperson; to align itself with the University's Waksman Institute of Microbiology, some of whose researchers would also become MBB faculty members; and to appoint additional new faculty with strong research credentials. After the search for a department chair had gone on for nearly three years, the University enticed a distinguished virologist at the Memorial Sloan Kettering Cancer Center to come to Rutgers in that role, effective September 1990.

From the moment of his arrival, the new chair was beset by opposition from several longtime members of the department who resented what they regarded as the University's high-handed transformation of their discipline. Before long, the dissenters became closely allied with several biochemistry faculty members at Cook College (the former College of Agriculture), and together they objected to everything done by the new chair and by faculty who were loyal to him. The points of contention included the undergraduate curriculum, the departmental bylaws, the allocation of lab space, who could participate in department meetings, and even office furniture. The new chair, with his medical school background, may not have handled these issues as collegially as he could have, but in fairness he had opponents who were angry, relentless, and sometimes crazed. As their dean, I was drawn into the warfare by both sides. On some days I would receive a fax from the dissenters, then shortly afterward a rebuttal from the chair, then their reply to him, and it went on and on. To my deep frustration, I was unable to resolve the controversy, which persisted without relief throughout my time as dean. Tensions between the old and new

Rutgers could be found in many quarters of the University, but the scope and the venom of the war within MBB were utterly unique.

Teaching was the place where the budget cuts were felt most acutely. Then as now, many Rutgers courses were taught by untenured part-time lecturers, whose appointment renewals became especially vulnerable when departmental budgets were sliced. Each new semester brought a struggle to identify resources with which to meet our students' course demands, and we took pride in numbers demonstrating the measure of our success, despite the budget cuts. Because the undergraduates were actually enrolled in the colleges rather than in the FAS, I had less contact with students than I would have liked (except in my own courses, which I continued to teach as dean) and thus less access to their inevitable concerns and complaints about course offerings and availability. To address that problem I created the FAS student executive committee, composed of representative students from each department, and met with it regularly. Our meetings scarcely solved all the problems, but they provided me with far greater understanding than I otherwise would have had of the academic experiences and problems that our students encountered. One concern I heard about but, as FAS dean, could do nothing to address was the frustrating—and, to students, inexplicable—variation among the different colleges' curriculum requirements. More than a decade would pass before I had an opportunity to tackle that problem.

The members of the FAS student executive committee were peaceable and courteous, but other Rutgers students were angry about the tuition increases and the cancellation of courses. Carrying forward the long tradition of Rutgers activism, the aggrieved students began their protests in the spring of 1989 and soon organized themselves as the Campaign for an Affordable Rutgers Education (CARE). Over the next several years, they disrupted Board of Governors meetings when tuition was on the agenda, occupied University buildings, and made themselves widely seen and heard on the streets and across campus. CARE demanded a tuition freeze, three seats for students on the Board of Governors, and a tenured faculty appointment for the renowned African American playwright, poet, and book author Amiri

Baraka. The latter demand, voiced in the spring of 1990, was directed at me.

Soon after I became acting dean in 1989, the chair of the English department, Barry Qualls, informed me that Baraka, then a visiting professor in the department, would likely be considered by the English faculty for a permanent position as a full professor. I certainly knew of Baraka's literary achievements, had read *Blues People*, his acclaimed study of black music, when I was in college (Baraka's name was then LeRoi Jones), and had no concerns about his possible appointment. As things turned out, however, the full professors in the English department decided against Baraka, and all hell broke loose. Baraka unleashed a tirade comparing the English faculty to Nazis ("Ivy League Goebbels"), to the ruling whites of apartheid South Africa ("these academic Boers"), and to members of the Ku Klux Klan ("the Klaven"). His supporters, who soon included the students of CARE, took to the streets to demand that I override the department and appoint Baraka as a tenured faculty member. Of course, I had no power to do that.

As the furor over Baraka subsided, my office began collaborating with about a half dozen FAS department chairs on a multidisciplinary search for African American faculty who would study and teach African American subjects. We advertised in journals such as the *Chronicle of Higher Education* and *Black Issues in Higher Education* that we were looking for "a group of teachers and scholars with related interests in all aspects of African-American history and culture." And we were pretty forthright in announcing our intention to appoint African Americans to these positions, which is something you would not and could not do today. At that time, however, "minority" mainly meant "black," and our decision to focus on the recruitment of African American faculty met with considerable acclaim and encountered no criticism. Admittedly the words I wrote to the chairs of the participating humanities and social science departments in the summer of 1990 do not stand up very well today: "Although not all scholars of the African-American experience are Black and not all Black scholars study African-American subjects, there is a sufficient convergence to encourage us to try to meet two very real needs. . . . This initiative is *one* avenue for achieving both goals." But the concept looked good back then, and, believing that a more diverse university would also be a better one, we made a success of it.

The basic idea behind a cooperative, multidisciplinary search was that we would have greater success in recruiting outstanding faculty if the candidates for these positions knew they would be coming to Rutgers with like-minded colleagues in other departments besides their own. To the extent possible, we arranged for candidates in the different disciplines to meet each other, as well as to get to know diverse faculty already at Rutgers. I hosted a reception in the dean's office for each candidate who came to campus for an interview and invited members of all the participating departments to come and meet our visitor. The camaraderie that the chairs and I had forged through the budget crisis now pervaded the multidisciplinary search. A lot of communication went on between the departments, and some friendly rivalry emerged, too. "Has your African American candidate been to campus yet?" chairs asked each other. As a result of all this, from 1990 to 1992, we appointed ten outstanding African American faculty members. Many years later, when I was president, we utilized an appropriately updated version of this approach for a cluster hiring initiative that also brought a significant number of diverse faculty to Rutgers. As the FAS dean, I was prouder of this initiative than any other.

Despite our relentless budget cutting, I loved being dean and felt pride in my staff and in the department chairs for our collective good management during tough times and for the successes we enjoyed in protecting the educational programs and in recruiting excellent new faculty. But I had become ambitious for a wider sphere in which to provide academic leadership and was keeping my eyes open for such opportunities, none of which seemed to be available at Rutgers. President Francis L. Lawrence had become president in the fall of 1990, and a year and a half later, although I had made many efforts to engage him, I hardly knew the president. As far as I could tell, few deans or faculty really did.

Sometime late in 1991, I became a candidate for the position of provost and vice chancellor for academic affairs at the University of North

Carolina at Chapel Hill, and the following March Chancellor Paul Hardin offered me the job. I'll never forget his phone call, which I took in my dean's office. "How soon can you come?" Paul asked, and I said very soon. A few days later we agreed that I would start on June 1, 1992. Expressed in crass career terms, this was a double jump for me: from dean to chief academic officer and from a very good state university to one of the nation's finest and most revered institutions. I was overjoyed to receive this chance, but I felt guilty about leaving Rutgers. It was, after all, my childhood home and was still my parents' home. For sixteen years, from the time I had arrived as a lucky assistant professor in 1976 until this moment in 1992, Rutgers had afforded me one opportunity after another to teach and write and lead. I knew that and felt very grateful. That spring, as I moved with my wife and our two young children, now aged seven and three, to the lovely southern town of Chapel Hill, I had no idea whether, except for visits to see my parents, I would ever come home again. But I remember hoping that I would.

A DIFFICULT FIRST
YEAR AS RUTGERS
PRESIDENT

By the summer of 2002, I had been gone from Rutgers for ten years—three in Chapel Hill as provost followed by seven in Seattle as president of the University of Washington. At UNC's flagship campus, I served as the chief academic officer of a self-confident institution that was cherished within its own state and esteemed around the country and the world. To be sure, UNC–Chapel Hill had its share of challenges, roughly similar to the issues that faced all of America's top universities in the 1990s, but no problems would fundamentally erode its excellence or diminish the allure that it held for North Carolinians and for men and women from well beyond the state's boundaries. I was proud to be there, and the university flourished academically on my watch—just as it did before I arrived and after I left.

Becoming provost in the spring of 1992, I was thrust immediately into a growing quarrel between African American student activists and my boss, Chancellor Paul Hardin, over the students' demand for a "free-standing" facility to house the Black Cultural Center (BCC). In my three years at Chapel Hill, probably the most useful thing I did was to help defuse that quarrel and channel enthusiasm for the BCC in positive directions. Originally established in 1988 and situated in cramped quarters in the student union building, the BCC had been renamed in 1991 for a charismatic African American faculty member, Sonja Haynes Stone, who died that year, still in her early fifties and the idol of her students. I never met Professor Stone, although I became friendly with her parents. Several months before my arrival, a hundred or more students had gathered at the university's main administration building to demand construction of a centrally located freestanding facility for the Sonja Haynes Stone Black Cultural Center as a sign of respect for black culture, for Stone, and for black students at the university. (The students insisted that it had to be the *Black* Cultural Center, not the *African American* Cultural Center.) To Hardin and to many other well-meaning white liberals in the community, a freestanding BCC smacked of separatism and segregation. As a newcomer to the scene, I saw the matter somewhat differently and became sympathetic to the students' goal. To me there was nothing inherently separatist in idealistic young African Americans asking their university visibly to affirm their culture and history. Certainly the university affirmed the culture and history of white North Carolinians.

Paul Hardin and I quickly developed a close and mutually supportive relationship. I admired him enormously as a university leader, and he evidently placed confidence in me. Secure in my relationship with Paul, I set myself to the task of persuading him to accept a freestanding BCC. This took time, however, and the quarrel with the students worsened in the fall of 1992. In early September, several hundred of them assembled outside the chancellor's residence to demand the facility, and a few days later an even larger number paraded to his office. Several black football players, who were popular and prominent on campus, took leading roles in the protest marches. Not long afterward, filmmaker Spike Lee, a relative of Professor Stone, dramatically upped the visibility of the issue by coming to town and leading a rally of five thousand chanting for a freestanding BCC. As the drama unfolded throughout the months ahead, other high-profile visitors arrived in Chapel Hill to offer support for the cause. These headliners included

Jesse Jackson and, to my surprise, Amiri Baraka, with whom I had a brief but decidedly pleasant conversation about the BCC.

Even before Spike Lee's visit to Chapel Hill, Paul Hardin changed the conversation by signaling a new openness to a freestanding BCC and by becoming directly involved in resolving the dispute. His principled leadership in the face of hurtful criticism framed the controversy from this point forward and gave me a model for managing university crises that I would always remember. Paul announced that he was asking me to form and chair a working group to study the situation and make recommendations to him and the board of trustees about whether the BCC should have its own separate building and where it should be located. Among the working group's most engaged members were Deloris Jordan, the mother of former UNC basketball star Michael Jordan, and Harvey Gantt, a Chapel Hill alumnus who had been the first African American mayor of Charlotte. Paul and I wanted some of the activist students to be represented on the working group, but they were still distrustful of us and declined to serve. Soon after its formation, the working group reached a consensus that the university community should put to rest the debilitating controversy, and we endorsed the concept of a freestanding facility. Hardin publicly expressed his support for that position, and the crisis waned—for the moment. The working group henceforth met jointly with the BCC advisory board, a body of African American students and faculty who had long been the center's strongest advocates and supporters. I gladly handed the gavel to Professor Harry Amana, who ably chaired our joint meetings during the months ahead.

Together the working group and the advisory board tried to address all of the most important questions about the Black Cultural Center: the programs it would house, its relationship to academic departments, and its architectural design. Agreement slowly emerged around most of these issues, but one big question remained undecided and highly controversial: Where would the BCC be sited? The students favored a symbolically prominent location on the main campus quadrangle right next to the university library. Others favored a nearby site adjacent to the university's iconic bell tower. My working group believed that either of these two locations would be acceptable, but the students and some of their faculty supporters disagreed. By April 1993, the quarrel over the site had escalated to the point that students staged a sit-in for two weeks at the university's main administration building (that's when Jesse Jackson showed up), and sixteen of them were arrested for refusing to leave Paul Hardin's office. The charges against the students were later dropped. It was anguishing for me to be at odds with students whose ally I felt I had been since arriving in Chapel Hill. That July, the university's board of trustees voted to locate the Black Cultural Center near the bell tower, on the site the students didn't want. BCC activists reluctantly accepted the trustees' locational decision a few months later, and the planning and fund raising for the center went forward. The next year, I obtained a lead gift for the project, a $500,000 contribution from NationsBank chairman Hugh McColl. With many more such gifts in hand, and with generous support from the university itself, ground was broken for a 44,500-square-foot facility in 2001, and a little more than three years later the community joyfully dedicated a majestic and, yes, freestanding building for the (slightly renamed) Sonja Haynes Stone Center for Black Culture and History. I was now long gone from Chapel Hill, but I rejoiced with pride from afar.

Very far. On September 1, 1995, I became president of the University of Washington. The preeminent higher education institution in the Northwest, the UW ranked first among public universities in America in research support from the federal government, a reflection of its extraordinary strength in many fields of science and technology. Perhaps the most outstanding part of the UW was its school of medicine, a truly remarkable engine of biomedical research and the predominant provider of medical education for the entire region from Wyoming to Alaska. The medical school was also unusually collaborative with the rest of the university, including arts and sciences, engineering, law, and, of course, the other health science disciplines.

One story about the UW's research prowess is worth relating, both because it illustrates the excellence of that institution and because I ended up telling the story again and again as president of Rutgers. In 2001, following initial completion of the vast human genome project, the National Human Genome Research Institute, a component of the National Institutes of Health, conducted a nationwide competition to encourage the advancement of "new, innovative genomic approaches to address important biological and biomedical research problems." When the first three awards were announced, the UW had garnered two of them, and Yale got the third. Both of the UW awards were distinctly interdisciplinary: one involved collaboration between medicine and engineering and the other between medicine and arts and sciences. As president, I had nothing to do with these successes; they were owed to the UW's superb scientists and to a spirit of support for interdisciplinary research that the university had nourished for decades. I told that story in New Jersey to argue for locating medicine within the same university as engineering and arts and sciences and all the other disciplines, a goal that was prominently discussed and debated during my first year as president of Rutgers but not achieved until my last.

One area where I helped make a difference as UW president was racial diversity. In 1998, the voters of the state of Washington were asked to consider Initiative 200 prohibiting government entities, including public universities, from giving preferential treatment based on race, sex, color, ethnicity, or national origin. I spoke out against the initiative, at least to the extent the university's lawyers would let me, by pointing with pride to the UW's multicultural student body and to the educational benefits of diversity for everyone who studied there. But the voters overwhelmingly approved it. The results of the initiative were immediately bad for diversity, just as we had anticipated. If you had been a UW freshman in the fall of 1998, just before the passage of Initiative 200, approximately one in eleven of your classmates would have been African American, Hispanic/Latino, or Native American. By the very next year, that ratio had dropped to only one in eighteen.

Forced to abandon the consideration of race in admissions decisions, commonly called affirmative action, the UW mustered an aggressive, multipronged strategy of recruitment and outreach. Faculty, students, and alumni fanned out across the state to talk with disadvantaged students in community colleges, high schools, and middle schools. We invited many of these students to campus, showed them the exciting educational opportunities they would have if they enrolled at the UW, and explained how they could obtain the financial aid they needed. The application for admission was rewritten to enable students to describe their personal experiences with diversity and adversity (experiences that people of any color can have), so this information could be used in a holistic evaluation of each applicant. Within five years, UW student diversity returned to its pre–Initiative 200 levels, and a recent study confirmed that the UW has maintained that success to the present day.

During the decade I spent away from Rutgers in Chapel Hill and Seattle, I had the opportunity to learn and apply university leadership skills: connecting with the many constituencies having a stake in the institution, communicating with public officials upon whose support the university depends, strengthening the ties between the institution and its local communities, raising funds from individuals and foundations, identifying and appointing outstanding members of a leadership team, modeling open and transparent administrative practices, and expressing university goals in inspiring words. I learned that while academic initiatives are usually best left to the schools and their faculties, there are a number of important areas where leadership from the central administration is essential to progress. These include the development of interdisciplinary programs, the internationalization of the university, the application of new technologies to teaching and research, and the racial and ethnic diversification of students, faculty, and staff. At both UNC and the UW, I saw at firsthand the value of successful big-time intercollegiate athletics, although I should have taken more time to appreciate the importance of close presidential attention to athletics. The chances are good that I would have learned—or, in the case of athletics, failed to learn—these same lessons almost as well (or badly) at any fine public research university where I happened to serve between 1992 and 2002. In addition, however, I acquired two particular convictions that Chapel Hill and Seattle were notably capable of imparting. First is the importance of having an academic medical center located within the same university as all the other educational disciplines and fully collaborative with them. Second is the emotional value of campuses and buildings that are beautiful, to which students and faculty are powerfully drawn, and where they feel safe, secure, and inspired. UNC–Chapel Hill and the UW took enormous pride in creating and maintaining such campuses, and from those physical surroundings I learned a lesson that I brought with me back to Rutgers. And now I must tell the challenging tale of how it happened that I returned home.

In early February 2002, Fran Lawrence announced his decision to step down as president of Rutgers, and Gene O'Hara, chair of the Board of Governors, made known the process through which the board would choose Lawrence's successor. I probably learned of these developments from my parents and from Rutgers friends soon after the news became public, but I didn't think much about them until May when the chair of the presidential search committee, John Colaizzi, dean of the Ernest Mario School of Pharmacy, got in touch with me to inquire confidentially about my possible interest in the position. I remembered John well and fondly from our days as Rutgers deans together back in the late 1980s and early 1990s. The vice chair of the search committee also called me. He was someone I knew even better than I knew John—my old history colleague, Lloyd Gardner, the one who taught his students about global war and peace while I was teaching mine about meat inspection. By this time, newspapers in New Jersey were beginning to speculate about possible candidates for the Rutgers presidency, and my name came up in most of the articles. There was even a report in one of the Seattle newspapers about Rutgers and me. By July, seriously interested in the Rutgers position, I accepted an invitation to visit New Jersey to talk with Gene O'Hara and John Colaizzi, and in mid-September I flew eastward again, this time to meet with the full presidential search committee. At some point in September, a delegation from the Rutgers Board of Governors visited me in Seattle. All of these contacts were supposedly confidential, although numerous leaks about the search somehow made their way into the newspapers. As my conversations with Rutgers became more serious, I informed Gerald Grinstein, chair of the UW board of regents, about them. Jerry thanked me for telling him and, so far as I know, kept the news to himself.

Now the story becomes more difficult. Soon after my September meetings with the search committee and the delegation from the Board of Governors, Gene O'Hara phoned me in Seattle and offered me the presidency of Rutgers. As a step in that direction, Gene asked me to return to New Jersey to meet with Governor Jim McGreevey at his home in Princeton, a meeting that became the lively Drumthwacket encounter I described at the beginning of this book. From that occasion, I derived admiration for the governor's energy and intelligence and, over dinner that evening, relayed my observations to a group of Rutgers board members. They, in turn, urged me to accept the Rutgers presidency. Returning to Seattle the next day, I thought long and hard about the choice before me and was deeply uncertain what to do.

But I knew I needed to make a decision soon—and I did: the worst decision of my life. By this time, old friends from Rutgers who had gotten wind of the situation were sending me e-mail messages asking me to accept the presidency or, in some cases happily believing that I had already done so, welcoming me home. Alas, I should have listened to them, but I went the other way. On the afternoon of Sunday, September 29, I phoned Gene O'Hara and, with emotion and with thanks, declined his offer of the Rutgers presidency. I gave him two truthful reasons for my decision. First, I was happy in my work at the University of Washington and believed that I had much more to accomplish there in the years ahead. And second, I had become alarmed about the impending report of Governor McGreevey's Commission on Health Science, Education, and Training, a report that was expected to recommend a radical restructuring of higher education in New Jersey, with uncertain implications for the position I had been offered. Gene accepted my decision graciously, but he was clearly disappointed. A week later, acting on behalf of the Board of Governors, he announced suspension of the search for president while the university community took time to examine the implications of the commission report. He also announced that Norman Samuels, formerly provost of the University's campus in Newark, would become acting president. Gene thanked and discharged the presidential search committee. I was having uneasy second thoughts about turning down the presidency of Rutgers but felt that, all things considered, I had made the right decision.

Then the hammer fell. On the afternoon of Friday, October 18, at the end of a long day of meetings of the UW board of regents, the chairman of the board, Jerry Grinstein, came to my office, closed the door, and told me that the board had lost confidence in me because I had had an affair with a university employee. I could stay on as a tenured faculty member if I wished, but my presidency had to wind down quickly with my resignation sometime in the next few weeks. I was humiliated and frightened. To this day, I don't know what the board members actually knew about the affair or whether they had other unstated reasons for ending my presidency. But they had lost confidence in me, and Jerry's stated reason, the affair, was true. I drove home, shared the life-changing news with my wife, who was deeply hurt and enraged at me, and spent the weekend in sorrow and terror not knowing what to do. On Sunday, following a phone conversation with Jerry Grinstein, I called Gene O'Hara and asked if I could still become president of Rutgers. I did not tell Gene the story of what happened at the University of Washington; I just said that, after living for three weeks with my decision to decline the Rutgers presidency, I had come to feel, both in my heart and my head, that I had made the wrong choice and that I hoped there was a chance I could still have the position he had offered me in September. I was humiliated then, and, as I write these words now, I am humiliated again to reveal that I asked Gene for the Rutgers presidency without telling him the truth about the circumstances in which I was doing so.

Gene seemed pleased by my call, but he was noncommittal. The Board of Governors, he told me, had a retreat scheduled for the next day. He would share my news with the board members and then call me on Monday afternoon with their answer. It was a long twenty-four hours. On Monday, Gene called and on behalf of the board again offered me the Rutgers presidency. This time I joyfully accepted. He told me that the University's Boards of Governors and Trustees would meet jointly and publicly, as required, to approve my appointment on

Friday, October 25, just four days hence. We agreed that my term of office would begin on December 1, 2002.

The next four days were a blur. I told my children that the UW board of regents had asked me to resign, but not why, and that I had accepted the presidency of Rutgers. I told the same to two of my closest associates in the UW president's office, and I told them why. I finished negotiating my compensation package with a representative of the firm that had assisted the Rutgers Board of Governors with the search and made plans for my family and me to fly to New Jersey on Thursday, in time for the joint board meeting and big announcement on Friday. And I had the helicopter conversation with Governor McGreevey. I still do not know why he was so angry with me that day or so opposed to my becoming president of Rutgers. He could not have known the circumstances in which I was leaving the UW, and, even if he had known, that would not explain the feelings he expressed. My best guess is that he now realized that Rutgers was going to give him trouble over the health science commission report and that I was going to be an agent of that trouble. If that's what he was thinking, he was right, but the story is complicated and will be told shortly.

On Friday morning, the Boards of Governors and Trustees formally selected me as the nineteenth president of Rutgers University, and I accepted with gratitude, pride—and submerged guilt. My family was present for the occasion, of course, and my father sat directly behind me as I addressed the boards. He had suggested to me the words with which I opened my remarks: "It's good to be home." Governor McGreevey's office issued a friendly and supportive statement on his behalf (and the governor would later speak graciously at my inauguration). My chief memory of the day is the remarkable joy with which I was greeted by faculty, staff, and students. Old colleagues exuberantly expressed their gladness that I had returned to Rutgers, and others who knew me only by reputation welcomed me warmly. The next day all the newspapers in New Jersey featured glowing stories about me and my Rutgers roots.

In the years that have passed since the fall of 2002, I have often wished that I had accepted Gene O'Hara's offer when I first had it.

So much that followed for Rutgers and for me would have been different and better. But that's the easy part—wishing I had said yes when I said no. More troubling is thinking about what happened next. What if I had told Gene the full truth about why I changed my mind? Would the Board of Governors still have offered me the presidency of Rutgers? We will never know. But I was wrong to conceal the truth. I should have told it and accepted the consequences.

In the days and months after my appointment as president, there was little time or reason to dwell on what might have been. I was grateful to have this opportunity, happy to be home in New Jersey, and ambitious for Rutgers. I did all the usual new-president things: greeting students in the dining halls, traveling about the campuses to meet with faculty and staff, hosting receptions for alumni around the state, and addressing the legislature in Trenton. On April 13, 2003, I delivered my inaugural address expressing an aspiration "to move Rutgers to the top tier of America's public research universities" but giving even more attention to the ever-elusive goal of becoming fully and completely New Jersey's state university. My title was "Affirming Our Values—Serving Our State." Like any new president, besides talking I did a lot of listening, and in consultation with deans and faculty began to identify transformative steps that would make Rutgers an even better university. In this endeavor, I was wonderfully fortunate to gain a brilliant top teammate, Philip Furmanski, a biologist whom I recruited from New York University to serve as executive vice president for academic affairs. Phil arrived on September 1, 2003, and for the next eight years we collaborated on a varied and adventuresome academic agenda, a story I'll tell in the next chapter. Little on that agenda got done during my first year as president, however, not only because I was still listening and learning, but also because the report of Governor McGreevey's Commission on Health Science, Education, and Training contained a momentous vision of its own for Rutgers, which the governor and the commission's chairman, P. Roy Vagelos, pressed relentlessly upon us.

Released in mid-October 2002, after rumors of its contents had been circulating for a month or more, the commission report was bold, farsighted—and exasperating. It recommended creation of "a single

New Jersey research university system" comprising all the schools and programs then within Rutgers University, the University of Medicine and Dentistry of New Jersey (UMDNJ), and the New Jersey Institute of Technology (NJIT). Within the overall system, tentatively named the University of New Jersey (UNJ), there would be three universities, each having "significant academic and administrative autonomy." In Newark, UNJ-North would include all of the elements of both Rutgers and UMDNJ that were located in that city, as well as NJIT; in New Brunswick and Piscataway, UNJ-Central would encompass everything that belonged to Rutgers and UMDNJ within those communities; and finally in Camden and Stratford, UNJ-South would similarly embrace all the elements of Rutgers and UMDNJ situated there. UNJ-North and UNJ-Central would be fully comprehensive research universities, each having (most of) the broad range of disciplines, including medicine, that are commonly found within such institutions. UNJ-South, including the Stratford-based School of Osteopathic Medicine, would be a rather smaller and less comprehensive university and, because Camden and Stratford are eleven miles apart, would be somewhat geographically challenged. In contrast, the campuses of the Newark and New Brunswick/Piscataway universities would be geographically proximate if not completely contiguous. The system as a whole, which was modeled on the highly regarded University of California, would be headed by a chancellor, whose office would be located in the state capital of Trenton and who reported to a board of regents. Each of the three universities would be headed by a president who reported to the chancellor. The report placed great emphasis upon the synergies that would be obtained within each of the three universities by associating the health sciences with all the other academic disciplines and upon the economic as well as educational benefits for the people of New Jersey. Finally, the commission report called upon the governor to appoint a task force on review and implementation to work out the many details of the far-reaching transformation it envisioned.

The document, authored by Roy Vagelos and released to great fanfare, was both visionary and superficial, sweeping in its breadth but startlingly neglectful of many critically important considerations. For one thing, the report had little to say about academic fields other than medicine, and, even in regard to medicine, the report, though its title included the words "education" and "training," was nearly silent about the actual production of physicians. Would there be more of them or fewer, and in what ways would they be better or worse? If you were a student or a faculty member in the arts, humanities, social sciences, law, engineering, agriculture, or business, the report had practically nothing to say about whether and how its recommendations would affect you. It is tempting to speculate about the reasons for these and other gaps in the report. As its name suggests, the commission was initially charged by the governor to study "medical and allied health care education" in New Jersey and to focus on UMDNJ; then somewhat belatedly the commission expanded its work to develop recommendations far transcending its original spotlight on the health care fields and to cover Rutgers and NJIT, as well. Originally expected to complete its work by December 2002, the commission evidently speeded up its deliberations in order to finalize and publicize its product prior to the appointment of the new Rutgers president. The report bore the unfortunate imprint of both of these midstream decisions. Most important, there were mountainous problems with the content of the commission's recommendations, about which significant questions immediately arose. To achieve its admirable goals in education and research, why did there have to be such vast and inevitably controversial changes in the structure and governance of the universities? How would New Jersey, which had never been disposed to provide adequate funding for even a single comprehensive research university, now find it possible to afford three such institutions? How much would it cost to implement the commission's recommendations and realize its goals? Over the course of the year ahead, as discussion and debate over the report proceeded, these core concerns about structure, governance, and funding were endlessly reviewed but never resolved.

For all its limitations, however, the Vagelos report was a major force to be reckoned with and received extremely serious consideration by hundreds if not thousands of higher education professionals, business leaders, and government officials. It was probably the most pervasive single subject of newspaper coverage in New Jersey from September 2002 through December 2003, and was widely noted around the country. There were any number of reasons why a flawed report gained such traction, but the place to start is with its two talented, driven protagonists: Governor Jim McGreevey and Dr. P. Roy Vagelos. Still in his first year as governor and still highly popular at the time he released the report, McGreevey was boundlessly energetic and ambitious. The proposed reorganization of the research universities constituted his most dramatic and conspicuous policy initiative, and it focused attention in an arena that had not seen any significant state governmental activity since the higher education advances of the Tom Kean era back in the 1980s. McGreevey made abundantly clear, in both public and private, that he wanted the report's recommendations to be enacted. The governor's partner in this endeavor, Roy Vagelos, was even more talented and accomplished, a truly distinguished biological scientist, and for many years CEO of Merck & Company, the New Jersey–based multinational pharmaceutical company. During Vagelos's time at the helm of Merck, *Fortune* magazine named it year after year "the most admired company in America." The designation was deserved. Vagelos drew upon his own considerable scientific experience to engineer a true transformation at Merck by swelling the pipeline of research-based pharmaceutical products and bringing many of them successfully and remuneratively to market. He also became an international humanitarian hero for his decision to donate unlimited amounts of Merck's drug Mectizan to combat a dreaded disease called river blindness, which afflicted tens of thousands in Africa. Through Merck's generosity, river blindness was practically wiped out. The advancement of health science education in New Jersey could not possibly have had a more distinguished and respected leader than Roy Vagelos.

Besides the strength that the commission report drew from its brilliant author and its powerful chief advocate, the report also derived influence from its irrefutable insight that New Jersey's three medical schools should not be cordoned off in a bloated, bureaucratic health sciences university, UMDNJ, but should be integrated with the academic disciplines located within the state's premier public research

university, Rutgers. Practically no one who took part in the deliberations of 2002–03 disputed the educational, scientific, and economic advantages of such unification. Many of the most distinguished scientists
at Rutgers praised Vagelos's vision and offered persuasive testimony
that their own teaching and research would benefit from adoption of
the recommendations in his report. They knew from direct experience
how frustrating, sometimes impossible, it was to collaborate with medical school colleagues in a separate university. Despite opposition to the
report from the top brass at UMDNJ, some of that university's best
scientists courageously expressed support for it. So did key business
leaders around the state. Advocates for the report repeatedly observed
that almost every medical school in America was part of a comprehensive research university and that most of the nation's top public
and private research universities included medical schools. Though
hardly a biomedical scientist myself, I knew from my time at UNC
and the UW the advantages of bringing medicine into Rutgers, and I
drew upon my experiences at those institutions, including the human
genome anecdote, throughout the debate over the Vagelos report.

There was one additional reason why the commission report, for all
its weaknesses, found support within Rutgers, and that was because its
adoption would remedy a terrible and politically motivated decades-
old injustice: the state's ripping from the University its medical school
in 1970. Under the leadership of President Mason Gross, Rutgers
Medical School (RMS) had been established in 1962 with a two-year
educational program and high hopes for expansion into a full-fledged
four-year medical school. RMS recruited an outstanding dean and faculty, admitted its first class of students in 1966, and moved into its new
facility at University Heights in Piscataway in 1970. That same year, for
sorry political reasons reflecting in part the civil disturbances that had
broken out in Newark in July 1967 and in part dissatisfaction in Trenton with Mason Gross, Governor William T. Cahill proposed and
compelled adoption of a law consolidating RMS with the Newark-
based, state-owned New Jersey College of Medicine and Dentistry.
Together the two schools would form a new entity called the College
of Medicine and Dentistry of New Jersey (later to become UMDNJ).

Rutgers leaders strenuously opposed Cahill's legislation, but when the state removed all funding for RMS and transferred it to the new institution, the Boards of Governors and Trustees and the president had to accept the reality that their medical school was lost. Still located on the Rutgers campus in Piscataway, the medical school curiously retained its Rutgers name until 1986, when it became Robert Wood Johnson Medical School. By then it was fully part of UMDNJ, an institution that had proved to be very responsive to the political urges of Newark and Essex County. At last, in 2002–03, the Vagelos report presented an opportunity to restore the medical school, widely considered to be the best of the eight schools that comprised UMDNJ, to its rightful place within Rutgers.

In December 2002, Governor McGreevey created the Review, Planning, and Implementation Steering Committee, chaired by Roy Vagelos and having twenty-one members altogether, including me. The committee's name suggested that it would "review" the work previously done by the commission, but because the governor and the chairman were fully satisfied with the commission's product, the task of review quickly gave way to full-scale planning for carrying out the commission's recommendations. Over the course of the next twelve months, the steering committee would meet many times; would spawn three university committees charged with making plans for UNJ-North, UNJ-Central, and UNJ-South; and, with the assistance of a high-powered consulting group, would delve into the complicated subjects of human resources, information technology and library services, hospitals, and finance. The organizational structure that had been recommended by the commission—three semiautonomous universities headed by a chancellor and board of regents in Trenton—was the only model ever considered by the steering committee. At no time did its chairman countenance discussion of alternative ways of achieving the commission's ambitious goals.

Roy Vagelos, though brilliant, was not well suited for guiding a controversial project across the rough-and-tumble terrains of New Jersey politics and public higher education where lots of people felt they had good ideas that deserved to be heard and considered. Back in October, shortly after release of the commission report, Vagelos, whom Governor McGreevey had recently appointed to the Rutgers Boards of Governors and Trustees, presented his plan to the trustees. Following his talk, several fellow board members praised Vagelos's farsighted vision for higher education in New Jersey but asked if there would be opportunities for discussing it and refining the details. No, Vagelos replied; he and the governor had already made the decisions. From that time forward, Vagelos was substantially alienated from the other members of the Rutgers boards—boards whose consent would be required for his plan to be enacted.

My own relationship with Roy began well enough but soon became troubled. At his invitation, the two of us had dinner together at a New Brunswick restaurant shortly after my appointment as Rutgers president. Roy told me that he had asked some of his acquaintances at the University of Washington about me and had heard from them that I had been a good president there. But I had not, he continued, ever done a "turnaround" as he had done at Merck. This was true: the UW was fundamentally the same fine institution when I left as it had been when I arrived. Adoption of the commission report, Roy said, would be my opportunity to do a turnaround, and he pressed hard for assurances of my allegiance to it. I replied by expressing strong support for his goals in education and research but also by wondering if the vast alterations he had proposed in organizational structure and university governance were all essential to realizing those goals. Could they not possibly be achieved without such wrenching changes? Roy did not like that question; he wanted the structure he wanted—three universities governed by a chancellor and regents in Trenton. By now I was beginning to believe that those organizational arrangements *had become* Roy's goals. On another occasion, I casually referred to the members of the Rutgers Board of Governors as my "bosses" and immediately regretted using that word. Roy objected strenuously, saying that as president I had the power to convince the board to do whatever I wanted. He himself clearly lacked that power over the board and, whether he believed it or not, so did I. By the early months of 2003, Roy was angry because I had not made sufficient progress toward complete support of his plan. Thenceforth he seemed to treat me distrustfully, peremptorily, and condescendingly.

Perhaps it should have been unsurprising that a globally lauded CEO like Vagelos would be so insistent on having his own way. But I had not expected the same from Governor McGreevey. I had formed positive impressions of the governor in our early meetings and assumed that, as a practical politician who had reached the governorship of New Jersey in his mid-forties and harbored ambitions for even higher office, he was accustomed to compromising to get what he wanted. Early in the Vagelos process, the savvy *Star-Ledger* columnist Bob Braun observed that McGreevey was "astute enough both to leave the definition of victory sufficiently vague so that any reasonable reform will do and to set up a procedure that ensures some sort of change could occur without much rancor." McGreevey, Braun said, "has been vague about most details, and flexible about others." Unfortunately, as it turned out, Vagelos's inflexibility became the governor's own. If they had been willing to settle for three-quarters of the report, they probably could have had it. But instead of focusing on the true goals, they insisted on enacting precisely the mechanisms that the commission had recommended.

Seeing great promise in the Vagelos report, above all for restoring Robert Wood Johnson Medical School to Rutgers, and believing that the report's worst features could be eliminated through compromise, I spoke favorably about it on many occasions. Sometimes, indeed, I spoke more favorably than my new "bosses" liked. Members of the Boards of Governors and Trustees were greatly worried that the Vagelos plan, with its chancellor and regents in Trenton, would destroy the successful system of governance that Rutgers had enjoyed since 1956 and would introduce in its place a highly politicized system. They were also profoundly concerned about the proposed establishment of three largely autonomous research universities. It was pretty clear from the beginning that the New Brunswick/Piscataway institution would still be called Rutgers, but what about UNJ-North and UNJ-South? How would the three universities relate to each other, and how could all of them thrive in a New Jersey fiscal environment that historically had been so ungenerous to the state's colleges and universities? When Governor McGreevey proposed a 12 percent budget cut for higher education in February 2003, the board members' doubts about the feasibility of the Vagelos plan deepened. And the governors and trustees were not alone. The University Senate, composed of faculty, students, and alumni, wrote reports expressing serious reservations about the commission's recommendations, as did the New Brunswick Faculty Council. While many Rutgers scientists lauded the report, the same was not true of faculty in other disciplines or in the professional schools.

By the spring and early summer of 2003, a rough Rutgers consensus on the Vagelos plan had emerged, at least for purposes of negotiation. The academic vision was inspiring, and, depending on the details, three semiautonomous universities might be acceptable—but only if certain conditions were met. First, the governance of each institution had to be primarily local and free from significant political interference. Second, the chancellor in Trenton would mainly serve as an advocate for the research universities and would not attempt to run them. Finally, there had to be assurances of adequate state funding—for the costs associated with the structural changes, for the operations of the universities, and for facilities. As yet, there had been no breakthroughs on any of these issues. It remained to be seen whether through the steering committee process or, later, through closed-door discussions involving the governor's people and Rutgers representatives, those conditions could be met. For the time being, the conversation about the Vagelos report just went on and on.

✺

Challenging as the Vagelos process was, plenty of other difficulties also plagued my first year as president. Some of the worst were my own fault. But not this next one. Late in January 2003, Governor McGreevey phoned the university presidents and told us that, because New Jersey was facing a multi-billion-dollar budget gap for the coming fiscal year, he was going to reduce state support for our institutions by 12 percent. When his proposed budget emerged in February, Rutgers's cut was indeed $39 million, or 11.9 percent of our total state appropriation.

New Jersey's budget woes were no surprise, but the extent of the burden that the governor had placed upon higher education was shocking, and the size of the Rutgers cut was larger than any previous cut anyone could remember. I communicated this news to the Boards of Governors and Trustees and to the university community and shared with them preliminary estimates of how the budget reduction would damage our teaching programs and every other activity at the University. I called upon everyone "to work together to raise public awareness of the likely results of these budget cuts," and in the weeks ahead a remarkable Rutgers effort took shape to beat back the cuts. Students, faculty, and staff contacted legislators by phone and e-mail and wrote letters to the editors of New Jersey's newspapers. My administration supplied all the information that members of the Rutgers community needed to undertake these communications. On March 6, more than a thousand of our students traveled to Trenton to protest the reductions, and the next week the leaders of the student governing associations sent letters to thirty-eight thousand parents of Rutgers students giving them information about the proposed cut and urging them to communicate to their legislators the impacts it would have on the quality of their children's education. When the budget deliberations in Trenton reached their most critical phase in late June, I asked members of the university community to contact their legislators. "Please urge them," I wrote, "to identify appropriate revenue sources and to take the fiscal measures necessary to restore the funding for New Jersey's colleges and universities."

It all worked, up to a point. The final budget approved by the legislature and the governor restored almost half the funds that were to have been cut. Rutgers still took a large hit but had avoided a far worse outcome. In allocating the budget reduction across the University, we assigned the smallest cuts to instructional units and the largest to administrative functions. In July, the Board of Governors approved a 9 percent tuition increase and allocated $4 million of the new tuition revenue for need-based financial aid for students who could not afford the higher tuition. These developments would be repeated almost every year during my time as president: state budget shortfalls, proposed reductions to higher education, Rutgers efforts to counter the cuts (sometimes successful, sometimes not), allocation of the pain across the University, tuition increases, and added financial aid for students who needed it. I'll return to this subject in a later chapter.

While state-supported institutions like Rutgers were trying to make a case against budget cuts, various media outlets made sport of trying to show that those same institutions were actually wasting public funds. I got a taste of this during my first year as president when a New Jersey radio station reported one afternoon that the University was spending $8 million to build a house for me in Saddle River, an affluent Bergen County community quite distant from the University. It was a call-in radio show, and after the host shared with his listening audience the outrageous news about my house, the first caller said that he was a plumber working on the house and it was the most obscenely extravagant residence for which he had ever supplied the plumbing. The next caller identified himself as an electrician working there and made a similar remark about the opulence of my mansion. By this point, the Rutgers media relations folks had gotten wind of the radio dialogue and phoned the station to say that no such house existed and to ask why the station had not even contacted Rutgers to inquire about the house before launching the story. The next afternoon the radio host announced that due to public outrage inspired by the previous day's reporting, the Rutgers Board of Governors had voted to cancel the project.

The next crises of 2003 were in intercollegiate athletics. The Big East Conference, to which Rutgers had belonged since 1991, was losing three of its member universities to the Atlantic Coast Conference. First Virginia Tech defected, then the University of Miami, then a few months later Boston College. All three defectors were very successful in football, and their departures were expected to weaken the Big East severely. Conference Commissioner Mike Tranghese called it "the deepest, darkest period in the history of this league." Although the Big East would try to add institutions to replace the deserters, and, indeed, was able to announce five new members later in the year, the future success of the conference was in doubt. At risk were the Big East's automatic berth in the Bowl Championship Series (BCS) and considerable television revenue.

To understand what happened next, it is important to keep in mind two things. First, the football success that Rutgers would enjoy under Coach Greg Schiano still lay in the future (the team's record in 2002 had been 1–11, 0–7 in the Big East). Second, at this point there was still considerable opposition on campus to Rutgers's quest for "big-time" status in intercollegiate athletics. Debates over this subject that never would have occurred in Chapel Hill or Seattle, or for that matter in Ann Arbor or Austin, were still commonplace at Rutgers. One idea making the rounds during 2003 was that Rutgers should leave the Big East and join the Patriot League, a conference of academically fine universities that did not aspire to play football at the level of the BCS conferences.

In June, I provided an update on the Big East situation at a public meeting of the Board of Governors. At this juncture, formal defections from the conference had not yet occurred, but they were widely anticipated, and I knew that board members were concerned about the future of the Big East. During that same meeting, I had the unpleasant duty of reporting on another problem in athletics, namely that Rutgers was going to suffer significant penalties from the National Collegiate Athletic Association (NCAA) for forty violations, committed several years earlier, involving certification of the academic eligibility of student-athletes. Although Rutgers had self-reported the violations and they appeared to have been random and unintentional, the NCAA deemed the violations to be "major," to warrant significant punishment, and to indicate the need for reinventing Rutgers's system of athletic compliance.

Having in mind all of these circumstances—the Big East's perilous condition, Rutgers's continuing lack of success in football, disagreement on campus over big-time sports, and the embarrassment of NCAA sanctions—I later broached with board members a discussion of the future of Rutgers athletics. I said I believed it would be a good time for the University to pause, to evaluate its goals for intercollegiate athletics, and to determine how best to achieve them. I envisioned a public process, probably led by a representative committee that the board and I would appoint, and I assumed (although I could not be certain) that the outcome would be an affirmation of the University's current aspirations and directions and a decision to remain in the Big East. The air would be cleared, I believed, and Rutgers would move forward and surmount its troubles in athletics. Most members of the Board of Governors disagreed with me. They did not want to encourage a public discussion that would stir up questions about the future of Rutgers athletics. The program's fundamental directions had been firmly established, and on that basis commitments had been made to coaches, athletes, and fans. One board member poked his finger into my chest and told me heatedly that I should stick to academics and never again get involved in athletics.

Looking back, it was a mistake for me to offer the proposal I did, and it was understandable that the board rejected it. A public discussion of the future of Rutgers athletics could well have worsened the existing troubled circumstances without engendering the kind of air-clearing affirmation I hoped for—in other words, a lose-lose. Although I did not take the advice of the board member who told me to steer clear of athletics in the years ahead (as president, I could not possibly do that), I never renewed my suggestion for a public discussion of the future of intercollegiate athletics. Fortunately, although none of us could have known it at the time, Rutgers athletics was soon to experience greater success than it had ever enjoyed before. Success then brought problems of its own, which is a story I'll tell later.

Vagelos, budget cuts, troubles in athletics: What else could go wrong in 2003? Lots, as it turned out, including some deeply disturbing incidents during the fall involving our students. In September, the campus witnessed an ugly upsurge of anti-Semitism that frightened and enraged Jewish members of the community and embarrassed the whole University. Natan Sharansky, a revered member of the Israeli government, had accepted an invitation to visit Rutgers and was preparing to speak when a student threw a pie in his face. Just a day or two later, two facilities with strong ties to the Jewish student community, the Hillel House and the Alpha Epsilon Pi fraternity, were defaced by swastikas.

On behalf of the University, I expressed outrage and extended regrets to Minister Sharansky and to the members of Hillel and Alpha Epsilon Pi. The next month, outside a fraternity house in the early hours of a Sunday morning, an exceptionally brutal fight broke out that was unrelated to religious bigotry; two students were severely beaten with baseball bats and suffered grave injuries. Then in November, one of the independent newspapers published by Rutgers students, *The Medium*, printed racist and other deeply offensive language in its personals section. It was not the first time *The Medium* had insulted and enraged its readers, and unfortunately it would not be the last. In a message to the university community, I deplored the racist language and went on to observe that although "the First Amendment protects the paper's right to exist, and the courts have consistently upheld the right to print hate speech. . . . These restrictions do not mean that we are helpless to change the situation." Over a period of many weeks, a series of private meetings and public forums provided minority students with opportunities to express their hurt and anger and to engage in a dialogue with the editors of *The Medium*, who acknowledged and regretted the pain they had caused. I cannot be sure about the lasting impact of these incidents, but by the end of the fall it felt to me that the university community had been shocked into serious soul-searching about the value of having a campus environment in which everyone is respected and everyone feels safe.

While these ugly incidents attracted notice mainly within Rutgers and New Jersey, another student-related episode drew angry attention from around the world. During the summer, a registered student organization named NJ Solidarity–Rutgers Chapter applied to use the Douglass Campus Center to hold a three-day conference entitled "Third National Student Conference on the Palestine Solidarity Movement." NJ Solidarity's mission statement opposed Israel's right to exist and sanctioned violence in the struggle for Palestine. When news became public of the organization's stated beliefs and its request to hold the conference at Rutgers, literally thousands of people wrote to me demanding the University deny the request on the grounds that the sponsoring organization's beliefs were unacceptable. I responded to every letter and e-mail message by saying that although NJ Solidarity's views differed sharply from my own, Rutgers's commitment to the free exchange of ideas, including highly unpopular ideas, required us to permit the conference. Wanting to use the occasion to raise consciousness of the University's obligation to free speech, I encouraged those who disagreed with NJ Solidarity to "express their own opinions in a public and constructive manner." Jewish students belonging to Rutgers Hillel took seriously the opportunity to do exactly that, and they organized a wonderfully well attended yearlong series of events and presentations called "Israel Inspires." As things turned out, NJ Solidarity–Rutgers Chapter could not, or would not, meet even minimal expectations in preparation for its conference. When the organization declined to provide a speakers list, cost estimates, a registration process, or even a coherent description of the event, the University appropriately withdrew permission to use the Douglass Campus Center. Not wishing to be misunderstood, I used my annual address in September to state clearly that cancellation of the conference was unrelated to the students' views on Israel and Palestine. It simply reflected their inability to host a viable event. "If they can do so at a later time," I said, " . . . they will be welcome to hold the conference."

Now, once again, this story becomes painful to tell because, in a difficult time for Rutgers, I made matters worse. Three highly publicized events, each more embarrassing than the one before, put Rutgers and me in an unfavorable light and cumulatively may have weakened my ability to lead the University. One evening in August, I purchased a bottle of wine at a liquor store on Easton Avenue in New Brunswick and walked out toward my car with my wallet still in my hand, rather than in my pocket where it should have been. The wallet quickly attracted the attention of a person who had been lurking across the street. He rushed toward me, grabbed the wallet, took a huge swing at me with his fist, but missed, and ran away down the street. The incident made headlines in the New Jersey newspapers the next day, and some of the reports erroneously said that I had been injured. Every media report, whether exaggerated or not, called attention to the fact that the robbery occurred outside a liquor store where I had just made a purchase.

A little over a month later, I rose early in the morning and took a train to Washington, D.C., for meetings there beginning at 9:30 a.m. As the meetings wound down, I was on the phone with colleagues back at Rutgers who briefed me on the latest developments relating to the proposed NJ Solidarity conference. They recommended that because of the students' evident inability to provide basic information about the conference, Rutgers should announce cancellation of the event. I accepted their advice but knew the announcement was going to be tricky because the proposed conference had attracted worldwide attention and we needed to make clear that Rutgers's decision to cancel it was unrelated to the controversial views of the sponsoring group. Given the importance of getting our message right, my colleagues and I agreed that during my train ride back from Washington I would make a series of phone calls to reporters we knew would cover the story the next day. That done, I got off the train not in New Brunswick but in Trenton, because at 5:00 p.m. I had a meeting with staff in the governor's office to continue our unending negotiations on the Vagelos report.

Later that evening, I met my mother, sister, and brother-in-law for dinner at a restaurant in Bound Brook. Exhaustedly and foolishly, I ate little dinner but drank some wine. Driving home after dinner, I stopped at a convenience store, then got back in my car and continued down River Road toward my home. Now I noticed that the car behind me was flashing its lights, and, to my astonishment, it followed mine right down the driveway of the president's residence. When the other driver and I each got out of our cars, he said that my car had hit his in the parking lot of the convenience store. I did not think that was true, but he insisted it was. We agreed to call the police, and officers soon arrived from both Rutgers and Piscataway. The other driver told them that I had hit his car, and, indeed, there was a scratch on his back bumper and the license plate was a bit bent. Still doubting that a collision had occurred, I nonetheless assured him that I would cover the cost of any repairs. I gave him my phone numbers and urged him to call me.

Neither the Rutgers police nor the Piscataway police filed accident reports (perhaps because they shared my doubts that an accident had occurred), but the Rutgers officers wrote an internal report describing me as glassy eyed, having alcohol on my breath, and walking unsteadily. When the document was leaked to the press, the media widely reported what it said about my appearance. Once again, I was publicly embarrassed, and this time I knew that I bore responsibility for the embarrassment, having consumed wine without food and then driven home. The other driver never contacted me, but I phoned him several days later and repeated my offer to pay for any damage to his car, an offer to which he never responded. And still the worst was yet to come.

On Sunday, November 2, the *Seattle Times* published a front-page article saying that the board of regents of the University of Washington had been unhappy with my presidential performance for some time prior to my departure the previous year and, having learned about my affair with a university employee, encouraged me to leave the UW and to accept the presidency of Rutgers. The story went on to say that after denying the relationship for months in interviews with the *Seattle Times* reporter, I had admitted it very recently when I learned that the newspaper was going to publish the article about it. The story also reported my admission that the regents' encouragement was a factor in my departure from the UW. The article's author had been on the trail of the story for many months, during which he phoned me often and, as his article revealed, also gathered information from ten other people (none of whom would permit him to use their names). By the late summer, however, judging from the cessation of his phone calls, the reporter seemed to have dropped the story—until September, that is, when he saw the unflattering description of my appearance written by the Rutgers police following the alleged accident in the convenience store parking lot. At that point he evidently got back on the trail. His article was devastating to my family and to me.

A couple of days prior to its publication, when I learned for certain that the story was coming, I informed the members of the Rutgers Board of Governors—first the chair and vice chair and then, in groups of three, the other board members. I told them to the best of my ability, not yet having read the article, what I believed it was going to say, and I acknowledged that it was essentially true. Speaking with the board members, I expressed deep regret, both for my terrible lapse in judgment and for personal behavior that was going to bring embarrassment to Rutgers. I asked for their support.

Within hours after the story's publication, I sent an e-mail message to everyone in the Rutgers community informing them of the article's contents, acknowledging its accuracy, and, just as I had done in conversations with board members, expressing shame and regret both for my behavior and for embarrassing Rutgers. That same day, the chairman of the board, Gene O'Hara, and I held a press conference at which we both read statements and answered questions. Other members of the board were also there, as were my wife and father, for whose public presence and support I was very grateful. My statement again apologized for "the grave personal mistake" I had made, while Gene's statement strongly praised the job I was doing as president and affirmed the board's confidence in me: "He had the board's support a year ago and he has the board's support today." I was so very appreciative when I heard Gene's words and saw the same sentiment reflected on the faces of the other board members at the press conference. Both my letter to the community and my public statement admitted that the UW board of regents' knowledge of the affair had "played a role in my decision to come to Rutgers" but did not say directly that they had asked me to resign. (Nor, to judge from the *Seattle Times* article, did any of the reporter's informants.) The next afternoon, I convened a meeting of the University's vice presidents and deans and another meeting of faculty and student leaders. By this time, of course, the New Jersey newspapers had all published front-page stories about the *Seattle Times* article. At each meeting, I apologized for my behavior, expressed regret for embarrassing Rutgers, and asked for my colleagues' support.

Their responses, and those of the community at large, were forgiving, affirming, and affectionate. Hundreds of e-mail messages poured into my office from faculty, staff, and students. The general gist of them was: "We like you as our president; let's move on." A surprising number of the communications, mostly from people I did not personally know, thanked me for particular things I had done as president or characterized my leadership in generous terms such as "open," "energetic," and "visionary." There were also some negative messages, perhaps a dozen or so, some of which called on me to resign. It is likely there were others at Rutgers who believed that my actions disqualified me as president but who did not write to tell me so. Overall the campus community was in my corner, probably far more than I deserved it to be. By late afternoon on Monday, I was getting phone calls from board members and others saying that I had apologized enough. "Let's move on," they said.

From beyond the university community, response to the news was more mixed and harder to gauge. A number of New Jersey newspapers wrote critical editorials, although none called for my resignation. A half dozen members of the legislature sent supportive letters to me, but another legislator, who was widely respected, told a member of my administration that he had grave concerns about my inappropriate behavior. Governor McGreevey phoned me on the day of the *Seattle Times* article to express sympathy and support, and he urged me to reach out to him for help if I needed it. A few weeks later, a long *New York Times* article about me quoted the governor's chief of staff, Jamie Fox, saying that I had "deftly handled the issue" and, more generally, "He has proven to be a strong leader. In full partnership with this administration, President McCormick will be instrumental in moving higher education in this state to the next level." More worrisome was a *Star-Ledger* column by Bob Braun observing that in my weakened condition I would be unable to stand up for Rutgers as the deliberations on the Vagelos report neared conclusion. Fortunately that prediction proved to be wrong.

By October 2003, the Review, Planning, and Implementation Steering Committee, chaired by Vagelos, together with its numerous subcommittees, had produced hefty draft reports on each of the three proposed research universities—UNJ-North, UNJ-Central, and UNJ-South— as well as on several system-wide issues, including human resources, information technology and library services, hospitals, and finance.

All the reports hewed closely to the commission's original recommendations, although many of the earlier gaps were now filled in. Disciplines other than medicine were included, or at least mentioned, and the three university reports offered credible, best-case scenarios for the proposed institutions. Rutgers board members, administrators, faculty, and shared governance bodies such as the University Senate, the New Brunswick Faculty Council, and the Rutgers Council of AAUP Chapters eagerly consumed the reports and in many cases wrote reports of their own evaluating the voluminous output of the Vagelos process. Each Rutgers campus held open forums to discuss the restructuring plan.

Virtually all the Rutgers responses highlighted two central concerns: governance and funding. A university system with its chancellor and regents in the state capital would vest control in politicized hands, distant from the university campuses, and would jeopardize, if not destroy, Rutgers's historic Boards of Governors and Trustees. The university system, moreover, would require significant funding for three kinds of costs: the up-front, one-time expenses of merging the separate institutions; annual operating budgets for three research universities; and the cost of building and maintaining facilities. In the current fiscal climate—and with the latest round of state budget cuts still fresh in everyone's memory—few believed that answers would soon be found for these funding challenges.

Nor was it likely that further progress in either area of concern would come through the work of the steering committee, although Vagelos himself would certainly not have accepted that judgment. Others did, however, and, even before completion of the draft reports, two sets of confidential negotiating meetings had begun involving Rutgers leaders and the governor's office, one focused on governance and the other on funding. Jim Davy, a trusted friend of Governor McGreevey and his chief of operations, was the governor's main spokesperson in both groups; in the funding meetings Jim was joined by John McCormac, the state treasurer. Though completely loyal to the governor, both Jim and John were honestly and honorably seeking solutions to the problems. Representing Rutgers were Gene O'Hara, chair of the

Board of Governors, Pat Nachtigal, chair of the Board of Trustees, and me.

As Gene and Pat knew better than anyone else, members of the Rutgers boards harbored deep skepticism about the Vagelos plan. Board members rightly regarded themselves as the guardians of Rutgers's political independence and the guarantors of its financial well-being. Trustees in particular engaged in lively e-mail communications whose contents ranged from flat-out opposition to the plan to possible acceptance of it under certain demanding conditions. The trustees' opinions mattered, because the existing structure and governance of the University, enshrined in the Rutgers Act of 1956, had come about through a compact between the state of New Jersey and the Board of Trustees; the state could not unilaterally reorganize the University, as the Vagelos plan would do, without the trustees' concurrence. In November, a study group composed of three members of each governing board, chaired by Duncan MacMillan, issued its long-awaited report recommending against trustee approval of any reorganization plan that failed to resolve satisfactorily the issues of governance and funding. Despite continued confidential negotiations between the governor's office and Rutgers, those issues were not even close to being settled. On a Saturday in late November, Gene O'Hara, Pat Nachtigal, and I met cordially for two hours with Governor McGreevey and Jim Davy. The governor explained that he supported the Vagelos plan, in all its essential details, as the only workable organizational model, and he shared with us candidly the unlikelihood of additional state funding for higher education in the foreseeable future.

By early December, the end game of the Vagelos process was under way, although not all of the players were ready to admit it. Besides Vagelos himself, many of the best scientists at Rutgers and UMDNJ continued to support the plan, although I knew their real goal was actually different from his. Where he wanted three research universities, they cared above all about bringing Robert Wood Johnson Medical School (back) into Rutgers because of the enormous value such unification would have for biomedical research and teaching. They were right. In early December, 164 science faculty sent an open letter to both Rutgers boards and both university presidents endorsing the commission report as "a once-in-a-generation opportunity" which should not be jeopardized "by hesitation" and declaring that "the time for debate has ended." Reluctant as I was to differ publicly with faculty colleagues whose views I shared on the key issue of the medical school, I issued a statement disagreeing with their letter on the grounds of governance and funding. "The restructuring proposal," I wrote, "is too complicated and too important to accept before these issues have been resolved appropriately." As soon as the Vagelos process was over, I reached out to as many of the scientists as I could to assure them that Rutgers would strenuously pursue reunification with the medical school. For now, however, the challenge was to extricate all the parties from the process with the fewest possible hard feelings and the greatest likelihood of revisiting the commission's core objectives at a later time.

Sometime early in the second week of December, Jim Davy phoned me to say that the governor now recognized the impossibility of gaining Rutgers's approval for the Vagelos plan and to propose a joint announcement by Governor McGreevey and the Board of Governors setting it to rest. I was pleased by the news and concurred with Jim's suggestion. Over the next day or so, we drafted a statement lauding the commission's vision for elevating higher education in New Jersey, citing the value of the yearlong review of issues and challenges, and calling for increased collaboration among the state's research universities. Rather than say directly that the Vagelos plan was dead, the statement would euphemistically declare it unready for presentation during the 2004 legislative session because of unresolved "financial and structural issues," which meant the same thing. The joint announcement would praise all parties to the process, while blaming none, and would pledge the governor and Rutgers to continue their efforts for the improvement of higher education. I kept Gene O'Hara and Pat Nachtigal closely informed as the statement developed. They were pleased and relieved that Rutgers and the governor would make the announcement together, without rancor or recrimination. By careful prearrangement, at 11:30 a.m. on December 12, the Rutgers Board of Governors, in public session at its regularly scheduled meeting, adopted the statement by a vote of ten to one, and Governor McGreevey's office in Trenton also released it. Roy Vagelos, not having been informed by the governor of where things stood, first learned of the joint announcement shortly before the board meeting. When the vote was taken he supplied the single nay. The ordeal that bore his name was now over.

Unsuccessful though it was in 2003, the project begun by Roy Vagelos and Jim McGreevey revealed exhilarating possibilities that would be realized a decade later. Vagelos was difficult to work with, but he was a true visionary. The long debate over his commission's report gave Vagelos himself and all those who believed in restoring the health science disciplines to Rutgers a rich opportunity to spread widely an understanding of the benefits that would come from having medicine lodged in the same university as everything else. The Boards of Governors and Trustees superbly fulfilled their obligations of guardianship by standing firmly against a plan that Rutgers could not accept for many reasons, but they also proved open to new ideas and dramatic changes. When a better plan for achieving the same goals became available, Rutgers was ready for it, in significant part because of what had occurred and what had been learned during 2002–03. The second time around saw a process that was even more controversial and convoluted than the first. But with a different governor, who was stubborn in his own ways but ultimately willing to compromise, Rutgers and New Jersey got it done.

THE ACADEMIC HEART
OF THE MATTER

WHILE AWAITING a better opportunity to restore the medical center to its place within Rutgers, the University vigorously advanced other initiatives for improving education and research. In my inaugural address I declared that "our most important goal is to move Rutgers to the top tier of America's public research universities." By top tier I meant UNC–Chapel Hill, Michigan, UC–Berkeley, and a few others at that level. We did not get that far, but Rutgers is closer than before because we consciously and successfully pursued several major academic objectives.

The largest share of responsibility for any university's academic work rests in the hands of its deans and faculty. They educate the students, conduct research, and advance the institution's mission of service to the larger community—and they make the vast majority of decisions about how to do these things. What programs of study should be offered and what lines of research should be pursued? Who should be appointed to carry on that work? What knowledge and which skills should students be expected to acquire before they graduate? These questions, and many more, are properly answered by the faculty. In some cases, faculty tenure decisions for example, administrative approval is required before final action is taken, but the presumption in such instances is that the recommendations of provosts, deans, and faculty will be respected. As president, I was seldom directly involved in matters like these.

There are, however, some major academic issues on which the president, working closely with deans and faculty, must provide leadership. Nowhere is there a comprehensive list of such presidential issues, but they certainly include any decisions that add to or subtract from the core missions of the institution, reorganize the university, notably affect its external constituencies, require approval by high-level governmental authorities, or demand the allocation or reallocation of significant resources. Such initiatives as these would almost certainly also necessitate involvement and approval by the university's governing board. A university president, after consulting widely with all the appropriate groups and individuals, and after taking into account the needs, the opportunities, and the culture of the institution, has a responsibility to identify a small number of academic goals upon which to focus attention. They should be objectives whose achievement will truly advance the university and upon which he or she is prepared to stake time, energy, and reputation. Nothing a president does is more important than choosing goals that meet these criteria and leading the university toward their achievement.

In many of its parameters and characteristics, the institution whose president I became in 2002 was not all that different from the one I had first joined as a faculty member a quarter century earlier. It now had about 10 percent more students, some 51,000 altogether, of whom 70 percent studied in New Brunswick, 20 percent in Newark, and 10 percent in Camden—ratios that were virtually unchanged from what they had been in 1976. Undergraduates still made up about three-quarters of the student body, and 90 percent of them hailed from communities within New Jersey. The students' ethnic and racial diversity was now somewhat greater than it had been when I first arrived at Rutgers; almost 20 percent were Asian, 10 percent African American, and 8 percent Hispanic/Latino. There were now almost 2,600 full-time faculty members, about 3 percent more than in 1976, and about 1,000 part-time lecturers, several hundred more than before. The University's annual budget was about $1.3 billion, more than six times what it had been in 1976; in real dollars, of course, the budgetary increase was far less than that.

Compared to its peers among public institutions in the exclusive Association of American Universities (AAU), Rutgers tended toward the middle of the pack on most measures of academic achievement. There were some variations, however. In the percentage of faculty and students who were minority or female, Rutgers stood among the highest. In the number of faculty who had been elected to the prestigious national academies of sciences, engineering, and medicine, we ranked above average but far below the universities at the top of the list. In the SAT scores and graduation rates of our students, Rutgers scored about average. To me, the most worrisome comparison was in the area of funded research: Rutgers stood well down on the list of the AAU public universities, around the top of the bottom quartile, right alongside the other institutions that also lacked medical schools. It was imperative to increase the research support Rutgers faculty received from the federal government and other sources.

These statistical comparisons mattered, but other influences also contributed to shaping the agenda of academic issues upon which my presidency would focus. Unquestionably, I was affected by what I had learned and seen during my own earlier days at Rutgers. On the positive side, I remembered well the dramatic enhancement of the University's research distinction that Ed Bloustein, Alec Pond, and their collaborators among deans and faculty had achieved by dint of hard work and sheer will. During the 1980s, Rutgers had burst through old barriers, become a true research university, and landed in the AAU. That job was done, but the task of sustaining and improving the Rutgers research engine, in a world of competitors who were straining mightily to accomplish the same for their own institutions, lay before us. The comparative data on funded research underscored the urgency of attending to this goal. On the negative side, I knew from my previous Rutgers experience about the disorganization of undergraduate education on the New Brunswick campus where four separate colleges, all without faculties, were competing with each other, confusing students and restricting their educational opportunities. While I recognized that Rutgers had changed in many ways during the decade I was away, the knowledge I had gained previously about research and undergraduate education undeniably helped determine the tasks I set myself as president. So, too, did my experiences during the intervening years at UNC–Chapel Hill and the University of Washington, where I learned about the value of having the academic medical center situated within the same institution as the other disciplines and where I had witnessed the uplifting influence of beautiful campus environments upon students and faculty.

National trends in higher education and widely shared currents of thought about the condition of America's universities also influenced our academic agenda for Rutgers. Three developments seemed particularly relevant. First was the widespread concern about the quality and cost of undergraduate education. Politicians and parents alike wanted tangible evidence that students were getting good value for their tuition dollars. That expectation was reflected in growing demands for assessment and accountability, and increasingly, at least among accreditors and regulators, for evidence that graduates had achieved certain specified "learning outcomes." More than ever, universities were supposed to prepare their students for careers offering good jobs; midway through my presidency a severe economic downturn added even greater fervor to that expectation. Second was the demand for research that was practical and helpful in solving real-world problems. Compared to undergraduate education, the research mission of universities has never been widely or popularly grasped, but citizens and elected officials are appreciative when scientists contribute to useful outcomes such as curing diseases, boosting crop yields, or improving transportation safety. A third trend was the seemingly irreversible decline in state support for public universities and the resulting need to find other sources of revenue.

All of these considerations, and more, influenced my presidency's academic goals: comparative information about where the University stood in relation to its peers, my own observations and experiences both at Rutgers and elsewhere, and visible national trends in higher education. Like all new presidents, moreover, I spent much of my first year (when I wasn't struggling with the Vagelos report) talking with students, faculty, deans, alumni, and board members about the opportunities and challenges facing the University; few of those with whom I spoke were shy about letting me know what should be done. Inevitably almost everyone shared the needs they perceived in their corner of the University, but a rough consensus emerged about the most important goals for Rutgers.

Three stood out above the rest. First was elevating the quality of undergraduate education on all three campuses, a goal whose attainment in New Brunswick would require a dramatic and controversial reorganization of that campus. Second was significantly enhancing the University's excellence in research, measured both in the number of dollars obtained to support it and in the development of selected fields whose research outcomes would profoundly benefit people, within New Jersey and beyond. Third was bringing Robert Wood Johnson Medical School back into Rutgers. These ambitions became my top presidential goals.

However lofty and inspiring an academic agenda may be, it is difficult to construct and even more difficult to achieve. Each of our top three goals included numerous components, some envisioned from the outset and others that appeared unexpectedly. For example, the goal of improving undergraduate education always included, among its many purposes, developing new academic offerings and curricula, securing for students the advantages of studying at a research university, and improving nonacademic services for our students. Only later did we realize that the transformation of undergraduate education in New Brunswick presented a remarkable chance to bring about a long-sought reorganization of the entire body of Rutgers alumni. The undergraduate education initiative also contributed unexpectedly to the development and realization of a wholly new vision for the Livingston campus in Piscataway, for decades the forgotten stepchild among Rutgers campuses. Similarly, our focus on research led to a large increase in federal grants to our faculty, just as we had hoped it would, but it also steered us toward interdisciplinary initiatives that we had not originally envisioned but seized upon only later, based on new information and opportunities. Each goal had unique trajectories that took us down unanticipated pathways, including a few dead ends. The agenda continuously emerged and evolved.

Achieving our academic goals—including the many that lay within the purview of faculty and deans, as well as the far smaller number for which I assumed presidential responsibility—depended critically upon several kinds of resources: strong leaders, sufficient dollars, and appropriate facilities located on pleasing campuses. When I became president, many outstanding men and women were already serving as vice presidents and deans, and some of those individuals still are. Right from the start, however, with approval from the Board of Governors, I began authorizing national searches to fill many of the University's leadership positions with new individuals, some drawn from within Rutgers but even more recruited from elsewhere. I took these searches and appointments very seriously because I knew that the quality of our academic achievements would be directly proportional to the excellence of the vice presidents and deans. Over the course of a decade, I made a few mistakes, but I got the great majority of these leadership decisions right, starting with Phil Furmanski, whose 2003 appointment as executive vice president for academic affairs has already been noted. Phil became my main partner in academic leadership and joined with me in recruiting the other vice presidents and deans. By the time we stepped down from our respective positions, we had appointed almost all the deans of the schools and colleges, the true academic leaders of the University. These men and women shared some common characteristics: outstanding academic judgment, an ability to inspire their faculty colleagues, eagerness to collaborate with each other, and a spirit of innovation and entrepreneurship that led them to establish new programs and to generate new resources. They are responsible for much of what Rutgers achieved during my time as president.

The deans' entrepreneurship was one of the most important factors in obtaining the dollars we needed to realize our goals. Over the course of my presidency, Rutgers's annual budget grew from approximately $1.3 billion to more than $2.1 billion, an increase of nearly $100 million a year. Virtually none of this increase came from the state of New Jersey. It came largely from tuition and fees, enrollment growth, research support, and new revenue-generating academic programs. Philanthropic gifts crucially supported a number of our most important initiatives. Led by Phil Furmanski and several of the most entrepreneurial deans, the University revised and clarified its budgetary practices to incentivize schools to expand their programs and their dollars. Now deans could know exactly how much revenue their schools would earn from new online courses, off-campus and international offerings, summer school programs, professional master's degrees, and executive and continuing education programs. These offerings had the double benefit of enabling Rutgers to serve nontraditional students whom the University would not otherwise reach and of generating badly needed revenue. At a time when state support was declining in real dollars, Rutgers looked to itself for the resources required to support its soaring ambitions. We were far from the first American university to make this transition toward self-sufficiency, and indeed the shift was well under way at Rutgers before my time in office, but we accelerated it and thereby gained dollars we would not otherwise have had for our academic programs.

The University's budgetary growth was satisfying, but only up to a point: it came with costs and, sizable as it was, proved inadequate in several worrying ways. The biggest cost was felt by our students, whose tuition rose by an average of more than 6 percent a year. Despite the University's largely successful efforts to cushion the increases through need-based financial aid, some students and their families experienced real hardship. This is a national trend, not just a Rutgers problem, and it threatens to reverse the historic expansion of higher educational opportunities that Americans experienced in the second half of the twentieth century. Notable as our budgetary increases were, moreover, most of the dollars were irretrievably obligated for specific purposes and were not available for discretionary spending to improve the University. Above all, we lacked sufficient resources to recruit enough tenured and tenure-track faculty members, especially in newer academic fields where just two or three appointments, carefully chosen to exploit Rutgers's and New Jersey's comparative advantages, could have propelled the University into positions of national leadership. The shortage of full-time faculty hires also meant that ever-larger numbers of courses were taught by part-time lecturers. Excellent as many PTLs may be in the classroom, they are not paid to carry on the full range of faculty responsibilities in research and service upon which the life of the University depends. This, too, is a national trend. Finally, our budgets were insufficient to provide faculty and staff with the compensation increases they deserved. As a result, Rutgers, like other public universities in an age of declining state support, fell further behind its private counterparts in the average salaries paid to faculty. Although a mass exodus of top scholars from Rutgers to prestigious private institutions has not yet occurred, a number of star faculty were lost, and the public-private salary gap continues to place at risk the long-term quality of the University's greatest asset, its faculty. If the state of New Jersey had just maintained in real dollars its annual support for Rutgers, these risks and damaging trends could have been avoided.

Lastly, the achievement of our academic goals depended upon adequate facilities for teaching, research, and student life, all situated on attractive campuses. Here, too, the record is mixed. During my presidency, Rutgers constructed new academic buildings and residence halls on every campus. Most of them, such as the law school at Camden, the business school at Newark, and new science buildings on the Busch Campus in Piscataway, would have been proud additions to any institution in the world. The new apartment-style residence halls look jaw-droppingly beautiful, especially to anyone who ever lived in a traditional dormitory with tiny rooms, bunk beds, and the bathroom way down the hall. The University also spent tens of millions of dollars renovating existing classrooms on every campus and equipping them with state-of-the-art technology. Despite these achievements, however, so much more could have been done with greater resources. Particularly in New Brunswick, many of the buildings are old and shabby, and across all three campuses more than a half billion dollars is needed for deferred maintenance. The government of New Jersey provided virtually no support for the facilities of the state university.

Soon after becoming president, I advanced an ambitious proposal for remaking the University's oldest campus, College Avenue in New Brunswick. The home of thousands of students, most of the humanities and social science departments, the main library, and the University's central administration, College Avenue is the historic heart of Rutgers. But it was deteriorating and more than a little dilapidated and didn't look very much like the revered central campus spaces at many of America's most picturesque universities. Believing that beautiful campuses add immeasurably to the satisfaction that students, faculty, and staff find in their work, I made a bold but ultimately impractical suggestion for closing College Avenue to vehicular traffic and turning it into a pedestrian mall. I envisioned shaded pathways, cozy gathering spaces, and altogether a campus that evoked the emotion of a Polk Place at Chapel Hill or the Rainier vista on the UW campus in Seattle. Students and alumni, in particular, responded positively to my proposal, which soon became known as the "greening" of College Avenue. But it was not to be. Independent consultants advised us that closing the street to cars and buses (especially to buses!) was impractical, and over time we settled on a much more modest plan of landscape architectural improvements. College Avenue is now prettier than it was a decade ago but is not fundamentally different—except, that is, for the addition of the grand Barnes & Noble Rutgers University Bookstore, a project in which I took intense personal interest.

Ironically, perhaps, the College Avenue campus is soon going to see its most significant transformation ever, because Rutgers has recently acquired most of the property belonging to the adjacent New Brunswick Theological Seminary. Long sought on my watch and formally approved during my last month as president, the acquisition of the seminary land and the construction of several major academic buildings there will remake College Avenue just as spectacularly as I originally hoped, but in a very different way. My successor as president, himself a firm believer in the power of campus improvements, will proudly cut the ribbon on all that. Unexpectedly, it was the Livingston campus into which I ended up pouring my convictions about beautiful campuses.

As my College Avenue anecdote may suggest, as Rutgers president I focused most of my attention on the University's oldest, largest, and most distinguished campus in New Brunswick. Although this sometimes annoyed my colleagues in Camden and Newark, those campuses did not actually suffer because of any neglect. On the contrary, they thrived academically, and both exceeded the University's overall rate of enrollment growth. With my support, Camden established a nursing school; launched its first-ever Ph.D. programs; constructed a spectacular new law school building; and dramatically renovated and improved its dining, recreational, classroom, and library facilities, thus making that campus far more attractive to students and faculty. Newark established its new School of Public Affairs and Administration, acquired and meticulously renovated a majestic building for the business school, added significantly to its teaching and research facilities in the biological sciences, doubled its on-campus student housing capacity, and gained national acclaim as a model urban campus and the most diverse university in America. The credit for these achievements belongs, above all, to the campus leaders: in Camden, Provost Roger Dennis, Interim Chancellor Margaret Marsh, and Chancellor Wendell Pritchett; in Newark, Provost/Chancellor Steven Diner; and on both campuses, the academic deans. Although differences emerged between Steve Diner and me toward the end of my presidency, I had confidence in these leaders and took pride in their achievements.

⁂

All three campuses shared the twin goals of improving undergraduate education and research, but by far the greatest improvements were needed in New Brunswick. A research university offers students boundless opportunities to choose from among hundreds of subjects and thousands of faculty with whom they can experience the excitement of acquiring and applying new knowledge. This kind of learning will serve them well whatever they choose to do for the rest of their lives. But the riches of research universities are not always readily available

to undergraduates. These institutions tend to value and reward graduate and professional study above undergraduate teaching and are often
organized in ways that are inhospitable to younger students. Universities like Rutgers have to work conscientiously to keep their promises
to undergraduates, and in the early 2000s many research universities
were doing exactly that. Michigan and Harvard, for example, brought
forth well-regarded faculty reports on how to improve undergraduate
education. All these difficulties were compounded at Rutgers–New
Brunswick by the disorganization to which I have already referred, by
a patchwork quilt of undergraduate colleges without faculties and an
arts and sciences faculty without true responsibility for the students.
And so in April 2004, Phil Furmanski and I did what presidents and
vice presidents always do: we appointed a committee, specifically a task
force of faculty and students to make recommendations for addressing the problems of undergraduate education. Astonishingly, perhaps,
that's exactly what they did, and their bold proposals were overwhelmingly approved and enacted.

To lead the task force, we chose Barry V. Qualls, a much-loved,
longtime faculty member and dean of humanities who was Rutgers's
most respected advocate for protecting and defending the mission of
undergraduate education. Barry had chaired the English department
many years earlier when I was dean of the Faculty of Arts and Sciences, and we knew each other well. In the intervening years, he had
led several efforts to reorganize and improve undergraduate education
at New Brunswick, but entrenched interests, mainly in the colleges and
the alumni associations, had always beaten back the proposed reforms.
Fortunately, Barry was willing to try again, and, working with Phil and
me, he assembled an outstanding group of faculty, students, and a few
administrators. Besides Barry, a number of well-regarded faculty members played essential roles in crafting the report and recommendations
of the task force and then in leading the massive campus conversation
that followed. They included Michael Beals, Martha Cotter, Haym
Hirsh, Peter Klein, Richard Miller, Angela O'Donnell, Kathleen Scott,
Linda Stamato, Lea Stewart, and Carla Yanni, several of whom I knew
from my old days at FAS. Undergraduate students also made major

contributions to the work of the task force, chief among them David Cole and Adam Cooper. Many more students later assumed leadership roles in the campus community's lively deliberations on the report; among the bravest and ultimately most influential of these were two presidents of the Douglass College Government Association, Kelly Brennan and Celeste Barretto.

Trusting the task force, Phil and I refrained from interfering in its work or telegraphing the recommendations we wished to receive. Barry kept us pretty well informed, however, so that we would not be blindsided by the final report. By early spring 2005, his group had been at work for nearly a year, and its proposals, though still confidential, seemed likely to include phasing out the colleges and establishing a single school of arts and sciences. These recommendations would be highly controversial and would inspire significant opposition. Throughout the year, I had provided updates on the task force to the Boards of Governors and Trustees, but now I stepped up my communications with them. Remembering and regretting that I had gotten out ahead of the boards at several points during the Vagelos process, I was not going to let that happen again. At the end of the day, the Board of Governors would make the final decision on any major changes, but closer to the beginning of the process the Board of Trustees was even more important. The great majority of trustees were Rutgers alumni, and many of them had graduated from the New Brunswick colleges whose future was now in doubt. Trustee opposition could well doom the report, while trustee support would likely carry weight with alumni generally and with the Board of Governors. Well before the task force report became public in July, Phil and Barry and I, together with some of the key faculty, spent a lot of time sharing with board members the rationale for the anticipated recommendations. The incoming chair of the Board of Trustees, Robert Laudicina, promised me that the trustees would give the report the attention it deserved early in the next academic year.

Well behind the scenes and in deeply declining health was my father, with whom I talked often about the work of the task force. A veteran observer of Rutgers's eternal efforts to get itself organized, he had been a loyal critic of Ed Bloustein's campus reorganization of 1981, and his perspective on that previous effort was pertinent now. It was, he wrote at the time, "an awkward and intricate compromise between champions of collegiate autonomy and those who would institute a more conventional scheme of university organization. . . . There will be no faculties, in the proper sense of that term, governing the work of most of the undergraduates in New Brunswick." My father and I had discussed these issues over the years, and, although I admired the positive outcomes of the 1981 reorganization, I shared his misgivings about a system in which colleges without faculties controlled undergraduate education. Unbeknownst to me, Barry Qualls had shared a number of my father's writings on this subject with the members of the task force, and their final product unmistakably reflected his influence. Besides our frequent conversations, my father still kept up his longtime practice of expressing his thoughts in writing for me. His last note, typed as always by my mother, was dated October 15, 2005.

As the task force report neared completion and rumors about its recommendations began leaking out, the alumnae leaders of Douglass College laid plans for a vigorous campaign to "save" their college. They would appeal to the deep emotional attachments that Douglass graduates felt for their alma mater; would recall with pride the historic role that Douglass had played in advancing educational opportunities for women; and would warn that without Douglass fewer women would study math, science, and engineering or would attain preparation for lifetimes of leadership. Thanks to such advocacy, New Jersey newspapers carried the Douglass story even before the task force report was finished, and in Trenton dozens of legislators signed on to sponsor resolutions praising Douglass. The save-Douglass campaign avidly sought but never obtained active intervention on the college's behalf by United States senator and soon-to-be governor Jon S. Corzine. The campaign for Douglass had an ally in Maggie M. Moran, a 1996 graduate of Douglass, a passionate supporter of her alma mater, and one of Corzine's closest advisers both in Washington, D.C., and in Trenton. Influenced no doubt by Moran, gubernatorial candidate Corzine issued a statement of support for "the integrity and identity of Douglass as a college," but that's about as far as he went. On two occasions he promised me that he would respect the University's decision-making processes and would stay out of the fight. He was as good as his word.

Advocates for Douglass were utterly correct in claiming for their college a proud history of educating women at a time when no other institution in New Jersey was doing that, but the current realities were far different. On every Rutgers campus and everywhere around the state, women now had access to the same educational opportunities as men. Within departments and centers across the University, students and faculty were carrying on outstanding research related to women, and Rutgers's department of women's and gender studies was regarded as among the best in the world. Most college-bound women were now uninterested in attending single-sex institutions, and, with many fewer applicants than before, Douglass College's academic profile had been declining for years. Of the women who were admitted each year to both Douglass College and Rutgers College, only a handful chose Douglass. As for the claims about math, science, and engineering, just 9 percent of Douglass students graduated in those fields, compared to 17 percent of the women at Rutgers College. As for leadership opportunities for female students, plenty existed outside of Douglass: women held 60 percent of the executive positions within Rutgers College student organizations, including half the presidencies. Appeals to emotion and loyalty can be more persuasive than statements of fact, however, and the campaign to save Douglass mustered lots of support—on campus among Douglass students, around the state among those who believed its claims, and everywhere among loyal Douglass alumnae.

The Douglass question would prove to be by far the most contentious part of reorganizing undergraduate education. Thanks to the college's passionate and energetic alumnae, news coverage of Douglass continued to dwarf the attention paid to anything else and created the impression that the Rutgers administration had a vendetta against women's education. The advocates for Douglass continuously stirred the pot in Trenton and led legislators to ask me about this issue again and again. My efforts to explain the goals we were trying to achieve drew blank stares more often than I would have liked. At no point could I be certain that the state government would refrain from interfering with the University's process. Back on campus, the Douglass issue divided faculty, staff, and students and put me at odds with some people whom I had known during my earlier days at Rutgers and a few I had known for most of my life. It was particularly hurtful to disagree with Mary S. Hartman, an old friend, a history colleague, and a former dean of Douglass who was widely admired and well liked by everyone at Rutgers, certainly including me. But feelings and tensions ran high. One afternoon I found myself standing in a parking lot having an argument, maybe even a shouting match, with Carmen Twillie Ambar, then dean of Douglass, who was in a difficult predicament, unluckily caught between her alumnae and her president, and was trying hard to manage a difficult situation for her college. That was not a very presidential moment.

By early July 2005, the Qualls task force had finished its report. Though lengthy, the document offered recommendations for achieving two goals above all others: expanding the educational opportunities available to undergraduate students and reestablishing the faculty's responsibility for undergraduate education. There would be a single set of admissions standards for all arts and sciences applicants. Those who were admitted, either to arts and sciences or to one of the professional schools, and who wished to live in the residence halls would choose from among the five campuses in New Brunswick/Piscataway, except that only women could live on the Douglass campus. The University's academic programs, resources, and facilities would be open to all students, no matter where they lived. There would be a single core curriculum, a single honors program, and universal access to academic advising, student activities, and student services. And much more. As expected, the report called for replacing the colleges with one school of arts and sciences whose faculty would be responsible for the undergraduate curriculum and for all the educational decisions that lie within a faculty's purview. Although the proposed changes were momentous, the task force urged the university community to accept them and to begin implementing them so that first-year students arriving in the fall of 2007 would embark upon the new system of undergraduate education. Students who were already enrolled in the colleges could complete their degrees and receive their diplomas as though nothing had changed.

Meticulous planning lay behind our rollout of the report. Board members were sent advance copies along with eight pages of talking points to which they could refer when questioned. Alumni leaders and legislators received advance notice of the report and a summary of its recommendations. On July 18, Phil, Barry, and I, together with selected faculty members of the task force, held a well-attended press conference to announce and explain the report. A dedicated website went live that same day, and the document itself flew electronically to tens of thousands, including faculty, staff, students, alumni, legislators, and donors. Over the next several days, we met with the editorial boards of newspapers throughout the state. I personally phoned more than thirty members of the legislature and followed each call with a hand-written note. Most of my legislative conversations were substantive, brief, and cordial, but many legislators clearly had already heard from Douglass. Over the course of the rest of the summer, we met with representatives of all the key constituencies on campus, particularly students, and prepared for an academic year in which practically every unit and organization within the University would deliberate about the report. One August meeting I'll never forget was with Professor Martha Cotter, a member of the task force and also chair of the University Senate. Martha told me that the senate and its many committees would give undivided attention to the report and would deliver its response to me during the fourth week of February. I had no idea how Martha conjured up such a precise prediction, but I thanked her. The senate adopted its final recommendations concerning the report on February 24, 2006!

The 2005 fall semester at Rutgers–New Brunswick was unlike any other I ever experienced. Every department, every school and college, and every student governing association plunged into discussions of undergraduate education. My own relationship to this process was quite sensitive: I supported the proposals in the report, but I also had a solemn responsibility to listen carefully to the campus conversation and to consider the ideas it brought forth, even if they diverged from the report. In my annual address on September 16, the occasion on which I was questioned for so long by banner-bearing Douglass students, I acknowledged that I was sympathetic to the report and the directions it proposed, but I predicted that with the benefit of so much campus discussion my final recommendations would depart in some respects from those of the task force. I promised that I would not formulate my own report to the Board of Governors until "every group and person who wants to speak" has had an opportunity to do so. "Rutgers," I said, "is an open, deliberative community, and this is the way we do things. When the process is done and the decisions have been made, everyone will be able to say, 'I had an opportunity to express my views, and I was heard.' So let's have an exemplary discussion in the best Rutgers tradition." And we did.

The main events, out of many, were the open forums on every campus in New Brunswick and Piscataway. Held on weekday evenings from late September through the middle of November, these meetings each drew hundreds of students, faculty, and staff, and each lasted for hours. The discussions were lively, not just at Douglass but everywhere. Livingston College students, for example, observed that they felt inferior to other Rutgers students because their campus facilities were not as good and because Livingston's admissions standards were believed to be weaker than the requirements elsewhere. But for all that, Livingston students said how much they cherished their small college's atmosphere, and some worried that the proposed changes would take that away. I attended every forum but scarcely spoke because I was there to listen. The spirit was that of a university community coming together to grapple with big and important decisions about its future—and that's exactly what was happening.

As the campus conversation unfolded, many individuals found themselves torn within their own minds and cross-pressured by competing loyalties. The colleges, whose fate was now the most highly charged issue among the many under discussion, each represented proud, prized themes in the University's long history. Rutgers College symbolized our institution's founding before the American Revolution and its commitment to undergraduate education of the highest quality. Douglass College represented the University's enduring obligation to provide equal educational opportunities for women. Livingston College stood for cultural and economic diversity and for educating men and women regardless of their heritage or economic status. University College epitomized our long-standing promise to nontraditional students, whose work or family responsibilities precluded them from full-time college attendance, but who deserved and cherished a chance to earn a Rutgers degree. No one was proposing that Rutgers should walk away from any of these values and commitments—indeed, all of them were now embedded throughout the University, not just in the colleges that had pioneered them—although an uninitiated observer of the impassioned debates occurring in the fall of 2005 might have concluded otherwise. In such a circumstance, courageous women and men, whose prior allegiances could have inclined them toward silence or even toward resisting the proposed changes in undergraduate education, now stepped boldly forward.

Particularly notable were several strong women, each with deep Douglass roots, who played visible, valuable roles in advancing the task force recommendations, despite the censure they endured from Douglass women who saw things differently. These included Linda Stamato, a Douglass alum, former member of the Board of Governors, former acting dean of Douglass, member of the Qualls task force, and a professor in the Bloustein School of Planning and Public Policy; Martha Cotter, also a former acting dean of Douglass, a task force member, chair of the University Senate, and a professor of chemistry; and Bernice Proctor Venable and Christine Tiritilli, both Douglass graduates and both active, articulate, and respected alumnae. I know from private conversations with each of them how deeply they believed in the goals we were trying to achieve but also how much anguish they endured for the sake of their convictions. Another hero, although in a very different category, was Carl Kirschner, a longtime faculty member, now dean of Rutgers College, and an early advocate of the task force recommendations. This was not easy for Carl, first, because his own job, the deanship of Rutgers College, would be a casualty of the proposed reorganization, and second, because many of his loyal alumni hated the idea of losing their college and they let Carl know how they felt. These five individuals, and others, modeled bravery and selflessness as the campus conversation went forward that fall.

By late October, the results were already starting to come in. The Rutgers Alumni Association, by far the largest of the University's nineteen alumni organizations, weighed in first with a strong affirmation of the Qualls report. This was huge, because alumni had been unsupportive of previous efforts to reorganize undergraduate education and because we doubted the report would ever win approval from the Douglass alumnae body. Next the students began to be heard from, beginning with the Rutgers College Governing Association, which expressed its approval on November 15. The independent student newspaper, the *Daily Targum*, also voiced support early in the process. The month of December brought even more vital backing, first from the New Brunswick Faculty Council and then from the Board of Trustees. As would be expected from a body of faculty leaders, the council's opinion was long and thoughtful. It embraced almost everything in the Qualls report but suggested a number of detailed modifications, several of which ended up in my own final recommendations to the Board of Governors. The trustees' endorsement came on December 15, after months of deliberation led by an ad hoc committee of seven who commended the Qualls recommendations to their fellow board members. The trustees, however, were not unanimous in their support: the vote was thirty yes, seven no, and six abstentions. Given the lack of unanimity and the passion for Douglass among several board members, the collegial trustees could easily have dodged a decisive vote or postponed one until the new year. But led by Bob Laudicina and by the cochairs of its ad hoc committee, Gerald C. Harvey and Rochelle Gizinski, the board acted courageously and, as the fall term came to a close, imparted tremendous momentum to the task force report. I now knew that its major recommendations would eventually be adopted.

Sometime over the Christmas holidays, my father and I talked about Rutgers for the last time. I told him about the trustees' approval of the plan and reminded him that his own insights had helped inspire the dramatic changes we were undertaking. Sadly, I discerned from his brief response that he was not really following the story anymore. The man who once knew more about the history and organization of Rutgers than anyone else ever did, or ever will, died on January 16, 2006, at age eighty-nine.

As the Rutgers–New Brunswick community reconvened for the spring semester, the most significant body that had not yet rendered its judgment on the Qualls report was the University Senate, historically independent minded and protective of its prerogatives. Under Martha Cotter's leadership, the senate had apportioned responsibility for evaluating the report among its committees, each of which had taken seriously its tasks. The senate wasn't going to rubber-stamp anything. At last, in late February, just as Martha had foretold, the senate finished its work and approved an exceptional document containing thirty-eight recommendations. Most of them echoed the task force report, but there were some differences reflecting the senate's own deliberations, as well as the obvious attention that its members had paid to the campus-wide discussion. I would end up accepting the recommendations of the senate in several areas where it differed from the Qualls report.

Our Rutgers process had worked well. In quiet consultation with the chair of the Board of Governors, Al Gamper, and with the other members of the board, I learned they shared my belief that the University community had reached a broad and deep consensus. There was not unanimity, to be sure, but there was sufficient support on which to rest a final decision. Everyone had been heard.

Just one more thing remained to be done before I prepared my report to the board, and that was to meet halfway those who cherished Douglass College, without abandoning the fundamental changes we were trying to make. Fortunately, the reports of the New Brunswick Faculty Council and the University Senate had proposed a way to do that, which I now embraced. The Douglass campus would provide not only a single-sex environment for women who chose to live there but also, for interested women students, the Douglass Residential College would offer cocurricular and student-life programs consistent with the historic mission of Douglass and, with approval from the new School of Arts and Sciences, related curricular opportunities as well. This complex formulation largely solved the problem. Although they would have far preferred to maintain the status quo, Douglass alumnae and student leaders signaled their acceptance of the compromise. I was grateful to Martha Cotter and to Paul Leath, formerly provost when I was FAS dean and now chair of the faculty council, for helping to devise a satisfactory outcome for Douglass.

At a press conference on March 7, I announced my plan for undergraduate education and commended it to the Board of Governors for approval. It was the Qualls plan, but revised in a number of ways to reflect ideas that had emerged during the campus conversation, as well to meet the concerns at Douglass. Two areas in which I went beyond the task force report are worth mentioning: a proposal for seminars for first-year students to be taught by senior members of the faculty and a commitment to remedy the disparities between the neglected Livingston campus and the other campuses. My final recommendations were well received, both within Rutgers and beyond. Three days later, the Board of Governors, which had been engaged and supportive throughout the process, formally approved the reorganization of the New Brunswick campus and of undergraduate education. The *Star-Ledger* was supportive, too: "Making fundamental changes at an academic institution rooted in tradition requires patience, care, and transparency. The restructuring at Rutgers has been marked by all three."

So many good things would flow from the decision to reorganize the New Brunswick campus. But first a lot of work had to be done, and done fast, to establish the new system of undergraduate education in time for first-year students arriving in the fall of 2007. Most urgently, a single process of admissions and recruitment had to be created in place of the separate and competing collegiate processes, and information about it had to be communicated quickly and clearly to high school students, parents, and guidance counselors. That in turn meant, among many tasks, that a new curriculum had to be developed so that applicants to Rutgers would have information about the educational requirements they would be expected to fulfill in order to graduate. To meet this need, the arts and sciences faculty speedily adopted an interim curriculum blending the separate college curricula and then turned to the far more challenging task of devising a wholly new permanent curriculum that would meet the needs of twenty-first-century students. Acting with equal urgency, student affairs staff merged separate college-based programs and services into New Brunswick–wide organizations. Residence hall activities, recreational facilities, student centers, psychological counseling, and much more were now reorganized on the principle that services for students should be managed centrally but delivered locally, so that everyone would have nearby access to quality programs. Students themselves took responsibility for creating the Rutgers University Student Assembly, a student government body representing all undergraduates on the New Brunswick campus, something that had never been done before. All of this work found dramatic expression and fulfillment on the evening of September 1, 2007, when more than six thousand new undergraduates—including both first-year and transfer students—gathered for convocation in the football stadium. They were a single body of Rutgers students, all chosen according to the same high standards of admission and all welcomed to an institution that had just taken some giant steps toward expanding educational opportunity and diminishing both confusion and disparity.

Not for decades had an arts and sciences faculty at Rutgers–New Brunswick developed a new core curriculum. Now an interdisciplinary committee of twenty-two faculty members, working with four academic administrators and three students, imagined, debated, and, at the end of their labors, wrote down what they believed a college-educated person should know and be able to do. Traditional core curricula are based on distribution requirements that students fulfill by taking specified numbers of courses in the humanities, social sciences, and sciences. Rutgers students would still take courses in all those areas, but the new core was defined not by disciplinary divisions but by carefully chosen learning goals that students would achieve through courses specially designed to promote them. Several of the goals demand an understanding of twenty-first-century challenges, for example, the ability to "analyze a contemporary global issue from a multidisciplinary perspective." Other goals relate to particular areas of inquiry, such as understanding scientific principles and concepts. Still others demand the achievement of cognitive skills, including writing and quantitative reasoning. Many courses in the core are designed to meet multiple learning goals, including the hugely popular "signature courses" on such topics as "Human Nature and Human Diversity" and "Energy and Climate Change."

Acting on the committee's recommendation in the spring of 2008, faculty in the new School of Arts and Sciences adopted the principles of the proposed core curriculum. Over the next several years, departments and faculty devised new courses and redesigned old ones to promote the learning goals that would now form the basis of a Rutgers education. To the extent possible, faculty in the professional schools on the New Brunswick campus also agreed to require their students to meet the demands of the new core. Without a doubt, the nation-wide trend toward assessment and accountability in undergraduate education influenced these developments at Rutgers, but the curricular outcome our faculty produced was distinctly their own. They had reassumed responsibility for their students' education—and inspiringly so.

Among our top goals was securing for undergraduate students the unique advantages of studying at a research university. That meant, above all, access to the most distinguished faculty and opportunities to do research. Thanks to a generous gift from Jack Byrne, a 1950s-era Rutgers alumnus who remembered his alma mater as a smaller and more intimate institution where students interacted easily with the most accomplished professors, the University launched a program of seminars for first-year students taught by senior faculty members and limited to twenty students per class. Beginning in the fall of 2007, dozens of faculty eagerly offered these courses on a wide range of engaging subjects, and the program immediately attracted nearly half of the first-year class. It has grown ever since; by 2014, three-quarters of the newest students are expected to be enrolled. Young men and women arriving for the first time at a large university inevitably are wary of approaching faculty, especially because most of the professors they initially see are lecturing from distant platforms to hundreds of students.

First-year seminars break down that wariness by placing the professor at a table surrounded by a small number of students—or, as is often the case, on a field trip or in the faculty member's laboratory. Everyone present, teacher and students alike, has chosen to be there because they share a common interest. Through that experience, students begin to discover the riches within an institution that previously seemed forbidding and to become comfortable with faculty who formerly appeared remote. While president, I taught several first-year seminars and found them to be remarkably rewarding, for the students and for me.

At the other end of their undergraduate lives, juniors and seniors at Rutgers now have vastly expanded opportunities to become involved in research of their own, under the direction of faculty members. Like the first-year seminars, undergraduate research benefited dramatically from the generous philanthropy of a grateful Rutgers alumnus—in this case, Jerome Aresty, and his wife, Lorraine. That gift, coming right at the moment when we were reorganizing the campus, enabled the University to expand a small Rutgers College program for undergraduate research to students everywhere in New Brunswick. Many modes and models are available for students to get involved in creating and applying new knowledge: honors programs in their majors, summer research assistantships with faculty, or yearlong projects for which students can receive stipends to cover the cost of their research. Every spring, hundreds of students are chosen to present their findings at an annual undergraduate research symposium. Most students, whether or not they pursue postgraduate education and whatever careers they may choose, will spend much of the rest of their lives seeking, analyzing, expressing, and applying new knowledge. There could be no better preparation than learning to do these things under the tutelage of faculty who are accomplished in research.

As their undergraduate educations come to a close, the very best Rutgers students are now applying for, and receiving, distinguished fellowships for which the nationwide competition is exceedingly fierce: Fulbright grants, Gates-Cambridge scholarships, Whitakers, Goldwaters, Churchills, Mitchells, Trumans, Erteguns, and more. These awards, most of which support international graduate study, enable the recipients to have life-changing educational experiences. Because these opportunities are so competitive, a university's success in winning them has become a notable mark of prestige. Prior to 2008, only a dozen or so Rutgers students applied annually for these awards, and only about three were successful each year. Just a few years later, thanks to the talents of Arthur D. Casciato, whom we recruited from the University of Pennsylvania to head this program, nearly two hundred students were applying; in 2010 and again in 2011, nineteen Rutgers applicants succeeded in winning one of these fellowships, as did thirty-nine in 2012 and thirty-nine again in 2013. Before 2008, Rutgers didn't really figure among AAU institutions in securing these awards; now we rank not at the very top but among the best. The success enjoyed by Rutgers students was not directly due to the reorganization of undergraduate education, but it would not have occurred without the creation of a campus-wide support structure for identifying and nurturing potential applicants.

Nowhere was the transformation of undergraduate education more evident than at Douglass. In the early 2000s, new students enrolling at Douglass College lagged behind their classmates elsewhere at Rutgers on the standard measures of academic achievement, including high school grades and SAT scores. With the creation of the Douglass Residential College in 2007, Rutgers's all-women's campus became a more attractive destination for top students from within and beyond New Jersey and for outstanding minority students. The academic indices for Douglass students rose approximately to the level of the rest of the New Brunswick campus, and Douglass began enrolling higher percentages of out-of-state students, African Americans, and Hispanic/Latinos than the rest of Rutgers. Douglass no longer awards baccalaureate degrees, but owing in large measure to the loyalty and generosity of its alumnae, it offers unique living and learning communities in its residence halls, externships enabling young women to explore careers of all kinds, and attractive programs of international study.

Together these initiatives expanded the opportunities available to Rutgers students and diminished the confusion and inequality that historically had attended undergraduate education. But much remains to be done. Faculty are now far more involved than they were before in making fundamental decisions about their students' education and are engaged in many more conversations about it, but the University's reward structure does not yet fully reflect the new state of affairs or adequately incentivize professors to keep their focus on undergraduates. At the very least, there should be more recognition, even symbolic recognition, for this kind of work. The insidious, competitive hierarchy of the former colleges is now gone, but a new financial competitiveness among and between the professional schools and the arts and sciences has appeared, and the University has not yet solved the problem of adequately supporting the arts and sciences whose faculty provide basic instruction for all undergraduates. Many courses are taught by part-time lecturers and graduate students instead of by tenured and tenure-track faculty. Two kinds of solutions will be required to ameliorate these problems. The first, of course, is more resources from within the University and from the state of New Jersey. The second is willingness within the Rutgers community continuously to come together to address the University's organizational challenges—a willingness that was amply shown in the transformation of undergraduate education.

An unanticipated dividend of that transformation was the dramatic reformation and renewal of the Livingston campus in Piscataway. Burdened, at least ostensibly, with a late-1960s mission whose relevance had steeply declined, physically unattractive, and home to students who resented their lowly status within Rutgers, Livingston needed and deserved significant attention. In truth the campus had warranted help for a very long time, but several influences now converged to supply it. First were the students living there, who seized upon the debate over the Qualls report to highlight the inadequacies of Livingston's student center, recreation center, residence halls, and dining facility, and, more generally, the neglect of their campus. Their appeals set change in motion, but just as important was an academic vision for Livingston that Phil Furmanski first advanced. That campus, he proposed, should become the home of professional education in the fields of business, management and labor relations, social work, and education. These areas had much in common, including a focus on the fulfillment of human potential, one of the original goals of Livingston College. Their concentration at Livingston would promote synergies among them and provide that campus with the academic mission it sorely lacked. Livingston's transformation was also enabled by the availability of undeveloped land; the ease of transportation, thanks to the state of New Jersey's extension and improvement of Route 18; and the absence of local resistance in that sparsely populated section of Piscataway. In each of these respects, Livingston had an advantage over College Avenue as a site for growth and change. The final circumstance that promoted the transformation of Livingston was the steady increase of undergraduate enrollment on the New Brunswick–Piscataway campus, from 28,000 in 2002 to 32,000 in 2012. A critical component of our budgetary plan, the enrollment growth necessitated the provision of more residence hall beds and dining services. Everything came together to advance Livingston.

First were the student life centers, upon whose shortcomings campus residents initially fastened their attention. The renovated recreation center opened in 2007, and the student center, now doubled in size and with attractive new activity spaces, reached completion two years later. Next was the glorious new dining hall that threw open its doors in 2011. While these projects were under way, guided by Greg Blimling, vice president for student affairs, the University remade the landscape of Livingston by creating attractive gathering places for students, planting hundreds of shrubs and trees, and constructing a fountain that inspires awe and sometimes invites trouble. The students loved it. Consistent with Phil's academic vision and a growing demand for undergraduate business education, the architectural masterpiece of the Livingston campus is the stunning new facility for the business school, a project that was significantly aided by a gift of $10 million from a Rutgers alumnus. (The same donor, who wishes to remain anonymous, also contributed $30 million to endow faculty chairs across a wide range of academic disciplines.) In 2012, the residence hall apartments opened with two thousand new beds, student-friendly shops, and three large classrooms that double as movie theaters on the weekends. A final component of Livingston's transformation was the brainchild of Tony Calcado, vice president for facilities: the installation of almost thirty thousand solar energy panels, mainly atop parking lots, that supply 60 percent of Livingston's electrical power. An environmentally conscious generation of students loved that, too. Buildings for social work and education still remain to be built there, but the Livingston campus already has become a far livelier and more attractive place to live and learn because we listened to students, took advantage of unexpected opportunities, and pursued our academic goals.

The final big thing that got done because of the changes in undergraduate education was the establishment of a single alumni association to which all of Rutgers's living graduates now belong. That may seem like a farfetched outcome, but it really was not. Phasing out the New Brunswick colleges as degree-granting units meant that within a few years Rutgers, Douglass, Livingston, and University College would no longer be producing alumni and funneling them into the University's traditional alumni associations—of which there were nineteen, all associated with particular schools or colleges. Because the nineteen did not cooperate or even communicate much with each other, there had been several earlier efforts to bring their members together into one organization that would more fully meet the needs of both the graduates and their alma mater. Those efforts had always fallen victim to opposition from leaders of the largest associations who cherished their independence and autonomy. In March 2006, the Board of Governors' approval of the undergraduate reorganization reopened the alumni question. Over the course of the next several months, I conferred quietly with selected leaders from among the graduates of all three campuses and from many of the associations, and together we decided to take another run at creating better arrangements for Rutgers and its alumni.

From the beginning, this was a sensitive project because alumni have a perfect right to organize themselves in any ways they see fit. The University can provide advice and support, but alumni associations belong to the alumni. Fortunately, however, there were many well-respected graduates from all corners of the University who recognized the limitations of the existing system and wanted to change it. In

September 2006, I appointed a task force of twenty-seven representing all three campuses and most of the nineteen associations. Its chair was Gene O'Hara, an alumnus of Rutgers-Newark and former chair of the Board of Governors; its vice chair was Gerry Harvey, a Rutgers College graduate, a veteran of earlier efforts to reorganize the alumni, and most recently an architect of the Board of Trustees' support for the Qualls report. My charge to the task force was lengthy, but basically it came down to a request for recommendations designed to establish the best possible, mutually beneficial relationship between Rutgers and its then-350,000 living graduates. Everything was on the table.

Just under a year later, the task force presented a compelling report. It set forth the many benefits that Rutgers and its alumni could gain from each other, but it also laid bare the uncoordinated, wasteful, and confusing character of the University's existing alumni organizations. In their place, the task force recommended "a new partnership between Rutgers and its alumni" to be achieved through the establishment of a single Rutgers University Alumni Association (RUAA) embracing all of the University's graduates. The report's many recommendations dealt with governance of the new association, funding for alumni activities (the University should provide more money), membership dues (abolish them), and *Rutgers Magazine* (send it to all RUAA members). Some of the report's most important observations concerned the potential for developing a myriad of regional clubs and shared interest groups. There would be one overarching alumni association but no limit upon the ways in which Rutgers graduates could organize and engage with each other and with the University.

During the fall of 2007, in an echo of the deliberative process employed two years earlier on undergraduate education, the University sponsored well-attended gatherings in Newark, Camden, and New Brunswick, as well as an online forum, to elicit alumni response to the task force report. Though not unanimous, the verdict was overwhelmingly favorable, and in December 2007, I endorsed the recommendations and named an implementation team of alumni to develop detailed plans for establishing the RUAA. The team, chaired by Robert Stevenson, a graduate of the School of Engineering and a member of the Board of Trustees, finished its work a few months later, and, with approval from the Board of Governors, Rutgers achieved at last a comprehensive organization of its alumni. Under the RUAA's wing, and through the work of the University's vice president for alumni relations, Donna Thornton, Rutgers graduates are now more closely connected to their alma mater and more actively engaged with it than ever before. More than 400,000 receive *Rutgers Magazine* three times a year, and 200,000 for whom the University has e-mail addresses receive frequent communications from Rutgers and from fellow alumni. Around the country and around the world, nearly 150 chartered alumni organizations have sprung into existence, based on geography, academic background, and shared interests of all kinds. Each year these groups sponsor approximately 1,000 events, bringing their members together for socializing, professional networking, and fund raising to support scholarships for Rutgers students. (Among these chartered organizations are the nineteen original alumni associations, which continue to serve their members.) When Rutgers-Camden was severely threatened in 2012, a story I'll tell in a later chapter, the RUAA's communication network enabled Camden alumni to learn what was going on and to defend their campus.

These were the many and varied fruits of our focus on undergraduate education. On the research side of the academic agenda, the outcomes were equally important, perhaps even more so because of the national and international distinction they brought to Rutgers. This was true both because the overall size of the University's research engine grew significantly and because many of the particular research achievements were important, either scientifically or practically or both. Here, however, my role was more distant and my relationship to the action less direct than it was in undergraduate education. I was proud to articulate the University's goals in research and kept careful track of the results. But the real work was done by the faculty, of course, and much of the leadership came from others, including Phil Furmanski, vice presidents Michael J. Pazzani and Kenneth J. Breslauer, and the deans. So I'll recount Rutgers's research accomplishments more briefly, but with no less fervor than the foregoing narrative of our educational attainments.

Universities like Rutgers place great emphasis on excellence in research because the creation of new knowledge is among their core missions, because it contributes directly to the education of students and service to the larger society, and because outstanding research attracts top faculty, staff, and students. Research is very expensive, however, including compensation for the highly skilled people who do it, the cost of the equipment they employ, and the facilities in which they carry on their work. Funding commonly comes from several sources, including industry, nonprofit organizations, state and local governments, and the institutions themselves. But the most important source of dollars for research is the U.S. government, whose agencies spend tens of billions each year on the creation of knowledge to achieve national goals such as curing diseases, unlocking new sources of energy, increasing agricultural productivity, improving transportation safety, and defending America. Some of the money is spent on pure science, that is, research that expands what we know even if that knowledge has no immediate or obvious utility, but much of the funding is directed toward the attainment of specific goals and the solution of particular problems. Most of the federal support is awarded to faculty in fields of science and engineering, but some of it goes to social science research, and small, but still vital, grants assist research and creative activity in the arts and humanities. On the whole, federal agencies award their dollars competitively, through a process involving rigorous peer review of the proposals that are submitted for funding, but some of the support is allocated in response to political or geographic considerations. Most observers agree that the American system of federal government support for university-based research has been hugely successful in advancing the nation's health and prosperity, and other countries around the world have widely copied it.

For universities, these federal dollars are highly prized in their own right because of the research they enable, but also because, more than any other single index of institutional achievement, federal research support is a marker of prestige and distinction. Although Rutgers had been recognized since the 1980s as a major research university, it was not doing very well in obtaining federal dollars for research. As noted earlier, we were far down the list of AAU public universities in this area, and, more troubling still, we were going in the wrong direction on that list. For the decade from 1992 to 2002, Rutgers stood twenty-sixth out of thirty-four AAU publics in the increase of federal research support: ours went up by 61 percent compared to the average of 89 percent, which meant that we were farther down the list at the end of those ten years than at the beginning.

Phil Furmanski and I focused on this challenge immediately after he arrived at Rutgers in 2003, and we soon launched a search for a vice president for research whose top assignment would be increasing support from the federal government. In Mike Pazzani, a computer scientist who was then heading an important division of the National Science Foundation, we found the person we wanted.

Research is carried on by faculty, not by vice presidents, but there are plenty of things a university administration can do to assist faculty in obtaining dollars for their research, and Phil and Mike crafted a comprehensive strategy for that purpose. First they began appointing experienced grant facilitators to help faculty prepare their proposals for federal support. Facilitators would help write the funding requests and ensure that all the requirements were met; even more important, they would advise faculty on aligning their proposals as closely as possible to the scientific expectations of the granting agencies. Our administration also invested seed money in carefully chosen fields where federal funding was available in order to prepare Rutgers faculty to compete for those dollars. A great deal of the most important research today occurs across the boundaries of the traditional disciplines, because significant problems are seldom solved within the narrow confines of a single scientific field. Accordingly, the federal agencies identify particular interdisciplinary problems for research funding, and the most compelling proposals inevitably come from teams of scientists representing several disciplines. Here was another role that Phil and Mike played—learning about such funding opportunities and bringing Rutgers scientists together in cross-disciplinary groups to compete successfully for these awards. In many cases, Phil and Mike sent, or took, faculty to Washington, D.C., to talk with program officers at the agencies to learn everything possible about their areas of emphasis and their criteria for research funding. Such trips also served the old-fashioned purpose of enabling Rutgers faculty to get to know the people who would be awarding the money. The final element of the strategy was cultural, a shift in the expectations for faculty tenure and promotion: if federal research funding was available in a faculty member's field, he or she would be expected to obtain some of it—not only because faculty need resources to do their work but also because an award from a federal agency validates the quality of that work on a national and even global scale.

As we will see, these efforts were highly successful, but something else was afoot, too, and it predated my presidency. In the 1980s, Ed Bloustein and Alec Pond had decided to invest resources and appoint great faculty in life science fields such as molecular biology, chemical biology, cell biology, neuroscience, genetics, biomaterials and bioengineering, biostatistics, and, later, computational biology. Each of these disciplines had a different trajectory at Rutgers, and some came to distinction earlier than others. (Some of the best faculty appointments were made while I was dean of the Faculty of Arts and Sciences, but Alec had a lot more to do with them than I did.) By the early 2000s, all these areas were reaching maturity. Most of them were now lodged within the division of life sciences—headed by Ken Breslauer, himself a distinguished professor of chemistry and chemical biology—where world-class senior faculty were carrying on well-funded research, interdisciplinary collaboration found ample encouragement, and young scientists thrived within a culture of nurturance and mentorship.

Some life science faculty certainly benefited from the steps that Phil Furmanski and Mike Pazzani took to increase federal research support, but others needed no such help. Jay Tischfield is an internationally acclaimed geneticist and one of Rutgers's most prodigious generators of federal dollars. He came to the University in 1998 as the founding chair of the department of genetics, which he led until 2010, and serves as the CEO and scientific director of the Rutgers Cell and

DNA Repository, a leader in storing, processing, and disseminating biological materials for research around the world. Helen Berman was already a distinguished structural biologist when she joined the Rutgers faculty in 1989. Together with collaborators at the University of California, San Diego, she headed for many years the RCSB Protein Data Bank, a Rutgers-based archive of information about tens of thousands of proteins and nucleic acids with funding from the National Science Foundation, the U.S. Department of Energy, the U.S. Department of Health and Human Services, and several branches of the National Institutes of Health. Nobody at Rutgers had to show Helen Berman around Washington, D.C. Joachim Kohn is a professor of chemistry and chemical biology and the director of the New Jersey Center for Biomaterials, which he has led since 1997. A discoverer of revolutionary synthetic products for implantation in the human body, Joachim has received over $75 million in research support from the federal government. These brilliant individuals illustrate the success of the decades-earlier decision to elevate life science research at Rutgers, and similar observations could be made about other disciplines, including chemistry, physics, earth and planetary sciences, marine science, mathematics, computer science, and several fields of engineering. In these areas, too, initiatives set in motion long ago brought to Rutgers outstanding scientists who generated significant support for their research and who, in turn, appointed and guided younger colleagues whose scientific achievements, and funding, were flourishing by the early 2000s.

While faculty, deans, and vice presidents were seeking and winning research support from many sources, above all the federal government, my administration undertook a parallel effort to identify a handful of new fields, or fields worthy of reinvention, where Rutgers research could make a difference in the wider world. Here, too, Phil Furmanski was our leader, although Mike Pazzani, Ken Breslauer, several deans, and key faculty members also played essential roles. We identified a half dozen signature initiatives, of which I'll cite three: transportation, energy, and nutrition. These special fields had several characteristics in common. Above all, they drew strength from core academic disciplines in which the University was already strong. Second, they exploited some comparative advantages possessed by Rutgers or New Jersey, because of history, location, or the availability of nearby partners. Third, these fields of research met important human needs, or responded to significant opportunities, from beyond the boundaries of the University, whether the challenges were local or global or both. Next, these areas attracted ambitious students who wanted careers solving important problems. And finally, these were fields for which the necessary resources were potentially available, if Rutgers developed sufficiently outstanding programs. In all these areas, the real work was done by faculty members and their students, but the University administration brought participants together from different disciplines and provided dollars to get things started.

In transportation, Rutgers possessed long-standing strengths in several engineering disciplines and in public policy. Engineering faculty had achieved expertise and national acclaim on such subjects as highway safety and the infrastructure of roads, bridges, and ports; public policy faculty had become notable advisers of state and federal transportation officials who were making key decisions about roadways, tunnels, and ports. Now we brought these faculty members together across their different disciplines, and the whole became far greater than the sum of the parts. It made sense for Rutgers to become a national leader in transportation, given the crowding of New Jersey's highways and the heavy dependence of the state's economy on trucking, shipping, and air transport. On the subject of energy, specifically the study of global climate change and the development of alternatives to fossil fuels, the University formed the Rutgers Energy Institute in 2006 to coordinate research by faculty in science and engineering, business and economics, and public policy. Together they are carrying on influential studies of biofuels, solar energy, wind power, carbon capture, green buildings, and energy policy. Tens of millions of dollars in support for their work has come from the state and federal governments and from private foundations. In the area of health and nutrition, New Jersey and the world are facing unprecedented epidemics of obesity, diabetes, and heart disease—all serious ailments to which bad dietary habits contribute and to which healthy eating is an essential long-term

Growth of Federal Research Support at Rutgers
Compared to All AAU Public Universities

	1992–2002 PERCENTAGE INCREASE	2002–2012 PERCENTAGE INCREASE
Rutgers	61	230
Public AAU members	89	83
Rutgers rank in percentage increase	26	1

Source: Rutgers University Office of Institutional Research and Academic Planning, employing data obtained from the National Science Foundation.

response. The Institute for Food, Nutrition, and Health, established in 2008, draws together faculty and students from agriculture, nutrition, food science, the health sciences, and public policy in programs of research, education, and community outreach. In support of its work, the institute has received millions of dollars from individuals and foundations, including two $10 million gifts—one from an anonymous Rutgers alumnus who believes deeply in its mission and the other from the Robert Wood Johnson Foundation, the organization that has contributed more to Rutgers over the years than any other philanthropic donor of any kind.

Given the multitude of our research initiatives, only a sampling of which is reflected here, by how much did Rutgers enhance its federal funding, the measure that tells more than any other about a university's prowess in research? The answer is: a great deal. From 2002 to 2012, Rutgers increased its research support from the U.S. government by 230 percent, more than any other AAU public university and more than all but one of the AAU privates. Following a decade in which Rutgers had fallen further down the list of our peers, we now performed better than anyone else in moving up the ranks. In the field of chemistry, including chemical biology, Rutgers vaulted to first in the nation in both federal research funding and total research funding.

The turnaround reflected our specific efforts to assist faculty in winning such support, as well as the maturation of Rutgers's decades-old quest for distinction in research. At the end of 2012, the University was still in the bottom half of AAU universities in federal funding, but we had righted our direction and were rising. With the inclusion of UMDNJ the following year, especially the schools of medicine whose faculty garner tens of millions of dollars annually from the National Institutes of Health, Rutgers advanced nearly to the top third of the AAUs in research funding from the federal government. Anyone who believes that undergraduate education and research are inimical to each other will find no support for that position at Rutgers. We improved them both, dramatically and by design.

INTERCOLLEGIATE
ATHLETICS

DIRECTOR OF INTERCOLLEGIATE Athletics Bob Mulcahy was at his best on the afternoon of June 17, 2003. He and I held a press conference to explain the University's violation of the rules for certifying the academic eligibility of student-athletes, a "major" violation that the NCAA had formally announced earlier in the day. Although the announcement was embarrassing to Rutgers and the penalties (two years of probation and the loss of twenty scholarships in ten sports) were quite severe, the entire episode actually reflected well on Mulcahy, as did his handling of the press conference that day. The department of intercollegiate athletics had begun to uncover the violations several years earlier, not long after Mulcahy became AD, and had reported them to the NCAA. Suspecting that the problem went beyond the violations that were initially discovered, the department, in consultation with the NCAA, hired an outside counsel to perform a thorough audit of the eligibility of many hundreds of student-athletes, as well to examine the University's procedures for certifying eligibility. When the audit uncovered many more violations, Rutgers again reported them to the NCAA and proposed appropriate penalties. It appeared that over a four-year period approximately forty student-athletes in fifteen different sports had been certified erroneously through the University's flawed procedures, although if appropriate practices had been followed, most of the students would, in fact, have been eligible to compete in intercollegiate sports. The violations reflected ineptitude rather than fraud, and resulted from random errors, not from intentional foul play by coaches, students, or anyone else. They were the product, above all, of a two-decades-old certification system that was woefully inadequate to deal with the growing complexities of the NCAA's eligibility requirements.

Recognizing the severity of the problem and the inability of the existing staff to solve it, AD Mulcahy sought expert counsel on creating a whole new process for certifying academic eligibility, and in 2001 he installed the new system under the leadership of a freshly appointed, highly qualified compliance officer named Kathleen Hickey. Working with the university administration, Mulcahy also reorganized the staff and office that provided academic support for student-athletes and moved that operation out of the department of athletics into the Office of the Vice President for Academic Affairs. The NCAA report that was released on the morning of the press conference, though quite critical of Rutgers, also said that the University "deserves credit" for detecting, probing, and self-reporting the violations. Speaking with justifiable pride, Mulcahy noted that "my department and this institution took the right steps in identifying the problem, investigating the problem, and rectifying the problem." At the press conference Bob was also funny. Asked by a reporter if Rutgers had gained any competitive advantage from the violations, Bob replied, "You wouldn't ask that if you'd looked at our record." Everyone laughed, and the next day's newspaper reports gave Bob and his staff the credit they deserved. This was Rutgers's first and last major NCAA infractions case.

Robert E. Mulcahy III had had a long and successful career in New Jersey public life before becoming the director of intercollegiate athletics at Rutgers. Elected as a councilman in the town of Mendham at age twenty-eight, he became Mendham's mayor in 1970 and soon thereafter a member of New Jersey governor Brendan Byrne's inner circle. Under Byrne, he served as New Jersey's first commissioner of corrections and, for a time, as chief of staff to the governor. In the late 1970s, Bob began his successful nineteen-year tenure as president and CEO of the New Jersey Sports and Exposition Authority (NJSEA); there he managed the Meadowlands Sports Complex in Bergen County and soon gained responsibility for other major venues, including Monmouth Park Racetrack and the Atlantic City Convention Center. During Bob's time at the NJSEA, its facilities hosted not only the New York Giants and Jets but also many national and international sporting events, innumerable musical performances, and, in 1995, Pope John Paul II. President Francis L. Lawrence appointed Bob as athletic director in 1998, and by the time I became president four years later, Bob already had several significant Rutgers accomplishments under his belt, including the overhaul of the compliance process and the appointment of Greg Schiano as football coach.

Coming in as president, I knew that a successful program of intercollegiate athletics could be a major contributor to the quality of campus life and to a university's reputation. My time at UNC and the UW had shown me that. But because athletics is more visible and more closely scrutinized than practically anything else at a university, problems in athletics—for example, serious violations of NCAA rules, widespread academic failure by student-athletes, or unstoppable financial losses—can become embarrassing liabilities. I knew also that, with a few notable exceptions, Rutgers athletics had enjoyed rather limited competitive success in recent decades, and I had no reason to believe that a turnabout was imminent. Lastly, I was aware that many members of the community, especially some faculty, remained suspicious of "big-time" sports because they associated it with a compromise of academic standards and believed that athletics was draining resources from education and research. In truth, I shared some of these suspicions early in my presidency, having learned them from my father who doubted that Rutgers could succeed in reaching the top tier in athletics, especially in football, and who was not favorably disposed toward the large financial investments such an effort would require. I never publicly discussed my ambivalence, although it came through in June 2003, when I proposed to the Board of Governors a "pause" to evaluate our goals in intercollegiate sports. As previously recounted, the board dismissed my suggestion, and I never repeated it. A soft echo of my troubled feelings could, however, be heard in an observation I made again and again in the early years of my presidency, in stock speeches or in answer to questions from skeptics of Rutgers athletics: "If you could reinvent American higher education," I said, "you might not combine the best public research universities with semiprofessional athletics. But that bell was rung a long time ago, and it is beyond our power to un-ring it now."

With all these concerns in mind, and with my ambivalence under wraps and soon to fade away, early in our time together I suggested to Bob Mulcahy that we agree upon and announce four goals for intercollegiate athletics at Rutgers: (1) a clean program, consistent with NCAA rules; (2) academic success for our student-athletes; (3) competitive success by our teams; and (4) progress toward reducing the athletic department's reliance on financial subsidies from the University. These goals were not controversial, and Bob was quick to embrace them. We obtained approval from the Board of Governors, though not in a formal vote, and found opportunities to talk publicly about the goals on campus and around New Jersey. Bob and I believed that these goals would provide a structure for our work together and enable us to assess how Rutgers athletics was performing in the areas of greatest importance. In due course, a committee chaired by Executive Vice President Phil Furmanski developed a series of accountability measures for each of the four goals, and every year thereafter my administration and the department of athletics agreed on targeted outcomes for each of the measures. Annual reports from the department recorded the progress and the results. Much later, I added a fifth goal: accountability with transparency in the management of athletics. I wish it had been there all along.

Through a lot of hard work, much of it begun before my arrival as president, the University proved highly successful in attaining the first two goals: program integrity and academic achievement. In all the years following the major violation and the penalties announced in June 2003, Rutgers had nothing but secondary violations. There were perhaps fifteen or twenty of these a year, similar to other universities with comparable athletic programs, and in each case Rutgers self-reported the infraction to the NCAA. All but one of the violations was inadvertent and unintentional, and none of them gained, or was designed to gain, any competitive advantage for Rutgers. A typical secondary violation would be missing a deadline for the submission of a report or sending material to a potential recruit before he or she was eligible to receive it because the recruit's high school class had been miscoded in a database. One of the secondary violations was, however, intentional rather than inadvertent and was treated with immense seriousness within the department of athletics. The story is this: A coach facing a deadline for submission of a document forged an athlete's signature because the athlete was out of town. The document was otherwise accurate. For his extremely poor judgment and his laziness, the coach suffered a written reprimand, a three-game suspension, and a frozen salary. The penalties were actually assessed shortly after Mulcahy had departed as AD, but they reflected the system that he, his staff, and the coaches had created to bring a culture of compliance to Rutgers athletics. This was no small achievement, considering how many intercollegiate programs have embarrassed themselves and their universities when students, coaches, or boosters succumbed to temptation and broke the rules that govern the games.

To judge from every available measure of educational achievement, student-athletes at Rutgers performed well during Bob Mulcahy's time as AD, and their success continues to the present day. There are many reasons for this, including the work of a strong faculty committee that is empowered to review the high school record of every prospective athlete and to reject applicants who are unlikely to succeed academically at Rutgers, as well as coaches who demand classroom achievement from their players. The University's growing provision of academic support services, principally tutoring and advising, for student-athletes also contributed to the positive educational outcomes. Rutgers steadily increased its investment in these activities from several hundred thousand dollars a year in the early 2000s to more than $1.6 million by 2012. And the results of all these efforts and activities were pretty remarkable. From 2004 to 2012, the graduation success rate for all Rutgers athletes went up from 75 percent to 88 percent. For football it rose from 53 percent to 91 percent, for women's basketball from 73 percent to 89 percent, and for men's basketball from 42 percent to 80 percent. In 2004, the NCAA created and began publicizing the Academic Progress Rate (APR), a measure of eligibility and retention (and an early indicator of graduation rates) that is calculated every year for every Division I team in the country. With a few exceptions that were quickly rectified, Rutgers teams measured up very well on the APR scale compared to their peers, particularly football, which has consistently ranked among the top ten programs, has usually been in the top three, and in 2008–09 was number one. Behind the impressive and improving graduation rates lay the success that Rutgers athletes achieved in their academic courses; in the decade from 2002 to 2012, the overall grade point average (GPA) of Rutgers athletes rose from 2.8 to 3.0 and of football players from 2.5 to 2.8. The athletes' GPA is almost identical to that of the student body as a whole. The bottom line for our first two goals for intercollegiate athletics was this: Rutgers has a clean program made up of students who get an education and graduate.

Our third goal was competitive success. Did they win some games? They did, although this is not the place for a full review of the results compiled by Rutgers teams while I was president. In the nonrevenue sports, sometimes called Olympic sports, there were some highlights. The baseball team, led and inspired by its revered veteran coach, Fred Hill, secured winning records most seasons, frequently made the national rankings, twice appeared in the NCAA tournament, and had a number of its players named All-American. The Rutgers wrestling program, which had enjoyed many winning seasons across the decades, gained a new burst of energy and excitement beginning in 2007 under Coach Scott Goodale, who took his team to the NCAAs in 2009, 2010, and 2011. Coached by Glenn Crooks, women's soccer had winning records almost every year, competed successfully in the Big East, and produced an extraordinary midfielder named Carli Lloyd. Named to the Big East's First Team for four straight years while she played at Rutgers, Lloyd went on to compete both professionally and internationally. As a member of the United States Olympic Team in the summer of 2008 and again in 2012, Lloyd amazingly scored the gold-medal-winning goals both times, first in Beijing and then in London.

Sadly, the greatest visibility attained by the Olympic sports on my watch came not on the playing fields but from my administration's reluctant decision to eliminate six intercollegiate varsity programs: men's and women's fencing, men's swimming and diving, men's tennis, and men's crew (both heavyweight and lightweight). We made and announced the decision in 2006, and it became effective the following year. Rutgers athletes would still have opportunities to participate in all these sports, but now they would do so at the less intensely competitive level of club sports. As early as 1998, before my return to Rutgers, the department of athletics had quietly begun asking how many sports it could afford to support in a way that assured quality experiences for student-athletes: access to good coaching, appropriate equipment and facilities, academic support, medical care, safe and reliable transportation, and more. At that time, Rutgers had thirty varsity sports, more than most of our peers, which tended to have around twenty. Following a particularly massive reduction of state funding for 2006–07, a budget cut in which the department of athletics fully shared, Bob Mulcahy recommended, and I approved, eliminating the six varsity sports one year hence. No student would lose financial aid, and athletes who wished to transfer to other institutions in order to remain active at the varsity level would have Rutgers's assistance in doing so. As expected, the decision aroused intense criticism from athletes and their families and from alumni in these sports, criticism that endured for more than a year and that later fed into the media campaign against Rutgers athletics in 2008. I regretted the elimination of six varsity sports but agreed that the University could not mount thirty intercollegiate programs at the high level of quality to which Rutgers aspired in everything it did.

Sports fans and sports cynics alike know that competitive success in college athletics means above all victories in basketball and football, the sports that attract the most fans, garner the greatest media attention, and, owing to their popularity, can generate revenue for the institution. When Bob Mulcahy and I evaluated progress toward our third goal, the truth is we focused mainly on basketball and football. The quick summary is this: men's basketball had a rare but thrilling peak of success from 2004 to 2006; women's basketball posted winning records and made NCAA appearances every season and came close to winning the national championship in 2007; and football made a turnaround that overshadowed everything else, transformed Rutgers athletics, and brought headaches as well as hurrahs.

As practically every Rutgers fan knows, the men's basketball team went to the NCAA Final Four in the spring of 1976 (at the very moment I was landing my first teaching position at the University) and played several fine seasons in the years thereafter. Beginning in the mid-1980s, however, there were more losing seasons than winning ones, and the record worsened after 1995, when Rutgers began playing in the basketball-rich Big East. During the ten basketball seasons of my presidency, the Rutgers men had winning records only in two, both early on under the leadership of Coach Gary Waters. The highest point, and it was pretty high, came in the 2003–04 season, when Rutgers compiled a record of twenty wins and thirteen losses and made it to the final game of the National Invitation Tournament (NIT). Both the NIT semifinal game, in which Rutgers beat Iowa State, and the final game, in which we lost to Michigan, were played at Madison Square Garden. Those games generated immense excitement on campus. Dressed in red, thousands of Rutgers students boarded New Jersey Transit trains for the trip from New Brunswick to Penn Station and cheered all the way to the Garden. Together with my son Michael, then a high school freshman, I rode the trains to and from the games in New York and shared in the emotion that athletic success, though too rarely seen, could bring to Rutgers. The team's emerging star at the NIT was a slender freshman named Quincy Douby, who followed his performances in Madison Square Garden with two outstanding seasons during which he set scoring records that stirred fans in the Rutgers Athletic Center to screaming "I Douby-lieve." After his

All-America junior year, Douby declared for the NBA draft and signed with the Sacramento Kings.

While men's basketball enjoyed a brief era of winning seasons and cheers for Douby, women's basketball was always winning while I was president. Led by C. Vivian Stringer, already a renowned coach when Rutgers lured her from the University of Iowa in 1995, the program won twenty games or more every season but one, competed strongly in the tough Big East, and never missed the NCAA tournament. Stringer excelled at recruiting and inspiring talented athletes and then placing upon them demands and expectations the likes of which they had never seen in high school. Each year she introduced a new class of recruits that was heralded by sportswriters as one of the best in the country. Among the dozens of outstanding young women who came to play for Stringer during these years, none was better than point guard Cappie Pondexter. A high school All-American from Chicago, Pondexter led Rutgers to first-place finishes in the Big East in 2005 and 2006, and over the course of four years she scored more than 2,000 points. After graduation, Pondexter played both professionally and internationally and won an Olympic gold medal in 2008. But Cappie was gone from Rutgers, already a professional, by the time Stringer's 2006–07 team captured national attention with an improbable run to the NCAA championship game and then, just days later, enkindled an outpouring of acclaim and affection from around the world for the classy way in which they stood up to a crude radio bully named Don Imus.

By Stringer's own account, her team that year "was a disaster." The players, she later recalled, were injured, lazy, and inexperienced, "the worst team I'd ever coached." They lost four of their first six games, including Rutgers's home opener to Duke by the score of 85 to 45. For not living up to her standards, Stringer punished the players: no use of the locker room, no laundry privileges, no practice uniforms. And then, with some timely help, this team of mostly freshmen and no seniors turned it around. On New Year's Eve, Cappie Pondexter and several others who had formerly starred for Stringer showed up at a practice session to try to teach and inspire the young players—and they succeeded. Applying Stringer's heralded full court press, called the fifty-five, the team lost only four more games during the regular season, won the Big East tournament, and blew through the first two games of the NCAAs. Their next opponent, feeling almost at home in Greensboro, North Carolina, was Duke, ranked number one in the country, against whom Rutgers now played one of its greatest games ever. The Scarlet Knights were down by ten points early in the second half and by four with a minute to play when junior Matee Ajavon hit a three-point shot. Freshman Epiphanny Prince then stole the ball from Duke and went "coast-to-coast," as the sportswriters say, for a lay-up that put Rutgers ahead by one. With only a tenth of a second on the clock, Duke's star Lindsey Harding, the national player of the year, had two foul shots to win or tie the game, but she missed them both, and Rutgers had an unbelievable victory. The next two wins, coming easily against Arizona State and Louisiana State, brought Rutgers into the championship game against Tennessee, which had a habit of beating Stringer's teams at NCAA time. Now they did it again, by the score of 59 to 46. At the press conference afterward, a deeply disappointed Coach Stringer took responsibility for the defeat, while her numbed and stunned players seemed to be at a loss for words. The next day, however, the *Star-Ledger* got it right: Rutgers had gloried in "a month of postseason overachievement." They had almost won the national championship; they were heroes. Stringer later called the 2006–07 season "the most rewarding year I'd ever had coaching basketball."

The same players who were at a loss for words following the game distinctly were not when confronting Don Imus. They found their voice—and found admirers around the world. On April 4, 2007, the morning after the final game, Imus, a radio talk show host with a reputation for making degrading and offensive on-the-air remarks, chatted obnoxiously with his studio sidekicks about Tennessee's victory and about the physical appearance of the players on both teams. The "rough girls from Rutgers," he said, " . . . got tattoos," and a moment later he called them "nappy-headed hos." Commonly used in rap lyrics, "ho" is street language for whore. Difficult as it may be to believe, because Imus's racist and sexist words would soon become so well known, his ugly phrase was little noted for several days after he first uttered it. At a large campus rally celebrating the team's accomplishments on April 5, although some of us knew what Imus had said, no one mentioned it. On the following day, NCAA president Myles Brand and I issued a joint statement condemning Imus for his "disregard for the dignity of human beings who have accomplished so much," but not until early the next week, as the news of his words spread, did the firestorm erupt. On Easter Sunday, April 8, African American pastors began to denounce Imus and to call for his dismissal from CBS Radio and MSNBC. The following day civil rights leaders in New Jersey and around the country also demanded his ouster. Bob Mulcahy and I met with Coach Stringer and the players in her office on Monday morning to express our abhorrence of Imus's words and our strong support and affection for the team. After the meeting, I had an impromptu session with press and TV reporters on the sidewalk outside the Rutgers Athletic Center and, according to one newspaper, "unleashed a torrent of invective against . . . Don Imus." With the players' permission, I phoned their parents individually to express the University's support for their daughters and outrage against Imus. But it was Stringer and, even more, her players themselves who rose to the occasion with grace and courage beyond their years.

At a nationally televised press conference on Tuesday, April 10, the coach spoke passionately and at times tearfully of the pain inflicted on her players by "racist and sexist remarks that are deplorable, despicable, and abominable and unconscionable." Team captain Essence Carson expressed with great dignity the anguish and anger that Imus's remarks had caused. He stole from us, she said, "a moment of pure grace." Heather Zurich, a sophomore teammate, spoke similarly: "We reached what many would only dream of, the NCAA title game, but . . . our moment was taken away." "Mr. Imus knows not one of us personally," she continued. "Worst of all, my team and I did nothing to deserve [his] . . . deplorable comments." Carson also revealed that the team had agreed to have a private meeting with Imus "at an undisclosed location in the near future . . . to express our great hurt [and] the sadness it has brought to us." Neither the team captain nor the coach nor anyone else joined in the cry for Imus's dismissal; they had decided that

With my parents in Old Queens on October 25, 2002, the day the Boards of Governors and Trustees formally chose me as the nineteenth president of Rutgers (Photo by John Emerson)

Edward J. Bloustein, Rutgers's greatest president, who served from 1971 to 1989 (Photo by Nick Romanenko)

With UNC–Chapel Hill Chancellor Paul Hardin awarding an honorary degree to President Bill Clinton, 1993 (Photo courtesy of North Carolina Collection, University of North Carolina at Chapel Hill Library)

With Governor Jim McGreevey at my inauguration as president of Rutgers, 2003 (Photo by Larry Levanti)

Sharing a laugh with Board of Governors Chairman Gene O'Hara, 2004 (Photo by Nick Romanenko)

Gerald C. Harvey, a trustee and a governor who provided leadership again and again (Photo by Larry Levanti)

With Phil Furmanski and my father at my 2005 annual address; Douglass students with their banners are in the background. (Photo by Nick Romanenko)

Announcing my final recommendations for reorganizing undergraduate education, 2006; Barry Qualls, the task force chair, is standing behind me second from the left. (Photo by Roy Groething)

Bringing Robert Wood Johnson Medical School back into Rutgers was one of my top goals. (Photo by Roy Groething)

With Coach C. Vivian Stringer and the 2006–07 women's basketball team in front of Old Queens (Photo by Roy Groething)

With Governor Dick Codey and Coach Greg Schiano, 2007 (Photo by Nick Romanenko)

A favorable camera angle creates the illusion that I am as tall as these members of the 2008 football team. (Photo by Lauren Guiliano, Rutgers University Alumni Relations)

With Tim Pernetti at a women's basketball game, 2009 (Photo by Nick Romanenko)

With David Mechanic; Risa Lavizzo-Mourey, president and CEO of the Robert Wood Johnson Foundation; and Governor Tom Kean, 2010 (Photo by Patti Sapone)

Welcoming a new class of Rutgers Future Scholars, 2009 (Photo by Nick Romanenko)

With students at Rutgers-Camden, 2009 (Photo by Nick Romanenko)

Greeting Governor Chris Christie at the gala grand opening of our $1 billion fund-raising campaign, 2010 (Photo by Saed Hindash, *Star-Ledger*)

Newark Mayor Cory Booker and Professor Clement A. Price at the 2012 Marion Thompson Wright Lecture (Photo by Fred Stucker)

With Joan Barry McCormick at the president's house, 2006 (Photo by Nick Romanenko)

Leaving commencement, 2006 (Photo by Nick Romanenko)

With Katie and Joan on Rutgers Day, 2012 (Photo by Nick Romanenko)

At the Old Queens gate with Joan and Katie and the president's office staff, 2012 (Photo by Nick Romanenko)

was not their cause. The press conference made news everywhere, and brought forth an outpouring of love and support for the team from people both famous and unknown around the world. Ultimately the Imus incident generated a degree of interest and attention for which there was no precedent in the University's history. Altogether almost twenty thousand print, digital, and broadcast stories appeared, virtually all of them favorable to Rutgers, whose handling of the controversy drew widespread praise. For this, the University could thank the coach and her players.

The promised encounter with Imus took place two days later at Drumthwacket, the New Jersey governor's mansion in Princeton. Governor Jon S. Corzine had agreed to host the meeting, but rushing home he was critically injured in a car accident on the Garden State Parkway and taken by helicopter to Cooper University Hospital in Camden. I learned of the accident from my mother, who reached me on my cell phone moments before I arrived at Drumthwacket. When I entered and saw the stricken faces of the governor's staff, I realized that his injuries were far more severe than the news reports had yet revealed. Despite their terror that the governor might die, his aides did everything they could to accommodate the emotion-laden, hours-long showdown that now occurred between the players and Imus. Also present were Imus's wife, Deirdre, Coach Stringer, Bob Mulcahy, and parents of the team members. The young women expressed movingly the sorrow and anger they felt when they heard Imus's words and, more generally, the pain inflicted upon them by racism and sexism. So did Coach Stringer and the parents, several of whom told painful stories of racial discrimination they had experienced, stories that in some cases their daughters had never heard before and that brought tears to everyone's eyes. Imus, whose firing had been announced that day by CBS, repeatedly apologized for his cruel words, and most of those who were present seemed convinced of his sincerity. One unforgettable moment came when a player stood up, walked across the room to a spot right in front of Mrs. Imus, and asked her "Are you a ho?" "No, of course not," she replied. The next day Coach Stringer announced that the team had accepted Imus's apology.

Almost exactly two years later, C. Vivian Stringer was elected to the Basketball Hall of Fame, not because of the Imus incident but because of the lifetime she had spent as an exacting teacher, a moral leader, and a successful coach. Stringer's formal entry into the hall came in September 2009, in a class of inductees that included Michael Jordan. His presence, no doubt, explained the extraordinary crowd of basketball luminaries that gathered that evening, including Dean Smith, Jordan's former coach at UNC. In accepting the honor, Jordan talked at length about himself. When her turn came, Vivian Stringer spoke more briefly and about others: about her family which had seen more than its share of tragedy, about her mentors, and about her "basketball daughters," none of whom ever exceeded the splendor of her players of 2007.

While the agonies and triumphs of women's basketball were unfolding that spring, it was becoming clear that football's success the previous fall was now working a profound transformation upon Rutgers athletics—and Rutgers. That 2006 season, whose defining moment came in the glorious victory over Louisville, has already been recounted. But it is worth observing again what a remarkable transformation had occurred: from a football program that was sometimes called the worst in the nation, a program that won only a single game in 2002, to a program that was now successful enough and prominent enough to gain respect around the country, both for football and for the University. Football's turnaround and its far-reaching impact speak to several realities. Americans are obsessed with football, and the victory over Louisville, cheered in living rooms and sports bars across the country, was one of the most conspicuous events in the centuries-long history of Rutgers. There is nothing the University could realistically do that would attract anywhere near the attention garnered by a successful football program. Academics and intellectual purists may lament this truth, but it is inescapable. A top-ranked philosophy department and pioneering research on HIV/AIDS, both of which Rutgers has, may be more important than football, but they have never attracted a fraction of the attention football commands. Those who observe that athletics in general and football in particular are the windows into the institution, or its "front porch" as some say when making the same point, are absolutely correct. The Rutgers community, which had not previously experienced success in big-time football, was now deeply appreciative, even ecstatic, for it. As we were to discover, however, the University was in some ways unprepared for the results of that success.

Its architect, of course, was Greg Schiano. Born and raised in New Jersey, Schiano attended Bucknell University, where he excelled as a linebacker, and in 1988 he began a coaching career that would include experience at Ramapo High School, his alma mater; Rutgers, where he served as a graduate assistant; Penn State; and the Chicago Bears. By the time Bob Mulcahy found him and hired him in late 2000, Schiano had risen to the position of defensive coordinator for the University of Miami, then the fifth-ranked program in the country. At the time he returned to Rutgers as its head football coach, Greg was thirty-four years old. Every young coach who inherits a losing program wants to turn it around and gain national kudos for his team; this guy actually did it. After a couple of seasons that were no better (maybe even a little worse) than the ones before he arrived, Schiano's team won five games in 2003, four in 2004, seven (and a bowl invitation) in 2005, and then came the Louisville season of 2006. At its conclusion, several organizations chose him as the national coach of the year. The program's new-found success rested heavily upon Greg's hard work and good values: his relationship-building with high school coaches, especially in New Jersey and Florida; his rock-solid integrity and sincerity when appealing to potential recruits and their parents; and his demands for a clean program and academic success for his players. This was a solid foundation upon which to build a winning football program, and Greg built it. Over the years, he worried whether the demanding curriculum that was established following the reorganization of undergraduate education would impair his players' academic progress, but he never disputed the faculty's right to set the educational requirements.

No one with a weak personality could possibly have achieved what Greg did in the hyper-charged, super-competitive world of inter-collegiate football. Those who encountered him quickly recognized his relentless drive, his passion for winning, his high expectations for everyone around him, and his determination to overcome every obstacle. These characteristics might not have succeeded in the English department, but in the hierarchical world of football, they worked very well. Added to them was Greg's charisma: people wanted to be around him, to support him, to help him win, and to share in his success. Personal integrity also increased Greg's influence: no hint of wrongdoing ever touched him; on the contrary, his values and his behavior were known to be exemplary and were widely admired. If Greg asked you to do something, there was seldom a reason not to do it. Greg wanted what he wanted, whether it was the improvement of his own compensation, access to a helicopter for recruiting, or expansion of the stadium. And he had the strength of personality to get what he wanted from a University and a state that were long starved for football success and deeply enamored of him.

In February 2007, following several months of discussions with the coach and his agent, Bob Mulcahy announced, with my approval, that Greg's annual compensation would increase to $1.5 million, plus a house loan and a longevity bonus, and that his contract would be extended through 2016. (Unfortunately, the press release did not state as clearly as it should have that the house loan and the longevity bonus would come to Schiano as additional payments, beyond the $1.5 million.) In a state where politicians and pundits make a sport of criticizing the high salaries of public figures, Greg's pay hike drew only praise. A year and a half later, as a result of developments that I will describe shortly, it was revealed that Mulcahy's announcement had omitted one important component of Schiano's compensation and that several side letters from the AD to the coach had never been made public. Those revelations, along with others, caused a furor within the University and around the state, and heavy blame for the lack of transparency fell upon Mulcahy, me, and the Board of Governors. It scarcely touched the coach, whose compensation was widely, and accurately, considered to reflect his worth in the big-money marketplace of college football.

The biggest thing Schiano wanted was a major expansion of Rutgers Stadium, a project that proved to be much more difficult and controversial than raising his salary. I knew that expanding the stadium was essential if Rutgers was going to continue to make progress in football, but not everyone agreed. Before it was done, the project suffered bizarre twists and turns over its finances and became the catalyst for a venomous newspaper campaign against Rutgers athletics.

There were good reasons for expanding the stadium. With only forty-three thousand seats, the facility's capacity was far below that of comparable programs. Among the thirty-seven AAU universities playing football at the highest level, only three, Vanderbilt, Duke, and Buffalo, had smaller stadiums than Rutgers. Even with the addition of twelve thousand seats, as proposed—approximately eleven thousand bench seats at the south end of the stadium and one thousand clubs seats on the mezzanine level of the east side—the stadium's size would still place it in the bottom half of that cohort and with barely half the capacity of the largest stadiums in the group, Michigan's and Penn State's. Football's success during the 2005 and 2006 seasons had dramatically driven up interest in attending the games, and there was now a waiting list of thousands of fans who wanted to buy season tickets but could not be accommodated within the existing stadium. Some of them were eager to pay extra money for the comfort of club seats, which would also afford them access to food and beverages and a friendly space in which to socialize with other fans. In addition to the paying customers, there were also many more Rutgers students who now wanted to attend the games and who would continue to be admitted for free. Besides these reasons, as Greg Schiano persuasively argued, expanding the stadium would help him recruit better football players, which in turn would bring more victories on the field and still more fans wanting seats. With all this in mind, and knowing that a winning football program was uniquely capable of focusing wide and favorable attention on the entire University, my administration and most members of the Board of Governors favored expanding the stadium. Initially the project was estimated to cost $120 million but was later scaled back to $102 million. Financing that amount would not prove easy.

Sometime early in 2007, Schiano and Mulcahy persuaded Governor Jon Corzine to agree to provide $30 million from the state of New

Jersey toward expansion of the stadium. Senate President Richard J. Codey was also supportive of the deal. I had a hand in these conversations, too, but Greg and Bob took the lead. Rutgers would borrow the balance of the money for the project and would repay the debt over a period of many years using revenue generated by the sale of tickets for the new seats. Then in November, the state's voters rejected a proposed $450 million bond issue for stem cell research, an outcome that quickly came to be viewed as a popular rebuke of governmental borrowing and spending. Shortly after the vote, Corzine decided that the state could not afford to provide $30 million for the stadium. Wanting to keep his commitment to Schiano, however, the governor teamed up with State Senator Raymond J. Lesniak and together they publicly pledged to lead "a fundraising campaign to raise 30 million dollars in contributions" for the project. Toward that goal, Corzine promised to give $1 million of his own money. Alluding obliquely to the governor's successful career in investment banking and his vast personal wealth, Lesniak famously declared that "all I have to do is go through Jon Corzine's Rolodex one time, and we'll get the commitment for the 30 million dollars." If only.

Now Rutgers had a tough decision to make: Should we proceed with the stadium expansion in anticipation of the governor's successful fund raising or should we wait until the money was in hand? Sentiment on campus was divided, as it was on the Board of Governors. Only the press seemed to be of one mind—negative. One distinguished biology professor wrote to me saying, "If this is funded you and the BOG risk a very serious rift with the faculty and students." Another senior faculty member, an economist, warned that if the University's attendance forecasts for the stadium did not hold up, Rutgers "will be stuck with long-term debt service costs . . . [and] the difference will come out of classroom budgets." He added what everyone knew: the University had recently experienced major reductions in its state-appropriated funding, and more cuts were expected. In such an environment, how could Rutgers afford to expand the stadium? In late January 2008, after faculty and students had returned to campus for the spring semester, my administration sponsored a well-attended campus forum for an airing of these concerns. We also answered the concerns with spreadsheets showing that the expanded stadium would generate enough revenue to repay the debt and with expressions of confidence that the governor would raise $30 million in private support. At the end of January, the Board of Governors voted to approve the $102 million stadium expansion and to authorize construction of the club seats before the beginning of the 2008 football season and the bench seats by the following year. Only one board member voted no, and that was George Zoffinger, a longtime critic of Mulcahy's management of Rutgers athletics. Despite fervent doubters and relentless scrutiny at every phase of the project, we kept to the budget and the timetable the board had authorized. But the bumps along the way were severe.

Unfortunately, Governor Corzine and Senator Lesniak proved unable to keep their pledge to raise $30 million. For about six months following their commitment, the governor's office scrutinized the relevant state laws and ethics rules in an attempt to devise a clean, clear process for soliciting gifts that would avoid even the appearance that donors might receive favorable treatment from the state in return for their generosity. He was the governor, after all, and this was the right thing to do. Members of my administration, including lawyers and fund raisers, worked with the governor's people to develop solicitation guidelines that could pass ethics muster, but without success. In July, Senator Lesniak acknowledged, "This was far more difficult than we could have thought. It really didn't get off the ground." Only $250,000 of the $30 million was ever raised, a gift from the governor himself.

The next blow to the stadium fell early in the summer when bids for concrete, steel, and fuel came in far higher than expected. To keep within the $102 million budget, the project would have to be scaled back by eliminating elements that were not essential to the core goal of increasing the stadium's seating capacity. And that's what we did: over the course of the project, a planned new locker room for visiting teams, a recruiting lounge, a media room, and a stair tower all were scrapped. Print, broadcast, and digital media widely reported the stadium's woes, and there was no shortage of commentary declaring that it would never be finished on time, would never be finished within budget, and should never have been started in the first place.

On July 9, 2008, Josh Margolin and Ted Sherman, the *Star-Ledger*'s crack investigative reporters, met with me and several members of my administration to confirm what we already knew: they were about to launch a series of articles that would severely criticize intercollegiate athletics at Rutgers, including the troubled stadium project, the high cost of big-time football, other instances of soaring expenditures, and alleged mismanagement within the department of athletics. Josh and Ted told us that they intended to rely upon the state's Open Public Records Act to demand thousands of pages of documents from us and that, if Rutgers resisted providing the information, they would not hesitate to take us to court. They reminded us of the series of articles they had published several years earlier on the University of Medicine and Dentistry of New Jersey, articles that had thoroughly destroyed the reputation of that institution by laying bare its waste, mismanagement, and even corruption. That's what we could expect, they said, especially if we did not cooperate with them.

Josh and Ted were true to their word: their series began the very next day, with a focus on the stadium, and soon spread to other aspects of Rutgers athletics, including Coach Schiano's compensation. This would be New Jersey media hardball at its meanest. Here are the headlines of the stories with which Margolin and Sherman began their series:

July 10 "Cost Woes Might Trim Stadium at Rutgers"
July 11 "Rutgers Stadium Bids Come in $18M Too High"
July 20 "Fewer Sports Teams, but Costs Still Rise"
July 22 "Rutgers Hid Part of Its Deal with Schiano"
July 23 "Rutgers Gave Coach a Secret Guarantee"
July 24 "The $2 Million Coach Says He's Focused"
July 27 "Shy on Funds, Rutgers Rethinks Stadium Strategy"
July 29 "State Examining Rutgers Finances"
July 30 "Rutgers Marketing Deal Stirs Review"

And that was just July! Margolin and Sherman would continue their investigative reporting throughout the rest of the summer and the fall. Not to be outdone by the *Star-Ledger*, other newspapers in New

Jersey, as well as in New York and Philadelphia, now piled on. Some reprinted stories written by Margolin and Sherman; others wrote their own. The (Hackensack) *Record*, the (Trenton) *Times*, the (East Brunswick) *Home News Tribune*, the *Asbury Park Press*, the (Bridgewater) *Courier News*, the *Philadelphia Inquirer*, the *New York Times*, and others all weighed in.

These stories revealed a great deal that was embarrassing to Rutgers and to its department of athletics. Margolin and Sherman's series of articles began with the high cost of the stadium expansion and its uncertain financing, a juicy topic to which they frequently returned, but they also moved on to other subjects. Their stories revealed that when Bob Mulcahy announced the increase of Coach Schiano's compensation in February 2007, the announcement failed to include an annual $250,000 payment that the coach would receive from Nelligan Sports Marketing, the University's exclusive marketing agent for athletics, a payment that the University later guaranteed to cover if Nelligan did not. The stories also disclosed the existence of other side letters from Mulcahy to Schiano, including one that covered his use of a helicopter for university business, mainly for recruiting football players. Margolin and Sherman revisited the University's controversial cost-saving decision to eliminate six varsity sports, a decision that had been made, announced, and widely protested in 2006 and then carried out in 2007. The elimination of the six sports, they now claimed, not only failed to save money but actually proved costly to Rutgers because, for reasons associated with Title IX of the federal higher education act, the University was now obligated to spend many more dollars than before on scholarships for women athletes. Toward the end of July, Margolin and Sherman had the pleasure of reporting that the Office of the State Comptroller had opened up an inquiry into athletics finances at Rutgers, an inquiry that was "triggered," they said, by their own investigative stories. It was a big mess for Rutgers, just as Josh and Ted and their editors intended.

Besides the stories, there were the inevitable editorials and opinion columns. "The [stadium] expansion was ill-advised from the start," declared a columnist in the *Record*. A few days later, an editorial in the same paper suggested that "perhaps McCormick or the members of the Board of Governors ... should be removed." The *Star-Ledger* said, "The issue is about Rutgers's leadership being honest with the public." The *New York Times* called me "a shameless cheerleader for the high-stakes football program" and urged Rutgers leaders to "swallow their egos and admit that their football fantasy was ill conceived." The *Times* of Trenton said, "It's time to come clean. There's too much 'official' silence about what's happening with Rutgers football."

Yes, the coverage was alarmist and repetitive; it sometimes employed verbal tricks to create impressions that were worse than the reality; it was not always completely truthful. But these are the ways of investigative reporting. Margolin and Sherman got a lot right. They uncovered problems that urgently demanded to be fixed, and they revealed areas in which the University's long-accepted ways of doing business were inadequate to manage an athletics program that now was much larger, more complicated, and more visible than ever before.

The media onslaught alarmed members of the Board of Governors, many of whom shared their concerns with me, usually over the telephone, employing language that was quite direct. They were embarrassed by the revelations and felt uninformed. They wondered why Rutgers couldn't get out in front of the *Star-Ledger*, voluntarily reveal everything, and shut down the newspaper's investigation. They questioned whether the department of athletics had been fully honest with my administration and whether I, in turn, had given the board all the information it should have had. Some were angry because important decisions had been made, for example about the coach's compensation, without sufficient board input or approval. A number of them agreed with board member George Zoffinger that a full and complete audit of the athletic department had to be done. All of the board members noted areas where the University must improve its policies and procedures and become radically more transparent. They asked me: "Is everything out there now?" "What other shoes are going to drop?"

In late July and early August, in response to the still-mounting media criticism and in consultation with the leadership of the Board of Governors, I appointed the Athletics Review Committee (ARC), a body of prominent individuals from within Rutgers and around the state to conduct a "complete and candid" review of the policies and practices of the department of athletics. Heading the ARC were two cochairs: Alfred C. Koeppe, an alumnus of Rutgers-Newark, a respected leader in the state's civic and business communities, and a hard-edged Jersey guy; and Albert R. Gamper Jr., also a graduate of Rutgers-Newark, a highly successful businessman, now retired, and a former chair of the Board of Governors. I charged the ARC with investigating all the issues that had been raised in regard to intercollegiate athletics and any additional matters they considered important, and I promised the committee full and complete access to information and individuals. The two Als and I agreed that the ARC would carry on its work confidentially and would deliver its report and recommendations to me. Then I, in turn, would make the report public. We also agreed that the Rutgers administration should not wait for the ARC report to begin reforming its policies and procedures in ways that were indicated by the ongoing revelations but should begin immediately to make needed changes. Not surprisingly, the ARC's appointment brought forth suspicion that the committee would do a whitewash of the problems, a concern that gained credence from the composition of the ARC, which included not only Al Gamper but also several other members of the Rutgers Boards of Governors and Trustees. The critics need not have worried.

In the late summer of 2008, while Margolin and Sherman were still deep into their Woodward and Bernstein thing and while the ARC was launching its strictly confidential work, the first phase of the stadium project was completed—and it was beautiful. Nearly a thousand club seats, every one of them sold, stretched from goal line to goal line, high upon the eastern side of the stadium. Behind the seats was a spacious, comfortable area for socializing and refreshment that was quickly judged to be one of the most attractive interior spaces in New Jersey. Seeing it for the first time, fans and their guests expressed admiration and delight. Everyone who had predicted that the club seating area wouldn't get done on time and on budget—and wasn't worth it anyway—was wrong.

As the fall wore on and while we waited for the ARC report, I began noticing what seemed to be a divergence between the department of athletics and me. Publicly and repeatedly, I acknowledged the problems in the administration of athletics and as president accepted responsibility for the mistakes and for making sure they did not occur again. I used a portion of my annual address to recognize that Rutgers had not managed the transition to big-time sports as well as it should have and observed that there were many administrative areas where we ought to have "done things better and more transparently." At a public meeting of the Board of Governors in October, I carried the point further by reporting a lengthy list of changes in policies and practices that were already under way, or soon would be, in response to the problems that had been identified. Some of the changes were unique to athletics, but many affected the entire University. These included staff training in ethics and conflicts of interest, professional development for business managers, and the writing of entirely new policies for high-level employment contracts, sponsorship agreements, and signatory authority for contracts. The department of athletics seemed less open to acknowledging the mistakes or changing our ways of doing business.

On November 18, after working confidentially for nearly four months, the Athletics Review Committee delivered its thirty-five-page report to me. I released it publicly the next day, together with my thanks to the committee and praise for its work. The report was extremely critical of the director of intercollegiate athletics, the president, and the Board of Governors for the isolated and unconstrained ways in which the department of athletics operated—and had been permitted to operate, by me and the governing board. The ARC's detailed narrative covered the University's successive contracts with Nelligan Sports Marketing and its contracts and side letters with Coach Schiano. Although the ARC found no criminal wrongdoing by anyone and did not fault the substantive outcomes of the decisions it reviewed, the report offered a harsh assessment of the University's processes and procedures, the lack of transparency in the management of athletics, and the failure of the president and the board to establish appropriate controls. By giving inadequate attention to decisions regarding athletics and by failing sufficiently to engage the board in those decisions, the senior management of the institution had tacitly endorsed the department's "increasingly insular manner of doing business." Some of these failures, the ARC recognized, were owed to the swift, recent growth of intercollegiate athletics at Rutgers, but the time had come to regularize the management of the department and bring it fully within the bounds of university governance. To this end, the report made a long series of recommendations and noted "as a positive step" the new policies and procedures that I had already announced. In making the report public, I listed eleven actions I would take immediately to implement its proposals. These included not only measures to strengthen administrative oversight of athletics but also steps to invigorate compliance, risk management, and audit activities throughout the University. Over the course of the next year, I reported regularly to the Board of Governors about our progress in enacting the ARC's recommendations. In due course, everything they proposed was done.

I should have paid closer attention to the management of athletics. There was no excuse for the University's failure to announce all the components of Coach Schiano's compensation or to release the later side letters. I was aware, after all, that the governance of Rutgers athletics had historically been somewhat irregular; my father had researched that and written it up. The decisions that had taken Rutgers over the years toward "big-time" sports had been informal, to say the least, and I had access to that history. Until November 2002, just a month before I became president, the Board of Governors did not even have a committee with responsibility for overseeing intercollegiate athletics; a body of athletics-boosting trustees named the Athletics Trustee Advisory Committee had claimed that honor. I was aware, moreover, of the potential for athletic problems to embarrass the University. That was the reason behind the four goals that Bob Mulcahy and I had agreed to early in my presidency: programmatic integrity, academic achievement, competitive success, and financial progress. My mistake was in failing to anticipate that administrative problems in athletics could also embarrass the University and in neglecting to articulate that fifth goal of accountability with transparency until the damage had been done. I had observed Bob Mulcahy's success in reinventing the athletic compliance process, had admired the academic achievements of our student-athletes, and, along with everyone else, had celebrated the improvement of the football program. As a result of these developments, I was too trusting and insufficiently attentive to management of the department. When football success arrived, the University was not fully prepared for it because governance practices in athletics had not kept up with the realities of the program. At the time Bob became AD, his department's budget was around $20 million a year; by 2008–09 it was $55 million. When Mulcahy began his tenure, no one paid much attention to Rutgers sports; by 2008, they did. Together we should have brought the administration of athletics into line with its enlarged budget and its newfound success, without waiting until we were forced to do so.

Three weeks after release of the report, I announced my decision to remove Bob Mulcahy as director of intercollegiate athletics, effective December 31, 2008, and issued statements reciting and applauding his accomplishments over the course of the decade during which he had served in that position. My action was consistent with strong advice I was receiving from members of my administration, from some board members, and from some legislators, but the decision was solely my own. I accepted responsibility for it then, and I accept it now. I believed the University needed new leadership in athletics that would join with me and the board in addressing the governance problems, while maintaining the progress to which Bob had contributed so much.

In dismissing Bob, I acted swiftly and without giving him advance notice because I knew that he was well connected in Trenton and around the state. Any delay would bring enormous pressures down upon me not to dismiss him, perhaps even enough to prevent me from doing so. Despite my precaution, a strong reaction on Bob's behalf emerged in several quarters: from sports fans who appreciated what he had accomplished, from some Rutgers board members who told me they supported my decision but didn't like the way I had carried it out, and from several elected officials who publicly criticized me for dismissing Mulcahy. The speaker of the assembly, Joseph J. Roberts, sent me a strongly worded letter expressing surprise and disappointment in my decision and stating bluntly that he did "not want to see Mr. Mulcahy become the scapegoat." "After all," he continued, "the commission [meaning the ARC] didn't find problems with Mr. Mulcahy, but with the failure of top university officials to adequately oversee critical issues." Some newspaper columnists similarly implied that the wrong person had been fired, although others, including one sportswriter who had covered Rutgers athletics for years, said it was time for Mulcahy to go. (The same writer was also critical of me.) Some of Bob's supporters urged Governor Corzine to step into the fray on the AD's behalf, but, just as he had done in the case of undergraduate education, the governor resisted pressure to get involved. State Senator Stephen Sweeney did not: "It's time for a real change," Sweeney said. "President McCormick should announce his resignation so we can begin the process of looking for new leadership." Fortunately, the chair and the vice chair of the Board of Governors came swiftly and publicly to my defense. On the day after Senator Sweeney's statement, the Office of the State Comptroller announced that based on the results of its preliminary inquiry into the department of athletics it would now undertake a full-scale audit of Rutgers's university-wide procurement and contracting processes. That investigation would go on for almost two years. Criticism of me for dismissing Mulcahy continued without relief until late February, when I announced the appointment of his successor.

Exactly at the moment when the pot was boiling over my removal of Bob Mulcahy, the University faced yet another difficult decision in regard to the stadium expansion. Just as before, the critical issue was how to finance the project. To recap: in January, the Board of Governors had approved the $102 million stadium expansion, to be completed in two phases (one of which was now done), and had authorized the University to borrow $72 million. The other $30 million was supposed to come from private fund raising, but by the fall of 2008, amidst a significant economic downturn and the inability of Governor Corzine and Senator Lesniak to realize their philanthropic goal, it was obvious that the original financial plan was in collapse. To make matters worse, the construction bids for phase two of the project had come in much higher than expected. So what to do? Should the University complete phase two, the most important component of which was the construction of seating in the south end zone, and, if so, how should we pay for it?

Quietly, my administration undertook an analysis of several options. One was to scrap the elaborate superstructure that would house the new seating and instead build eleven thousand bleacher-type seats at the south end of the stadium. That option would reduce the cost of the project, but only to about $86 million. Another option was to "power down" the stadium expansion, wait for a year or more, and then with money in hand, from what source we knew not, resume the construction of eleven thousand seats as originally planned. The more we studied these options, and one or two others besides, the clearer it became that by far the best choice was to go ahead with the original project, which would mean asking the Board of Governors for authorization to borrow the full $102 million. Bleacher seats would make the stadium look like a high school football field. Powering down had significant costs of its own and would have sent all the wrong messages to every constituency from fans to recruits. And when and how would we ever "power up"? Most important, without the eleven thousand new seats, the University would be unable to cover the debt service on the money it had already borrowed for the stadium. In full consultation with members of the Board of Governors, we went back to the drawing board, and the department of athletics developed a plan to both raise ticket prices and require annual "donations" for sideline seats. In December, the board voted, unanimously this time, to expand the seating as originally planned, to eliminate several proposed features of the stadium that were unrelated to seating capacity, and to borrow the full amount required. Just as before, the project came in on time and within budget. On September 1, 2009, Rutgers Stadium, at last forming a complete oval, was a sea of fifty-four thousand fans, clad in red and cheering Rutgers on against the University of Cincinnati. We lost that particular football game, but from that day forward few failed to agree that Rutgers had made the right choice to expand the stadium.

With the stadium decision made, we now had to find a new director of intercollegiate athletics. I appointed a diverse search committee of fifteen people headed by Phil Furmanski, and my administration issued a request for proposals for an executive search firm to assist us. Within a week or so, we received half a dozen proposals and chose Parker Executive Search, an Atlanta-based company. In mid-January 2009, Phil and I and several others met with a contingent from Parker who shared with us a proposed plan for identifying qualified candidates for the position. The Parker team also brought with them a timeline for the search that indicated we would announce the appointment of the new athletic director on February 26, and that he or she would assume the position on April 1. I was impressed by the Parker people but, knowing that successful searches took far longer than six weeks, did not initially give much credence to their timeline. The important thing, we agreed, was to make the best possible appointment, no matter how long it took, and so most of our discussion that day focused on the pool of individuals who were potentially available and highly capable of filling the position. The Parker team estimated that there were about a hundred people nationwide who should be considered and asked Phil and me for a commitment that, at the appropriate time, we would personally interview about ten of them. Of course, we said we would. As the search developed, it turned out that Parker really did have a Rolodex. Phil and I interviewed ten semifinal candidates for an hour and a half each on three successive days in mid-February, and from among them we selected three finalists. A week later, thanks to superlative choreography, all three candidates were on campus simultaneously, but without ever encountering each other. Each of them had a substantive meeting with the full search committee and approximately twenty separate meetings with individuals and groups whose advice I wanted to have before making the final choice. On February 26, precisely as Parker's timeline had foretold, the Board of Governors approved my recommended appointee, and a few minutes later I convened a press conference to introduce Rutgers's new director of intercollegiate athletics, Tim Pernetti. He started the job on April 1.

Just thirty-eight years old, Tim had grown up in New Jersey, played four years of football at Rutgers before graduating in 1993, and earned a master's degree, also from Rutgers, the following year. He began his career in sports television at ABC, and in 2003, together with several friends, he created College Sports Television, an enterprise that later became CBS College Sports Network, where Tim served as executive vice president. For the past eight years he had also been the color commentator for the Rutgers Football Radio Network. The *Star-Ledger* called the search "a sham," on the grounds that Tim was a Rutgers football insider and a close friend of Coach Schiano and wasn't ready to lead a troubled, money-losing athletics department. An editorial cartoon in the same newspaper portrayed me announcing Pernetti's appointment "after an exhaustive search of Coach Schiano's living room." Other New Jersey newspapers also initially disparaged the search, and Tim, on the same grounds. Their description of the appointment process was inaccurate but, more important, they had underestimated Tim. After he became AD, criticism quieted quickly and soon died altogether. Indeed, thanks in large part to his leadership and communication skills, the media assault on Rutgers athletics faded away during the spring and summer of 2009, as did the sniping from politicians. On campus, Tim proved to be exactly the athletics leader we needed. Reaching out immediately to faculty and deans and working collaboratively with all parts of the University's administration, from human resources to facilities to legal services, he accomplished, and personified, the reintegration of athletics with the rest of Rutgers.

Tim and I met face-to-face almost every week and spoke on the telephone more often than that. Right from the start, he assumed responsibility for ensuring that phase two of the stadium expansion came in on time and on budget, which, as we have seen, it did. Working with Phil Furmanski and me, Tim developed measures for evaluating progress toward his department's new goal of accountability with transparency, and he took over the task of implementing the management changes that the ARC had recommended. Together he and I reviewed the coaches, prepared for meetings with the now-invigorated Board of Governors Committee on Athletics, and discussed Tim's ambitious plans for upgrading the athletic facilities, especially the cramped and worn Rutgers Athletic Center, home of our basketball teams. But for all this, the two most important subjects that Tim and I discussed were conference realignment and his department's finances—and these were not unrelated.

Although superficially stable in 2009 and 2010, the Big East Conference to which Rutgers belonged was a strange creature among the nation's top six athletic conferences. Its sixteen members varied widely from small Catholic institutions whose main sport was basketball to large state universities, like Rutgers, whose future in athletics was prominently tied to football. The heterogeneous Big East also suffered from the immense geographic dispersion of its member institutions. Put simply: the many differences within the conference cast doubt upon its long-term viability, especially at a moment when conference realignment was becoming rampant everywhere. A number of Big East members were known to be looking quietly for better conference homes, and one of them was Rutgers. Right from the beginning of our work together, Tim and I were focused on this subject.

We knew that the best place for Rutgers would be the Big Ten. That conference included most of the top public research universities in the northeastern quadrant of the United States, exactly the group with which we wanted Rutgers to be aligned. The Big Ten institutions were all academically outstanding; all gave robust and ambitious interpretation to the traditional missions of teaching, research, and service; all had shown for decades that wildly popular sports teams could be part of the fabric of universities whose primary purposes were teaching and research. In mid-December 2009, the Big Ten announced that its presidents and chancellors believed the time was right to "conduct a thorough evaluation of options for conference structure and expansion" and that the Big Ten commissioner, James E. Delany, would be gathering the information needed for such an evaluation. Through his earlier work in the field of sports television, Tim knew Jim Delany well. Following the Big Ten announcement, Tim and Jim began confidential discussions about Rutgers's potential membership in the conference, discussions that were rewarded with success a little less than three years later. Whenever Tim and I talked, we never failed to review our most recent information about the Big Ten's expansion plans.

In May 2010, Tim and I and three of our colleagues in the Rutgers administration accepted an invitation from Delany to meet with him and several members of his staff for a confidential exchange of information about Rutgers and the Big Ten. That daylong session was rewarding and encouraging but did not immediately lead to a Big Ten invitation for Rutgers. Instead the University of Nebraska got the nod, and Tim's conversations with Jim Delany went on and on. We still believed the Big Ten wanted Rutgers and that, when the stars were aligned, it would happen. Rutgers's academic excellence and our location in the New York metropolitan area made us an obvious candidate. The recent success of our football program, the integrity of Rutgers athletics, the academic success of our student-athletes, and our expanded stadium were also attractive to the Big Ten. Based on incomplete information, I surmised that the Big Ten was waiting for the University of Notre Dame to make a decision about its own conference plans. If Notre Dame had agreed to become a full (all-sports) member of the Big Ten, Rutgers probably would have been invited as well. That didn't happen, but what did occur was just as good for Rutgers. After Notre Dame announced its all-but-football alignment with the Atlantic Coast Conference in March 2012, the Big Ten invited the University of Maryland and Rutgers to become members, beginning in 2014. Both accepted. By the time the invitation came in October 2012, I was no longer president of the University but was thrilled by Tim's achievement of a long-sought goal.

Among the many benefits of Big Ten membership should be a significant improvement in the financial condition of Rutgers athletics, thanks to our share of television revenue from the Big Ten Network. If that proves true, the fourth goal that Bob Mulcahy and I announced at the beginning of my presidency, reducing the reliance of the department of athletics on financial subsidies from the University, will finally be realized. Regrettably, it was not achieved on my watch. When I became president, the University's annual subsidy of athletics was about $13 million, around 1 percent of Rutgers's overall expenditures. When I left the presidency, the subsidy was about $19 million, approximately 0.9 percent of total expenditures. Expressing the subsidy as a percentage of the institution's total annual outlay, we had made some modest progress in reducing it, but the real dollar amount of the sub-sidy had gone in the wrong direction. Tim Pernetti took this problem seriously and made diligent and, to some degree, successful efforts to move athletics toward financial self-sufficiency. By annually scour-ing his department's expenditures and cutting back as many of them as he could and by generating new revenue for athletics, such as the payments for naming rights to the enlarged stadium, Tim reduced his department's reliance on the University below what it otherwise would have been. But given Rutgers's commitment to be athletically competi-tive, he had few degrees of freedom. The only real solution was to radi-cally increase revenues by getting into the Big Ten, which we did.

Intercollegiate athletics is expensive. Salaries for coaches, scholar-ships for athletes, maintenance and debt service for facilities, and travel costs all go up and up. It's a national problem, not just a Rutgers issue. The Knight Commission, the faculty senates of many universities, and even the NCAA have expressed alarm about the "arms race" in athletics spending. The same warning was heard at Rutgers as recently as Feb-ruary 2012, when faculty in the School of Arts and Sciences adopted a resolution calling upon the University to reduce its subsidy for inter-collegiate athletics and to allocate the funds to academics. When the University becomes a member of the Big Ten, it will gain access to far greater television revenues than ever before, but expenditures for ath-letics will also rise. Travel costs will go up, and there will be healthy pressure to invest more in the Olympic sports so that Rutgers can compete with Big Ten universities in soccer, softball, and wrestling, as well as football and basketball. The best answers will lie in continued good management of the kind that Tim Pernetti embraced and in an unceasing resolve that intercollegiate athletics shall be fully one with the University's educational mission and values, not a thing apart.

Rutgers never actually had the open discussion of its goals for inter-collegiate athletics that I proposed to the Board of Governors in 2003. But unanticipated events, some of them quite painful, brought forth a kind of proxy for that discussion and resolved some long-standing questions about the future. Between November 2006, when the victory over Louisville gave Rutgers a taste of athletic success better than it had ever enjoyed before, a taste that it now wanted to keep, and the summer of 2009, when the stadium expansion was finished, the media ended its war on Rutgers athletics, and Tim Pernetti's leadership style began to make its mark, the University's intercollegiate program passed across a great divide. Now, at last, Rutgers had big-time sports that were not only clean and educationally sound (those achievements were not new) but also tightly bound to the rest of the University, widely respected, and athletically more successful than ever. Besides the dramatic elevation of the football program, other developments also had a part in that passage: the universal goodwill that enveloped Rutgers athletics when Vivian Stringer's players courageously answered Don Imus, the University's effective response to the *Star-Ledger*'s investigative reporting and the ARC report, and the leadership transition to Pernetti. Rutgers's admission to the Big Ten in the fall of 2012 confirmed the program's elevated status and its future prospects.

Unfortunately, just a few months later, despite the lessons learned from the events of 2008, and in stark contrast to the new and positive trajectory taken by Rutgers athletics in the years thereafter, a damning video disseminated worldwide caused as much pain and damage to the program and the University as anything that had come before. In April 2013, ESPN exposed taped evidence of Mike Rice, the third-year men's basketball coach, verbally and physically abusing his players during team practices, and for weeks afterward every news outlet rebroadcast the tapes. Watching them, I and everyone who witnessed the abuse felt very badly for the student-athletes, who should never have been subjected to such demeaning treatment by a coach. Rice, who had initially been suspended, fined, and ordered to undergo anger management therapy for his actions before the video became public, was promptly fired. The calamity quickly claimed others among its casualties: within days, resignations were received from Tim Pernetti and Acting General Counsel John Wolf, two of the University's most highly dedicated and principled senior leaders.

The program suffered further embarrassment when Rutgers erroneously claimed that the new head coach—Eddie Jordan, the much admired and accomplished star of the 1976 Rutgers team that had played in the NCAA Final Four—was a Rutgers graduate when he had not actually completed his degree. And there was one more jolt: a few days after the appointment of the new athletic director, Julie Hermann, former players accused her of verbally abusing them years earlier when she had been their college volleyball coach. Fortunately, the stories ran their course without further damage, and a subsequent independent review provided recommendations that will strengthen procedures within and beyond Rutgers athletics. But the furor gave my successor, Bob Barchi, a hard lesson in the intensity of big-time college athletics, the disproportionate media scrutiny it receives compared to anything else at a university, and the essentiality of relentless presidential attention to athletics. I had had my own hard lessons in all those things.

Despite these deeply difficult events, Rutgers *is* going to continue playing big-time collegiate sports, and over the years will likely achieve considerable competitive success. Many of its victories will be won in the now-enlarged football stadium, the most visible symbol of Rutgers athletics. For the University to realize the benefits of these triumphs, the sports program must remain clean and honorable, and its student-athletes must continue to receive a good education and to graduate. The program must continue to be managed well and transparently and to be accountable to the university community and the people of New Jersey. Attaining these lofty outcomes will require great effort and great faith, perhaps occasionally in the face of adversities as severe as those of 2008 or 2013. Impetus to keep up that work may sometimes come from the taunts of critics, on campus or in the media, who remain skeptical of Rutgers athletics. But the great divide that was crossed will not have to be traversed again. For Rutgers, at last, the bell really has been rung. Through trials by fire that no one wanted or foresaw, the University now has, and is committed to, an intercollegiate athletics program that is as good as Rutgers itself. Maintaining that excellence will demand not only hard work but also discipline to resist the pressures that could put success at risk. Among these, the most worrisome is competitive pressure toward unbridled spending.

RUTGERS AND
NEW JERSEY

WITH HIGH HOPES, I devoted most of my inaugural address on April 13, 2003, to the subject of Rutgers and New Jersey. Invoking the ideal of the great American state universities that had grown up in partnership with the people of their states, I committed Rutgers more fully to become that kind of institution for New Jersey. My speech pointed with pride to our graduates' readiness to contribute to the state's economy, gave examples of Rutgers research focused on New Jersey's needs, and cited prominent instances of our University's service to the people of the state. But it acknowledged that, compared to great institutions in the South and Midwest, Rutgers historically had not always fulfilled the obligations of a true state university. Now, directly addressing Governor Jim McGreevey and the other elected officials who were present that day, I pledged that we would do so. "Rutgers," I said, "will be your state university. We will work with you to meet the needs of the people of our state, to provide outstanding education to our students, to discover and apply new knowledge, and to serve. And we, in turn, will expect you to help us and to support us with adequate funding." Elsewhere in the speech I made the same point: "If we do our part, the people of New Jersey will do theirs." It was a bold formulation, perhaps even foolhardy. But I believed that Rutgers should connect more deeply with the people of New Jersey and that they would reciprocate our embrace. The influences upon me as I set forth this goal came from all the usual places: my own earlier associations with Rutgers; my father, whose history of the University had chronicled the uneven development of its relationship to New Jersey; my experiences at the state universities of North Carolina and Washington; and countless conversations within the Rutgers community and around the state since I returned as president.

Making headway against the ambitious objective I expressed in my inaugural address would require numerous and parallel efforts. We would need to learn as much as we could about how the people of New Jersey perceived Rutgers and what they expected from us. We would have to expand programs of teaching, research, and service that were related to issues facing the state and establish new programs where there were needs and opportunities to do so. Progress toward the goal would also require spreading accurate information about Rutgers widely across New Jersey and dispelling popular confusions about the University. Finally, our success would necessitate communicating effectively with many constituencies, none more important than elected officials at the state capital in Trenton.

Earlier in this book I summarized the findings of our 2004 Constituency Research Project, a massive survey of thousands of New Jerseyans whose opinions of Rutgers provided grounds for both satisfaction and concern. Although most respondents knew that Rutgers was the state university of New Jersey, few of them were aware of any attributes that distinguished it from other public colleges and universities in the state. The ideas and images with which they associated Rutgers were highly varied and alarmingly vague; recognition of the value of Rutgers research was distinctly limited. One component of the project was a series of in-depth interviews with twenty-three New Jersey government leaders, including current and former legislators, former governors, and other state officials. All of them expressed positive feelings about Rutgers, and three-quarters of them ranked Rutgers above the state's other colleges and universities in providing high-quality

education and service to the people of the state. Even these government leaders, however, showed only a limited understanding of the
University's role in research. They felt Rutgers needed to do a far better
job of keeping officials like themselves, as well as state residents generally, aware of what was going on at the University. In particular, they
wanted to see evidence of Rutgers's usefulness in their local communities. The Constituency Research Project provided a lot of information
to work with. It helped my administration to devise a multipronged
communications effort on the University's behalf, and it guided us in
developing relationships with members of the legislature and other
government officials.

But first to the substance of the matter: What would Rutgers do to
fulfill more completely its mission as the state university of New Jersey? Rutgers was no stranger to the concept of service to the state. For
well over a century, the Rutgers New Jersey Agricultural Experiment
Station had been offering science-based assistance to farmers in every
county; across the decades its programs had expanded beyond agriculture to include food safety and nutrition, environmental protection,
and the management of natural resources. Since the 1960s, Rutgers law
students in both Newark and Camden, working under the close super-
vision of faculty members, had furnished free legal services to low-
income clients in such areas as housing, child advocacy, civil justice, and
tax law. Almost all of the University's professional schools provided
opportunities for continuing education for practitioners in their fields.
Faculty and students on all three Rutgers campuses were engaged in
advising and supporting state and municipal officials through the work
of the Bloustein School of Planning and Public Policy in New Brunswick, the Walter Rand Institute for Public Affairs in Camden, and the
National Center for Public Performance in Newark. Several noted faculty members, in particular, had become highly respected advisers to
New Jersey's governors and legislators of both political parties. They
included Joseph J. Seneca and James W. Hughes, whose counsel was
regularly sought on the New Jersey economy; Carl E. Van Horn, the
state's foremost expert on workforce development; and Martin E. Rob-
ins, who had similar stature in the field of transportation. For decades,

the Eagleton Institute of Politics, and especially its revered former director, Alan Rosenthal, had forged essential bonds between the University and state officials by providing regular speaking and teaching opportunities for political leaders and training grounds for students pursuing careers in government. Activities such as these characterize state universities across America, and Rutgers could be proud of its programs of outreach to New Jersey.

Then suddenly there were many more of them. A burst of Rutgers endeavors to serve the state and its people coincided with my presidency, but, like all other academic initiatives, it owed most to deans and faculty members. In an earlier chapter, I pointed with pride to some of the characteristics shared by the deans whom Phil Furmanski and I recruited; now I will mention another of their attributes: commitment to the ideals of a state university. Many of them came to Rutgers from big-time public institutions whose values they brought with them. Richard L. Edwards arrived here from the University of North Carolina at Chapel Hill to become dean of the School of Social Work. Thomas Farris came from Purdue University to head the School of Engineering. Robert M. Goodman left the University of Wisconsin to become dean of our School of Environmental and Biological Sciences. William L. Holzemer arrived at Rutgers from the University of California, San Francisco, to lead the College of Nursing. Jorge Reina Schement departed from Pennsylvania State University to serve as dean of the School of Communication and Information. Kriste Lindenmeyer arrived here from the University of Maryland, Baltimore County, to head the Faculty of Arts and Sciences at Camden. Others came to Rutgers with public service backgrounds, such as John J. Farmer Jr., dean of the School of Law at Newark and formerly attorney general of the state of New Jersey. Still others arrived here with accomplishments in research and scholarship that inclined them toward the public-serving ideals of a state university. These included Wendell E. Pritchett, chancellor of the Camden campus, and Todd Clear, dean of the School of Criminal Justice. Yet still others among the deans had been at Rutgers for many years and had acquired along the way the full mind-set of state university academic leaders: Marc Holzer (School of Public Affairs and Administration), Richard De Lisi (Graduate School of Education), George B. Stauffer (Mason Gross School of the Arts), James M. Hughes (Bloustein School), and Rayman L. Solomon (School of Law at Camden). Together they moved Rutgers in the direction I had pledged it would go, and their impact will be felt for decades to come.

Following his arrival in 2005, Dick Edwards reoriented a sleepy social work school toward solving problems faced by ordinary people in New Jersey and around the world. The Institute for Families, the Center on Violence Against Women and Children, and the Center for Gambling Studies all sprang into existence just two years later; all provide opportunities for faculty and students to engage with partners in the community, the private and nonprofit sectors, and the government; and all are using the capabilities of a public research university to improve life for individuals and families. Soon after Richard De Lisi became dean of the Graduate School of Education (GSE) in 2003, we agreed that service and support for New Jersey's public schools should become one of the University's signature commitments. Now, thanks in large part, but not exclusively, to faculty and students in GSE, every single one of New Jersey's forty legislative districts has multiple Rutgers programs in partnership with local K–12 schools. George Stauffer created an extension division within the Mason Gross School of the Arts; each year it provides teaching and training in dance, music, theater, and visual arts for thousands of men, women, and children, both online and around the state.

At Rutgers-Camden, Provost Roger Dennis and the faculty launched their campus's first-ever Ph.D. programs with community needs as well as academic considerations in mind: childhood studies in 2007 and public affairs in 2010. While serving as dean of arts and sciences, Margaret S. Marsh became the driving force behind the childhood studies program; Roger Dennis himself, together with Richard A. Harris, then director of the Rand Institute, provided the leadership for establishing the program in public affairs. Roger's successor, Wendell Pritchett, now called chancellor, drew upon his own scholarship and hands-on experience in urban public policy to create the Office of Civic Engagement, which supports more than two dozen programs of outreach in education, economic development, and law and public policy serving the city of Camden and much of South Jersey. In 2006, Rutgers-Newark established the School of Public Affairs and Administration, its first new degree-granting school in decades, to prepare students for careers in public service. Led by its founding dean, Marc Holzer, the school also runs programs of professional development for city and state officials. In its research, as well as in education and service, Rutgers is doing more than ever for the state of New Jersey. As noted in an earlier chapter, when my administration chose to invest in such interdisciplinary research initiatives as transportation, energy, and nutrition, their relevance to our state's needs was a key consideration.

As New Jersey and the nation entered into a severe economic recession in 2008, the University launched Rutgers Against Hunger (RAH), a program combining the Agricultural Experiment Station's experience in sharing science-based information about nutrition with a new and urgent commitment to collecting and donating food for needy New Jersey families. Conceived by Leslie Fehrenbach, who also serves as secretary of the University, and Larry S. Katz, director of cooperative extension, RAH distributes food and nutritional information in partnership with sixty hunger-fighting agencies, mostly food banks and homeless shelters, located in every region of the state. While New Jersey is a relatively wealthy state, consistently ranking near the top in median household income, its prosperity is far from universally shared. Thousands of men, women, and children, urban and rural alike, have insufficient access to healthy, nutritious food. As unemployment rose and family incomes declined, sometimes to nothing, the problem worsened. RAH's response to this challenge expressed the university community's sense of obligation to the people of New Jersey, while it also drew upon the institution's long-standing strengths in nutrition, food science, and agricultural extension. More than 150 departments, student groups, and alumni organizations now actively participate in RAH.

As we had learned through the Constituency Research Project, it was not enough just to do these things: we also had to share information about them across the state and especially with its most influential citizens. I have already described two of our endeavors to spread the word about Rutgers: a week-long faculty bus tour of New Jersey and our annual Rutgers Day. Regrettably, after five successful years, the bus tour fell victim to budget cuts, but Rutgers Day is now more successful than ever in attracting tens of thousands of New Jerseyans to the New Brunswick campus on the last Saturday of each April. We took other steps, as well, to brand Rutgers, to sharpen its identity in the minds of state residents, and to disseminate news of its achievements. The University crafted a new slogan—"Jersey Roots, Global Reach"—that efficiently communicates Rutgers's deep ties to the state and the world-wide ambitions of its work. Schools and colleges across the University incorporated the new tagline into descriptions of their own programs, and the Office of University Relations, led by Vice President Kim Manning, made these words ubiquitous around New Jersey through television spots, billboards, bus wraps, and print media. Whatever the communication vehicle, these ads are designed to increase popular appreciation for Rutgers by spotlighting individuals who exemplify its proudest achievements: students who win the most prestigious fellowships or participate in significant research projects, faculty such as neuroscientist Wise Young who make important discoveries or receive major awards, and other Rutgers leaders, like Coach Vivian Stringer, who have brought honor to the University.

Besides buying space and time in other people's media, Rutgers also developed a suite of new communications instruments of its own—online, in print, and sometimes both. In 2009, the Office of Public Affairs established an electronic publication, *Friends of Rutgers News*, which it sends each Friday to a still-growing group of several thousand influential citizens (and anyone else who wants to receive it). The newsletter offers brief articles about and pictures of the most interesting and timely happenings at Rutgers, all designed with our external constituencies in mind. At the same time, the Office of University Relations created a parallel online publication, *Rutgers Today*, which continuously provides news of University events and achievements, both for internal audiences and for outside media, often yielding hundreds of placements in online and print publications around the world. In an earlier chapter, I recounted our decision to begin sending hard copies of *Rutgers Magazine* to four hundred thousand worldwide alumni, approximately half of them in New Jersey. Besides these publications offering a broad spectrum of information about the University, we also created several pieces intended for business and government leaders whose opinions carry particular weight. In 2009, with the recession at its peak, we published and disseminated *Solutions from Rutgers: New Jersey's Partner for a Strong Economy*, an attractive compilation of hard data and human stories about the University's myriad contributions to the state's well-being—through the multiplier effect of its spending, the out-of-state resources its attracts, workforce development, research, and targeted economic services of many kinds. I'll mention just one more communications effort: Rutgers's ongoing enumeration of its activities in each of the state's forty legislative districts. These handy pages (in print or online) reveal that in addition to the pervasive K–12 school partnerships noted earlier, Rutgers offers economic assistance, continuing and professional education, and support for agriculture and nutrition virtually everywhere in New Jersey. I rarely met with a legislator without having one of these documents in my hand.

I would like to tie a bow around this narrative of our efforts to serve and to reach the people of New Jersey by relating exactly how much difference our initiatives made. Unfortunately, however, we launched these many endeavors, and more, without determining exactly how we would measure progress toward the goal of deepening the University's ties to the state. At the least, we should have replicated the Constituency Research Project to test our success in improving popular attitudes toward Rutgers and promoting greater knowledge of its missions. There is plenty of qualitative and anecdotal evidence suggesting that New Jerseyans understand and admire the University more than they did a decade ago. But by how much? And what caused the improvement of Rutgers's reputation? Surely the deans' new programs of service to the state made a difference. Certainly the University's new vehicles of communication also helped. But so did the success of the football team, as did the reorganization of undergraduate education by easing the burden of explaining Rutgers to prospective students and their parents. How does Rutgers stack up today in fulfillment of its role as New Jersey's state university, compared to the very best public institutions whose ties to their states I noted in my inaugural address? As Rutgers enters the Big Ten, which is chock-full of such institutions, and joins the conference's Committee on Institutional Cooperation, there will be greater opportunities than ever to answer that question.

※

Predictably, inevitably, and with determination, we carried our goals for Rutgers and the news of its usefulness to New Jersey into the realm of politics and government. There we encountered in full measure the realities of the state's rough-and-tumble public life. Least problematic and, indeed, largely satisfying were Rutgers's relationships at the local, municipal level, especially in the University's four hometowns of Newark, Camden, New Brunswick, and Piscataway. The provosts, later called chancellors, and their staffs who led the Newark and Camden campuses forged strong ties with their mayors, council members, and school district leaders. Steve Diner, Roger Dennis, and Wendell Pritchett believed that Rutgers should aggressively support its host communities, and, in collaboration with local officials, they created program after program through which faculty and students reached out to help meet the needs of city government, public safety, social welfare, and K–12 education. More than just wanting to help, however, Steve, Roger, and Wendell regarded the location of their campuses within struggling cities striving to reinvent themselves as a distinct strength because it fostered the development of innovative teaching and research that attracted faculty and students with a special commitment to urban America. All three of them exhibited the Rutgers trait of turning local circumstances, even difficult ones, into comparative academic advantages. Not surprisingly, Steve, Roger, and Wendell all gained national reputations for knowledge and advocacy of urban universities.

In New Brunswick and Piscataway, too, Rutgers established productive partnerships with local officials. This was especially true in

New Brunswick, a small city with its share of problems, but also with a long tradition of clean and stable government, headed throughout my presidential years by Mayor Jim Cahill, and with the active presence of an innovative nonprofit agency called the New Brunswick Development Corporation (Devco), which worked closely with both the city and Rutgers. That three-way partnership led to the financing and construction of a number of outstanding facilities in the heart of New Brunswick, none more vital to both the University and the community than the Barnes & Noble Rutgers Bookstore that opened in 2012. Devco's energetic CEO, Rutgers alum Christopher J. Paladino, who could always find an obscure tax credit or a state subsidy when he needed one, also engineered the deal that enabled Rutgers to obtain most of the property belonging to the New Brunswick Theological Seminary. Just as in Newark and Camden, Rutgers faculty and students became actively engaged in New Brunswick–based service and research. Working with local officials and city residents, a faculty committee developed guidelines and best practices for research partnerships between the University and the community, grounded in mutual respect, cultural understanding, and shared authority. My administration launched a program of annual grants to support that kind of research in New Brunswick. Finally, as noted much earlier in this book, hundreds of high school students in each of the University's four hometowns are preparing for college as members of the Rutgers Future Scholars Program.

Fulfilling as these local endeavors were, Rutgers's main political focus was, and is, the government of the state of New Jersey. Although the University possesses considerable statutory independence thanks to the act of 1956 that established the Board of Governors, the state still regulates many activities within the institution, plays an indispensable role in providing student financial aid, and, above all, controls more than $400 million that New Jersey appropriates annually for Rutgers. With all this in mind, I, like every other public university president, plunged into developing relationships with the members of the state legislature, the governors, and their staffs. I wanted to make them champions of Rutgers—to have them know and support our achievements and ambitions, to connect their public policy goals with our own programs, and, of course, to increase the state's investment in Rutgers. To these ends, members of my administration and I continuously met and talked with legislators—in their local district offices and in Trenton, on the Rutgers campus if we could attract them for dinners at my home or for conversations in my office or sometimes for athletic events, and on the telephone. When meeting with a member of the legislature, I almost always shared the summary of the University's activities in his or her district and brought up Rutgers programs that were related to the legislator's own priorities. Consistent with my state university ideals, I frequently asked what more we could do to meet the needs of the legislator and his constituents. Colleagues in the Rutgers administration helped me prepare for these meetings and usually accompanied me: in the early years, it was Sharon Ainsworth, director of state relations, and then, in sequence, two remarkably well-connected and talented vice presidents for public affairs, Jeannine F. LaRue and Peter J. McDonough Jr.

Meetings with legislators were nearly always friendly. Generally, they expressed high regard for Rutgers, although if we were doing something they didn't like I would hear about it. They might ask if the University could establish a particular teaching program in their district or wonder if Rutgers researchers could help with a certain problem their constituents were having. We tried to be responsive, and over the years the University greatly expanded its educational offerings around the state, usually on the campuses of community colleges and in partnership with them. Sometimes legislators would recommend particular individuals for admission to Rutgers or for employment. In response, I would promise to contact whoever was responsible for that decision within the University and ask that person to take a good look at the applicant, but I would tell the legislator that the final outcome would rest on the merits of the candidate. Following such requests, I would do as I had promised. With rare exceptions, legislators accepted that answer and did not press for politically driven decisions. It was probably enough to tell a constituent that the Rutgers president had promised to take a sympathetic look at the case.

My colleagues and I also used our meetings with legislators to deepen their appreciation of Rutgers's value to the state. We told them about our students, the vast majority of whom grew up in New Jersey, came from sufficiently modest backgrounds that 80 percent of them qualified for financial aid, and remained in the state after graduation where, owing to their Rutgers education, they contributed to New Jersey's knowledge-based economy. We spoke of the hundreds of millions of dollars Rutgers brought into the state each year to support faculty research and gave examples of how that research was creating jobs, solving problems, and saving lives. We proudly described the ways in which Rutgers was responding to the needs of New Jersey's businesses, protecting its environment, and improving its cities—often with examples drawn from the towns and industries that were most familiar to the legislator. Sometimes we cited the latest Rutgers accomplishment that had garnered national or international kudos. Because legislators were so busy, there was never enough time to say nearly all of these things in a single meeting. But we were always prepared to do so if we got the chance and always thanked them for their time and attention.

For all this, the main subject we discussed with legislators was the state's appropriation for higher education and for Rutgers. New Jersey's annual budgetary cycle begins in February or March when the governor proposes a spending plan for the coming fiscal year starting July 1. Legislative hearings and many heated conversations then follow throughout the spring, until the governor and the legislature exhaustedly agree on a budget for the state, often just hours before the clock runs out on June 30. The final result almost always closely resembles what the governor had originally recommended, although inevitably a handful of powerful legislators succeed in tweaking the state executive's budget in directions they favor. Over the years, the higher education community, meaning not just Rutgers but all the public colleges and universities, would like to have exerted more influence each winter on the governor's proposed budget, but we never found a way to do that. So my fellow presidents and I, along with our state relations officers, would spend the spring talking with legislators, testifying at their hearings, and trying to improve upon what the governor had recommended for us. In some years, we urged faculty, staff, and alumni to send e-mail messages to their legislators seeking a better budget for Rutgers; sometimes our students organized rallies in Trenton, usually in concert with students from other universities around the state. All of this activity usually made little difference, although in 2003, as I have already recounted, and again in 2006, the higher education community managed to ameliorate, but did not come close to eliminating, deep cuts that the governor had proposed.

Several invariable themes ran through our budget discussions with state officials. Most prominent was the truth that New Jersey was broke. Its rising obligations for K–12 schools, health care, aid to municipalities, debt service, and pensions, together with the political unacceptability of raising taxes, meant that the state had, and still has, a more or less permanent structural deficit and an enduring need to rely on one-time sources of revenue to balance the budget. In such a context, unfortunately, higher education was not politically strong enough to withstand the inevitable annual search, by both governors and legislators, for lines in the budget they could reduce. To elected officials, there was no penalty, no price to be paid for cutting higher education, compared to, say, the public schools or the cities or the seniors. As legislators said to me more than once, "Your students don't vote." That statement wasn't strictly true, of course, but it expressed the perception that no sizable bloc within the electorate had higher education as its top priority. No public official ever lost reelection for approving a budget reducing the allocation to colleges and universities. State officials were pretty honest in acknowledging these truths: "We're out of money and you don't have much clout."

To those in elected office, moreover, higher education wasn't in any kind of crisis. Colleges and universities did not appear desperately to need additional revenues, as, for example, city schools, prisons, and worn-out bridges so obviously did. To be sure, legislators would complain about such things as our allegedly low graduation rates or the growth of our students' indebtedness due to rising tuition, but no one perceived these ills as fatally flawing higher education. And it was true: we were not broken. In year A Rutgers graduated 11,000 students; then our budget was cut, and in year B we awarded 12,000 degrees; then our budget was cut again, and in year C 13,000 men and women collected their Rutgers diplomas. What's to complain about? Our productivity seemed to go up and up, irrespective of how much state support we received.

These realities made for frustrating and repetitive budget conversations with legislators. My colleagues and I would do our best to make the case for improved funding for Rutgers, and the legislators with whom we were speaking, having no money and no political incentive to help us but no particular ill will toward Rutgers either, would reply in one of several ways. Perhaps the most common response to our pitch for a better budget was something like this: "Well, *I* would like to increase the funding for higher education, but my fellow legislators don't agree. You'll have to talk with Assemblyman Smith and Senator Jones and see if you can persuade them. If you do, I'll be with you." A somewhat similar reply to our request went along these lines: "Rutgers is clearly doing great work, but you haven't *communicated* it well enough. You and the other presidents simply must tell your stories better. Then we will have to increase your funding." Those were the nice responses. Sometimes the answers got rougher, along lines like this: "We're cutting your budget because of the bad things your university is doing. You are driving students into debt and then not graduating them. You are insufficiently accountable for the state money you already have. Until you fix these problems you won't get any more." Unpleasant words like these were seldom spoken in our face-to-face meetings. They were generally reserved for press releases and for legislative hearings (of which I'll say more below). As one assemblyman put it in a public statement: "It is shameful that the heads of our four-year schools refuse to see that their internal practices . . . are the real problem. . . . Until they can prove to us that they have learned that lesson, they shouldn't expect any special favors."

These rhetorical thrusts were difficult to parry. Added to them was a dilemma I always faced when arguing for more state support for Rutgers. Again and again, I pointed with pride to the University's achievements in education, research, and service—our fine and deserving students, our faculty's laudable accomplishments, our contributions to New Jersey and the world. And then I asked for more money. How to reconcile these things? The obvious reply, which I sometimes heard but usually went unspoken, was this: "If Rutgers is doing such great work, you must not really need more state support." I could avoid the dilemma, of course, by saying nothing about the University's achievements and focusing only on its needs and problems, but that was no solution, and indeed it was an inconceivable approach. There were only two truthful ways to reconcile the bragging with the begging, and I employed them both from time to time. One was to observe that all of Rutgers's fine achievements were "at risk" without more state support. The other was to describe exciting new initiatives in education and research that the University could undertake if only it had additional resources. But neither approach was politically compelling in an environment of severe budgetary scarcity and of needs that appeared far more urgent than ours. Worse, the purposes for which Rutgers most needed additional state funding were not very appealing to elected officials: money for faculty and staff salaries, for underfunded educational programs, and for maintenance of our facilities. Nobody ever won reelection by championing appropriations for those things.

Legislative hearings can be great theater. Every spring, the budget committees of both the assembly and senate hold multiple public sessions to discuss the proposed state budget. As Rutgers president, I participated each year, together with some of my fellow presidents, in the budget hearings devoted to higher education. Following our brief opening remarks, we answered questions for as long as the legislators were inclined to ask them. The tone and tenor of these hearings varied greatly from year to year. Sometimes they were entirely friendly and mild. On these occasions the legislators would observe how fortunate New Jersey was to have such fine colleges and universities, and we presidents fielded mainly softballs. In other years, the hearings were nastier, and at those times we and our institutions fell under suspicion of all kinds of nefarious practices. In one particularly difficult hearing, a member of the assembly budget committee directed his fire for several long hours mainly at Rutgers and me over issues I have mentioned already, graduation rates and student debt. These were subjects I knew well, and I did my best to respond to his angry questions, but I could not shake the feeling that something besides those two issues lay behind his outrage. Soon afterward, I visited the assemblyman in his district office and asked him about the hearing. His response was surprisingly friendly but vague, and I never really learned the cause of his frenzy. Indeed, the ebb and flow of legislative cordiality did not seem to have much to do with Rutgers or higher education, but rather with political dynamics within the legislature and between the legislative and executive branches. It was seldom evident that anything occurring in the hearings actually affected the final budget.

So how did Rutgers fare in its annual quest for funding from New Jersey? Not very well. In fiscal year 2003, my first as president, Rutgers's state appropriation was $436 million; in fiscal year 2012, my last, the appropriation was $429 million. Over the course of the decade, it went up and down from year to year, but from one end of my presidency to the other, there was little change in the nominal dollars appropriated by the state to Rutgers, or, for that matter, to New Jersey's other public colleges and universities. Taking into account the declining value of the dollar, the real worth of the University's state appropriation fell by approximately 25 percent. Across these same years, the state's overall budget grew by nearly 30 percent in actual dollars, growth in which higher education shared not at all. The long-term national trend of declining state support for colleges and universities continued on my watch as president of Rutgers.

In compensation for the loss in real dollars of aid from New Jersey, the University turned increasingly to other sources of revenue, the largest of which were tuition and fees from our students. This, too, continued a long-term trend. Consider the following: For a New Jersey resident attending Rutgers in 1990, the state provided about 70 percent of the cost of education, while tuition and fees covered about 30 percent. By 2012, following more than two decades of declining state support and rising tuition, those numbers were almost exactly reversed. The state now furnished only a little more than 30 percent of the cost of education, while tuition and fees were required to do the rest. Fortunately for our students, the availability of need-based financial aid from the federal government, from the state government (New Jersey actually does this well by national standards), and from Rutgers has substantially reduced the impact of rising tuition. So far, there is little evidence that the economic profile of the University's student body is changing, and Rutgers continues to be accessible to students from economically disadvantaged families.

By 2012, the state of New Jersey was providing only about 20 percent of the overall Rutgers budget. Knowing this, well-meaning friends of Rutgers, usually businesspeople, often asked me why the University didn't just walk away from the state and "go private." It wouldn't be hard, they believed, to replace New Jersey's modest contribution to the Rutgers budget, and we could get rid of a lot of regulatory headaches at the same time. So what's wrong with that scenario? Three big things. First, there is no way the state government would permit it. Whatever the size of the state's budgetary contribution, elected officials believe that Rutgers belongs to the people of New Jersey. (So do I.) Second, while the state appropriation is "only" 20 percent of the University's budget, there is no realistic way to replace it. Doing so would take an endowment of approximately $10 billion, an amount that is completely beyond our ability to obtain, or a tuition increase of nearly 100 percent, a ridiculous figure. Finally, walking away from New Jersey—even if it were possible, which it is not—would mean abandoning Rutgers's mission as the state university. Complicated as Rutgers's relationship to New Jersey is and always has been, that mission is now at the core of the University's identity. "Going private" may be a well-meaning suggestion, but it is utterly fantastical.

Considering that the real value of the state's budgetary support for the University had been falling long before I became president and considering that the trend of declining state support for higher education was (as it still is) a nationwide phenomenon, it seems unlikely there is anything that I or Rutgers could have done to obtain a substantially better outcome in our quest for dollars from New Jersey. However true that may be, it never felt that way to me. I was always hopeful for greater success, against the odds, and believed that if I could do a better job of building relationships in Trenton and of advocating for Rutgers, the University would receive more money. Looking back on all those meetings with legislators, my personal style was probably not well suited to the job at hand. I was very earnest, very serious, very detailed. I was on message when I should have shot the breeze, uptight when I should have loosened up, polite when I should have been gregarious.

What's more, I was insufficiently appreciative of the time frame in which legislators operated. They were on political time, not academic time. Everything was urgent. They were impatient for results and intolerant of time-consuming reflection. The budget had to be adopted next week, the next election campaign was just around the corner, and competitive partisan strategies (about which I knew little) were always in play.

A single anecdote will make the point. One year, just after the senate budgetary hearing on higher education had wrapped up, Senator Stephen Sweeney called me over and asked how much it cost to educate a Rutgers student. It was a reasonable question for a legislator to ask a university president, and he asked it in a friendly way. I replied that I would find the answer and get back in touch with him. Unfortunately, I way overthought his question. It costs more to educate an engineer than a sociologist; it costs more to educate a graduate student than an undergraduate; it costs more to educate a student who requires a lot of university services than a student who is self-sufficient. There was no single answer to Sweeney's question. I relayed all this to my colleagues in the Rutgers budget office and asked them to try to come up with a number I could give the senator. They worked and worked on it. A couple of weeks later Sweeney phoned me and asked if I had the answer for him. This time he was a little less friendly.

Finally after about six weeks, my budget office friends, having employed who knows what methodologies to answer such a complicated question, came up with a number that I could give Senator Sweeney. It was around $19,400. I phoned Sweeney and gave him the answer, but he was clearly annoyed that I had taken so long to come up with it. I now realized what I should have done. Instead of all that nonsense about different kinds of students, I should have taken the dollar amount of the state appropriation for Rutgers, divided it by the total number of students of all kinds, and added to that figure the dollar amount of tuition. That's the cost of a Rutgers education. I could practically have done that calculation in my head, and in any event it would have taken less than five minutes. And do you know what? That simple arithmetic yielded a number within about a hundred dollars of the sophisticatedly derived figure I gave the senator! I was so stupid to overthink his question. The CEO of McDonald's knows off the top of his head how much it costs to make a cheeseburger. Senator Sweeney was understandably sore at me for making him wait so long for the answer to a simple question. Despite his annoyance, Sweeney became one of the legislature's strongest advocates for higher education. In 2012, by now the senate president, he championed a long-sought bond issue for college and university facilities. Placed on the ballot that year, it passed easily.

Senator Sweeney was, and still is, among the state's most influential legislators, but in New Jersey no member of the senate or the assembly comes close to matching the political power of the governor. The chief executive's authority derives from constitutional provisions crafted more than a half century ago for the purpose of strengthening that office, as well as from the successful exercise of gubernatorial powers by almost all of the individuals who have filled that position in recent decades. New Jersey's political culture is focused on the governor. As president of Rutgers, I wanted to have the kind of relationship with the governor that Ed Bloustein had had with Tom Kean in the 1980s. Personal friends, they collaborated in devising plans for the appointment of dozens of world-class faculty members (the WCSLs noted earlier) and for the establishment of successful research institutes such as the Center for Advanced Biotechnology and Medicine and the Environmental and Occupational Health Sciences Institute, both on the Rutgers campus in Piscataway. Bloustein and Kean also worked together to find resources for these endeavors—from, among other places, the higher education bond issue of 1988 and wealthy donors whom they jointly cultivated. The story of their relationship has acquired an aura of harmony and achievement that may obscure a somewhat grittier reality, but it is indisputable that support from Governor Kean played an essential role in Rutgers's ascent to distinction in the 1980s. I would have loved to develop a relationship like that.

Four men served as governor of New Jersey while I was president of Rutgers: Jim McGreevey (2002–2004), Dick Codey (2004–2006), Jon Corzine (2006–2010), and Chris Christie (2010–2012). I wanted Rutgers, through its research and faculty expertise, to support each governor's goals for New Jersey. That's what state universities do: they provide academic resources to assist governors in achieving their objectives for the state. When collaboration between a state university and its governor is successful, the university benefits, too. That was certainly true in New Jersey in the 1980s. The research institutes established by Kean and Bloustein enabled Rutgers to attract millions of federal dollars and to appoint distinguished scientists whose work contributed to achieving the governor's goal of technology-based economic growth. Rutgers got better and so did New Jersey.

My very first conversation with Jim McGreevey, the Drumthwacket encounter described at the beginning of this book, covered this exact ground. When I told him how much federal research support the University of Washington garnered each year and named some of the local industries that benefited from that research, he expressed great interest. We began, but only began, a conversation about how to bring more success of that kind to New Jersey. McGreevey was already thinking along these lines long before he met me, though. Research-based economic development was precisely the goal he wanted to achieve through Roy Vagelos's plan for reorganizing higher education in the state. Several weeks after my meeting with the governor, the Vagelos report became public and began its tortuous, ultimately unsuccessful journey through the state's and the University's public processes. My relationship with Governor McGreevey unfolded largely within the bounds of the deliberations over the Vagelos plan, and there it did not flourish.

McGreevey at least tried to get something really big done for New Jersey through the agency of its universities. Not until Chris Christie would another chief executive endorse a comparably grand vision for advancing the state by transforming Rutgers. Sometime during the fall of 2004, after McGreevey had announced his resignation but before he had left the governorship, he stopped by my office in Old Queens to chat for about an hour on a day when another obligation had brought him to the Rutgers campus. Our pleasant conversation was mainly personal. He and I were both going through divorces at the time, and he offered me some advice: "Be nice," he said. Although we didn't mention the Vagelos vision, it was certainly on my mind. I remember thinking wistfully that I could have enjoyed a kind of Ed Bloustein–to–Tom Kean relationship with this governor, who so plainly understood how states and their universities could become partners for prosperity.

Dick Codey, who completed McGreevey's term as governor and served only about fourteen months, had no particular plans for higher education. His policy priorities lay elsewhere, in care for the mentally ill and services for other disadvantaged New Jerseyans. In conversations with Codey's staff, I learned all I could about his policy objectives as governor and saw to the preparation of a series of documents outlining how Rutgers could support him in areas such as child health and welfare, adolescent mental health, school security, and prisoner reentry. In a cover letter to one of Codey's aides, I expressed my goal directly: "Rutgers wants to be The State University of New Jersey in fact as well as name." These efforts certainly built goodwill between the University and the governor's office, but I am not aware that they led to important policy initiatives in which Rutgers experts played key roles.

Governor Codey and I developed a friendly relationship. He was a sports fan and frequently attended Rutgers basketball and football games; at the latter, he prowled the sidelines and then came upstairs at halftime for a soda and a hot dog. Whoever approached Codey on these occasions got a warm response and likely a wisecrack. The only state budget for which Governor Codey was responsible, the one for fiscal year 2006, proved to be by far the best budget Rutgers had while I was president. Besides a rare and welcome increase in operating aid, it included $18 million in capital funds to assist the University in purchasing and renovating a building for the business school in Newark.

On my watch, that was the only significant contribution the state made for Rutgers facilities.

Next came Jon Corzine, whom I first got to know when he was a United States senator. We met on several occasions to discuss his legislative agenda, which included improving chemical plant security, a worthy objective for a New Jersey senator in the years shortly after 9/11. I helped put his staff in touch with appropriate Rutgers faculty in chemistry and chemical engineering and asked them to help the senator in any ways they could. During his 2005 gubernatorial election campaign, I met with Corzine and several of his advisers to discuss his prospective policy goals for the state and to share information about Rutgers people and programs that could assist him. (I had similar conversations with the Republican candidate, Doug Forrester.) Just as in the case of Codey, however, these well-intentioned efforts to put Rutgers resources behind Corzine's policy agenda did not bring any significant results. I was thinking about the experience of midwestern states like Wisconsin, where for more than a century state governments and their universities have worked in partnership. The dream of transplanting that ideal to New Jersey proved far more elusive than I had hoped it would.

At the very beginning of his governorship, Jon Corzine and I maintained the respectful relationship we had begun when he was a U.S. senator. He phoned me with condolences after my father died, and he stayed out of the fight over Douglass College, despite entreaties from members of his own staff to get involved. He seemed at least mildly interested when I urged him to take up the cause of bringing Robert Wood Johnson Medical School back into Rutgers (although nothing came of that during his governorship). Before long, however, Corzine developed, or perhaps revealed, what seemed to be an aversion to higher education. Early in his term of office, about a half dozen public university presidents met with him to discuss our proposal for a higher education facilities bond issue on which we had been working together for a couple of years and to which we had received positive responses from within the McGreevey/Codey administration and from key legislators in both political parties. Corzine listened, asked a few good questions that we answered in writing several days later, and then never said another word about the project to any of the presidents. We learned from his staff that the governor had no intention of supporting the bond issue, but he never told us why or whether there were any circumstances in which he might reconsider it.

In March 2006, Governor Corzine proposed his first state budget. It was disastrous for Rutgers and for the other public colleges and universities, by far the severest higher education budget reduction I had ever seen or heard of. Altogether the proposed cut for Rutgers came to nearly $100 million, including a 15 percent hit to our base budget, zero funding for previously negotiated salary and benefits increases, and a number of other major reductions. We had expected bad news owing to the state's fiscal difficulties, but nothing like this. Just as I did every year, I sent a message to the University community about the governor's proposed budget, and this time my language was pretty strong. The budget, I said, "would fundamentally affect our ability to educate students and would close the door on options for higher education to thousands of citizens of this state. . . . Rutgers would face layoffs, the cancellation of hundreds of classes, and reductions to services that our students require." I promised that the University would "mount an aggressive campaign to fight these severe and devastating cuts." A few days later, I received an unpleasant phone call from the governor's chief of staff, who chewed me out for criticizing his boss's budget and inciting the Rutgers community against the governor. Only later did I learn that Corzine expected university presidents, like the heads of state agencies who served in his cabinet, to accept his budget without complaint. I knew, however, that that was not what Rutgers faculty, staff, students, and board members expected of me.

A few weeks later I got myself into more trouble with the governor in a meeting to which he had summoned the university presidents for discussion of his budget. I described unsparingly what the loss of $100 million would mean for Rutgers and then observed, with reference to the multiple components of the cut, that the budget seemed to have been prepared by people who were working in different rooms without communicating among themselves. How else could such an immense package of reductions have been proposed for the colleges and universities? The governor was understandably offended by my implication that he was not fully knowledgeable about all the elements of his own budget. The next day I sent him a handwritten letter of apology acknowledging the inappropriateness of my remarks. He never replied, and my relationship with Governor Corzine never recovered.

Throughout that spring, Rutgers and the other colleges and universities lobbied hard to restore some of the funding the governor would take away. Our students rallied in Trenton, and members of the Rutgers community sent an estimated ninety thousand e-mail messages to members of the senate and assembly. Just as in every budget season, I met with dozens of legislators and testified at their hearings. All of this activity contributed to a restoration of about a third of the cut the governor had proposed. This result improved upon what might have been, but it was not enough to forestall the damaging outcomes I had predicted. It is instructive to place Governor Corzine's higher education budget policies in a national perspective. During the first two fiscal years of his administration, the prosperous years just prior to the onset of the recession, forty-one American states provided double-digit percentage budgetary increases for higher education, while eight states appropriated single-digit percentage increases. Only one state decreased its higher education funding during those pre-recession years: New Jersey.

In the summer of 2009, when Chris Christie was campaigning for governor against Jon Corzine, he visited with me in my office at Rutgers. It was a long and cordial meeting, in which Christie showed a great deal of knowledge of higher education and a firm commitment to it. Particularly encouraging was the candidate's understanding of how states and their universities could work together. A proud graduate of the University of Delaware, Christie had remained closely connected with his alma mater and recognized how much that institution contributed to the prosperity of its state. He knew, for example, that Delaware's historic excellence in the field of chemical engineering had benefited DuPont, and vice versa. I spoke of my admiration for Christie's political mentor, Governor Tom Kean, and of the investments Kean had made in Rutgers faculty and research as means of advancing New Jersey's economy. Christie was entirely familiar with all of that and told me with pride and amusement the story of how Kean had first drawn him into politics. Sensing Christie's receptivity to my thought that as governor he might undertake efforts similar to those of his mentor, I suggested for his consideration state support for targeted faculty appointments in areas where research would bring economic benefits. I gave as examples the fields of engineering and biological science, and Christie seemed interested in that idea. To my mind, we had a terrific first conversation.

A few weeks after Christie's election as governor, I made an appointment for lunch with Governor Kean, whom I knew well, to seek his counsel on developing Rutgers's relationship with the soon-to-be chief executive. The former governor cheerfully recounted the steps his administration had taken to advance the state's economy by investing in Rutgers research, and we agreed on the need for comparable measures at the current time. He made no promises, of course, about what I could expect from Governor Christie, but Kean affirmed my sense that the new governor shared a similar understanding of how states and their universities could be mutually supportive. I told Governor Kean of my plan to include in the University's budget request for the coming year a proposal for new faculty positions tied to economic development, and he thought that was a good idea. In May 2010, five months after he became governor, Chris Christie appointed the New Jersey Higher Education Task Force, gave it a broad mandate to develop recommendations for higher education, and named Governor Kean as its chair. Everyone connected with New Jersey's public colleges and universities felt a surge of optimism that the Kean task force would offer compelling proposals for state support of our enterprise.

Despite these bright portents, there were no early rewards for higher education from the Christie administration. Just a month into his term, in order to deal with a massive shortfall he had inherited from his predecessor, the new governor announced a midyear state budget cut, including $62 million to be taken from the colleges and universities, of which Rutgers's share was more than $18 million. The next month, Christie offered his budget for the following fiscal year; as we had been warned, it included a 15 percent reduction for Rutgers (compared to the original appropriation for the then-current year). Under his budget, the University would receive from the state approximately the same number of actual dollars it had received in 1994. The legislature passed the governor's budget essentially unchanged. Besides the 15 percent cut, it included zero funding for salary increases, language precluding the institutions from raising tuition by more than 4 percent, and, unsurprisingly, no mention of the special faculty positions the University had requested.

Amid the budget cutting, Rutgers did something that made the governor really angry. Besides an empty treasury, Christie had inherited from Corzine a recently adopted law authorizing the use of marijuana for medicinal purposes by chronically ill patients. The new governor did not like the marijuana legislation very much, but it had been duly enacted, and members of his administration were facing up to the complexities of executing it. Somewhere along the way, the idea emerged—probably from someone at the New Jersey Agricultural Experiment Station (NJAES), which is part of Rutgers—that the NJAES could become involved in marijuana research, education, and even production. On its face, the proposal seemed perfectly consistent with a public research university's mission of service to the state. In the discussions that followed throughout the spring and early summer of 2010, NJEAS staff raised expectations within the Christie administration that the University would indeed lend its expertise to the marijuana program. The governor himself was said to be enthusiastic about Rutgers's potential role. Not until July did senior members of my administration learn how advanced the discussions had become. They expressed concern that any involvement with marijuana, even research let alone production, would violate the federal controlled substances act and jeopardize Rutgers's receipt of hundreds of millions of dollars in research grants and student aid from the U.S. government. After considerable effort to find a way in which the University could legally participate, including consultation with experienced law firms and with other universities that had attempted similar initiatives in their states, we reluctantly determined that Rutgers could not engage in the marijuana program without grave risk to federal resources upon which we depended. Members of my administration informed the governor's office of this conclusion, and the University released a statement announcing its decision not to become involved with medical marijuana.

Governor Christie was angry that Rutgers had raised expectations it could not fulfill and had taken so long to recognize that fact. Speaking to the press, he personalized the matter by observing that "the lack of clarity and leadership at Rutgers on this issue is very disturbing to me, not only on the medical marijuana issue, but more broadly what that means for the leadership of the University." Unable to reach the governor directly, I talked on the phone with one of his closest advisers to whom I acknowledged the University's mistakes and apologized for Rutgers's handling of the matter. Within my own administrative circle, I expressed wonderment and annoyance that Rutgers officials had ignored for months the implications of a well-known federal statute, but I also recognized my own responsibility because I had failed to ask my colleagues enough questions about Rutgers's proposed involvement in the program. Following the medical marijuana embarrassment, I remained optimistic that the Christie administration would ultimately be supportive of higher education. But my hopefulness rested far more on the report that Governor Kean was going to write than it did upon my own relationship with Governor Christie. That had gone up in smoke.

Besides governors, two agencies of state government, each endowed with considerable independence and far-reaching investigatory authority, found great fault with Rutgers during my presidency: the State Commission of Investigation (SCI) and the Office of the State Comptroller (OSC). The SCI was created in 1968 to investigate organized crime and political corruption and to refer its findings, as appropriate, to prosecutors, as well as to the governor and legislature. Over the years, while it probed fraud and abuse within an astonishing array of state and municipal government entities, school districts, health care providers, and even private industries, the objective of uncovering crime and corruption remained central to the SCI's mission. In 2005, amid revelations of ethics violations, dubious spending and procurement practices, and Medicaid/Medicare overbilling at the University of Medicine and Dentistry of New Jersey (UMDNJ), the SCI launched an investigation of public higher education. The investigation included Rutgers, indeed, especially Rutgers. For two and a half years, SCI staff members and a team of forensic accountants hired by the SCI reviewed tens of thousands of pages and countless gigabytes of University records. They demanded and received cooperation from dozens of University employees who set aside their regularly assigned work for thousands of hours altogether to comply with SCI requests. As the work neared completion, SCI staff shared with Rutgers heavily redacted drafts of only selected portions of the report's many pages about the University and invited our response. Only very late in the process did I have an opportunity to talk with anyone from the SCI, and at no time did they meet with any members of the Rutgers boards, even though board governance turned out to be a significant subject of their report and recommendations.

In October 2007, the State Commission of Investigation released its report: "Vulnerable to Abuse: The Importance of Restoring Accountability, Transparency, and Oversight to Public Higher Education Governance." The opening sentence of the report's executive summary established its tone: "Public higher education in New Jersey has labored for more than two years under clouds of scandal and corruption." While acknowledging that most of the clouds had hovered over UMDNJ, the report quickly stated its central claim that the "entire system" of public higher education was vulnerable to "problematic governance, serious shortcomings in oversight, accountability and transparency and outright violations of the public trust." In light of these "complex problems," the report continued, "piecemeal change would be a grossly inadequate strategy. . . . Unless the state is willing to tolerate the risk of history scandalously repeating itself somewhere within this troubled system, wholesale reform is the only sensible and responsible course of action." Inflammatory language like that, familiar to readers of supermarket tabloids, continued throughout the report. The

Reverend M. William Howard Jr., mild-mannered chair of the University's Board of Governors, observed in a public statement that "the report is framed in a way that is more likely to gain sensational headlines than to provide the fair review of the operations of New Jersey colleges and universities that the public deserves."

So what had the SCI investigators uncovered about Rutgers? Basically they found a very large and complicated university, not all of whose processes and procedures they liked or understood, and a handful of embarrassing instances in which travel reports and meal expenditures were out of compliance with the rules. They found no examples of fraud or malfeasance. And they barely acknowledged the University's continuous efforts to review and improve its systems of internal control, risk assessment, and fiscal accountability. To fix the problems it claimed to have disclosed, not just at Rutgers but also at other institutions, the SCI offered many recommendations for reforming the governance of New Jersey's public universities. Most notably for Rutgers, the report urged the legislature to rewrite the 1956 legislation that had established the Board of Governors and had served for half a century as the foundation of the University's successful system of governance. Despite our deep disappointment in the SCI report, all of my public statements committed the University to take seriously its findings and recommendations and to keep up our continuing efforts to improve Rutgers's business practices.

Just as we had expected, the newspaper headlines about the SCI report were disturbing. "Higher Ed System Fraught with Waste, Abuse," said one. "Colleges Faulted for Heavy Debt, Fiscal Waste," declared another. "State Report Raises Alarm on College Spending," headlined a third. Political leaders issued statements decrying the universities' business methods and promising to enact reform. Legislative hearings predictably followed. A month before the report was to be released, I finally had my meeting with the chair of the State Commission of Investigation, W. Cary Edwards, a widely respected public figure who had served as attorney general in the Kean administration, and with several members of his staff. The SCI chair listened politely to my expressions of concern about the manner in which his organization had gone about its work and about the forthcoming report, so little of which I was allowed to review before its issuance. Edwards was dreadfully honest in his reply: "This is how we work, Dick. We cherry-pick the facts to make you look as bad as possible to support our recommendations."

Early in 2011, the Office of the State Comptroller issued its long-awaited performance audit of Rutgers's contracting and financial management practices. In its origins, development, contents, and outcomes, the OSC report bore some similarities to that of the SCI, but there were also crucial differences. Both investigations were born in controversy: the SCI probe grew out of the UMDNJ scandals of 2005, while the OSC audit emerged from the 2008 athletics embarrassments at Rutgers. Both investigations involved lengthy on-site quests for documents and data, with which University staff cooperated—for thirty consecutive months in the case of the SCI and twenty-two months for the OSC. Both reports were quite critical of Rutgers and offered substantive recommendations for change. Both provoked negative publicity and ill will for the University and inspired hostile comments from elected officials. The newspaper headlines generated by the OSC audit were by now wearyingly familiar. "Audit Slams Rutgers for No-Bid Contracts," announced the *Star-Ledger*. And again from the same source: "Rutgers Needs Integrity in Bidding Process."

The OSC's core conclusion was that while Rutgers was legally exempt from the state's public bidding requirements, the University's own policies for the procurement of goods and services failed to encourage competition and fairness. The audit found no fraud, waste, or abuse. We strongly disagreed with the finding that the University's procurement practices discouraged competition and fairness, and in the University's formal response to the report we explained why. Rutgers also observed that the OSC report offered no evidence that using the state's procedures, rather than the University's own, "would have resulted in better goods and services at lower prices." Notwithstanding all that, however, the University accepted sixteen of the OSC's eighteen recommendations for modifying our business practices and quickly implemented them. The biggest difference between the SCI and the

OSC reports was that the comptroller's findings were largely expressed in civil, noninflammatory language. My administrative team, led by Senior Vice President Bruce C. Fehn, developed a positive working relationship with staff at the OSC and kept in good touch with them during the follow-up process. Once again, board member Gerald Harvey, by then chair of the Board of Governors Audit Committee, played a particularly constructive role, in this case by communicating closely with key officials at the OSC and by providing calming reassurances to several Rutgers board members who were more alarmed by the report than they should have been.

*

So many conditions and circumstances had conspired against a dramatic improvement in Rutgers's relationship to New Jersey: the peculiar history of the University's connection to the state; a culture in which sharp words and hostile criticisms are commonplace; a political and economic environment, both nationally and locally, where public higher education was largely powerless; and the mistakes and limitations of many individuals, including me. I never found language sufficiently persuasive to overcome these circumstances or developed deep enough relationships with potential partners who might have been willing to rise up against these barriers. Unfortunately, with a few exceptions, nor did political leaders resist the commonplace urgencies of the moment by supporting farsighted goals whose benefits might not all be realized by the next election. Not since the decades immediately following World War II had university presidents expressed words that were sufficiently cosmic and compelling to advance their enterprise. Not since that same moment in time had political leaders, in both the states and the nation, placed their faith in colleges and universities to bring opportunity and prosperity to the American people they serve.

I continue to wonder what could have been done to increase Rutgers's political effectiveness in the early years of the twenty-first century. From the beginning of my presidency, I cited the ideal of a state university and exhorted Rutgers truly to fulfill that role, both because

I believed in it and because I thought that "if we do our part, the people of New Jersey will do theirs." Looking back, we probably placed too much emphasis on service to the state and too little on offering a larger vision for Rutgers as a national and international institution. We should have focused less on relations within New Jersey and more on the University's most ambitious goals and inspiring achievements, no matter where their impact was felt. That would have meant aligning Rutgers's identity with the brilliant professors we were appointing, the knowledge they were creating, and the outstanding students they were attracting from around the world. It would have meant defining Rutgers as a place where faculty members who belonged to the national academies of sciences and engineering were making pathbreaking discoveries, as the home of students who were competing successfully for prestigious international scholarships, and as the alma mater of alumni with globally acclaimed accomplishments. All of this material was close at hand. We continually celebrated these achievements within the University community; they should also have been central to our external relations. In pursuit of support and affection from the people and politicians of New Jersey, we may have parochialized Rutgers instead of universalizing it.

Taking this thought one step further, it may have been foolhardy in the early 2000s to try to become a traditional state university. That ideal had originated in the nineteenth century, attained great force in the twentieth, and still has some influence, to be sure. But in a world that is flat and wired, the concept of a "state university" is less compelling than it formerly was. Certainly it was naive to think that serving New Jersey better would bring Rutgers more money. That moment had passed. All the trends were going in the other direction, and the state's powerful people didn't seem interested anyway.

Except that a few of them did. One of them was Tom Kean and another was a guy he brought into politics named Chris Christie. On January 4, 2011, Governor Christie unveiled the report that Kean and his task force had been working on since the previous spring. My colleagues and I within the Rutgers administration had been waiting for it with great hope, but also with trepidation. So much was at stake, and there weren't many chances left for public higher education to obtain support from the people of New Jersey. As the members of my inner circle gathered around our small conference table that morning, we knew that the governor's office had promised to send us the document a few hours before its release. When the report arrived electronically, my office staff printed enough copies for each of us, and the room fell silent as we speed-read its 138 pages. And then the smiles came and then our cheers. This *was* the report we had been waiting for. One of its sentences expressed everything we had been trying to say for years: "For a state to be great, it must have a great state university."

GETTING A
MEDICAL SCHOOL,
CONCLUDING
A PRESIDENCY

NOT FOR DECADES, if ever, had New Jersey seen as compelling a study of higher education as the Kean task force now offered. It covered all the big issues: university governance, mission differentiation among the institutions, educational quality, financing, affordability, and higher education's indispensability to a thriving economy. The report placed its findings broadly within a national context, too often ignored in our state, and made more than seventy specific recommendations. The persuasiveness of the document's every feature—its factual observations, its lucid analyses, and its commanding proposals—was elevated by the universal respect its principal author enjoyed. More than any other single source of influence, the Kean report shaped the agenda of my presidency's final year and a half.

The report repeatedly called attention to the state's inadequate funding for its colleges and universities. New Jersey, it said, was "at the bottom of national comparisons" in support for higher education, a point amply documented by data in the appendices. "Greater funding for New Jersey's colleges and universities is critical," the report observed, "to expand college opportunity, decrease student costs, and ensure the prosperity of the state's economy." Achieving these goals would require increased annual appropriations for the colleges and universities, as well as long-term investments through the issuance of bonds to finance their facilities. Not since 1988, when Tom Kean was governor, had such a bond issue been available to support capital improvements in higher education. The state's college and university presidents had been seeking a bond issue for more than a decade; the Kean report now greatly boosted our hopes of getting one.

Just as we had anticipated, the report emphatically recommended returning Robert Wood Johnson Medical School (RWJMS) to Rutgers, the objective that Phil Furmanski and I had placed uppermost in our summer 2010 meetings with Kean and the other members of his task force. Here, too, the report situated its findings in a national higher education context: "Few great research universities do not have a medical school." In comparison to its peers, the report said, Rutgers's ranking as a research university was hurt by the "absence of a medical school." The University should therefore prepare to absorb RWJMS, as well as UMDNJ's School of Public Health (also located in New Brunswick/Piscataway), and "to establish a first-class comprehensive university-based health science center." Such an entity would benefit not only Rutgers but also the health of the state's citizens and the future prosperity of New Jersey's preeminent pharmaceutical and biomedical companies. The report went on to say realistically that many additional questions would have to be answered before this recommendation could be implemented, most notably questions about the other academic units that UMDNJ comprised and about the future of medical education in Newark and in South Jersey. Accordingly, the report proposed that an "expert panel should be convened as soon as possible" to deal with "the many complex issues" affecting health science education in the state. Everyone reading the Kean report knew that these issues would be excruciatingly difficult to resolve—and indeed they were.

The observation that Rutgers's national ranking in research ought to be improved was but one facet of the report's larger finding that although Rutgers had become a good and well-respected institution, it was not yet the "great university" New Jersey needed. That point stung, but it was factual and we knew it. My administration's recognition that Rutgers was "good but not great" lay behind our strenuous efforts, recounted earlier, to obtain increased funding for research, and it energized, as well, our long campaign to regain RWJMS, a goal the report now endorsed. In addition to the medical school, the Kean task force offered a number of other recommendations for making Rutgers great. These included sharpening the University's academic focus on "areas of excellence," eliminating redundancies across the three campuses, and working more closely with the state's business community. Consistent with the report as a whole, the task force urged the state to provide increased funding for Rutgers. "If the State demands more from Rutgers," the report said, "it is only fair that Rutgers demand more from the State." I would like to think that Tom Kean borrowed that thought from my inaugural address, but I am sure he didn't. The report also recommended, with a gentle but unmistakably accurate slap at me, that "the President of Rutgers should at times act as the spokesperson for higher education in New Jersey." As president I had focused relentlessly on my own institution and had given far less attention to speaking for all the colleges and universities in the state.

Much good would come from the Kean task force report, including measures affecting the statewide governance of higher education, relieving the institutions from some burdensome regulations, and improving student assistance programs. These causes gave me opportunities to advocate broadly for New Jersey's colleges and universities, not just my own. At Rutgers we were engaged in all of these developments, but we devoted most of our attention to obtaining a bond issue for higher education facilities and, above all, to reclaiming our medical school.

In placing health science education back on the state's agenda, the Kean report returned to the very subject that had achieved such prominence and generated such controversy nearly a decade earlier at the time of the Vagelos report. In truth, however, the goal of reorganizing health science education had never entirely disappeared from New Jersey's radar screen. The record of what had happened after Vagelos and before Kean is worth remembering because it foreshadowed some of the difficult problems and seemingly unresolvable conflicts that arose when Governor Chris Christie grappled with his task force's recommendation to reunite RWJMS with Rutgers.

In his 2004 state of the state address, just a month after the Vagelos process collapsed, Governor Jim McGreevey called upon the state's public research universities, namely Rutgers, UMDNJ, and the New Jersey Institute of Technology (NJIT), to break down the barriers between themselves and undertake more collaborative research, especially in areas that would benefit the economy. Responding to the governor's directive, the other two presidents and I, together with our chief academic officers, dutifully met and tried to agree upon new mechanisms for joint projects. In June, we sent the governor a long letter reporting on our progress, such as it was, and over the next few months tried to establish an entity we called the New Jersey Research University Foundation "to promote and manage major multi-institution research initiatives." It never really went anywhere, and looking back I can see that our efforts were only halfhearted. For one thing, nobody, including the governor, seemed very interested. For another, each of the three universities was mainly looking after its own affairs. In New Brunswick and Piscataway, substantial cooperation already existed between the life science programs at Rutgers and Robert Wood Johnson Medical School. Further progress was unlikely to be achieved until RWJMS formally became part of Rutgers. Many faculty members at the medical school shared that goal, but, of course, their bosses in the UMDNJ administration did not. As Governor McGreevey departed from office in November, the three universities' nominal efforts to enhance collaboration ground to a halt. Two years later, the presidents and chief academic officers of Rutgers and UMDNJ made another short-lived attempt to increase collaboration between their universities, but nothing much came of it.

The most visible effort to transform health science education during the years between Vagelos and Kean emerged during 2006–07, soon after the revelations of scandal and mismanagement at UMDNJ. Governor Jon Corzine showed little enthusiasm for the project, which he probably regarded as politically unattainable, but several legislators, most notably Senator Raymond J. Lesniak, became quite focused on it. In the fall of 2006, the leaders of both legislative houses appointed a ten-member joint Task Force on Higher Education and the Economy and charged that body with "finding the best way to create a world-class research university" in New Jersey. Cochaired by Lesniak and Assemblyman Wilfredo Caraballo, two legislators who had demonstrated far more interest in higher education than most of their peers, the task force considered a couple of models, both of which would have effectively eliminated UMDNJ. One option was a complete Rutgers takeover of UMDNJ (and perhaps NJIT, too), but with the Rutgers campuses in north and south Jersey gaining far greater autonomy from the University's central administration. The other option was to establish a University of Newark, composed of the Newark-based elements of all three existing universities, and at the same time to transfer to Rutgers the units of UMDNJ that were located in central and south Jersey. For a while, Lesniak advocated a variation on option two—moving the Rutgers School of Pharmacy back to Newark, where it had originated long ago—but Phil Furmanski and I firmly rejected that idea.

Senator Lesniak, with whom I communicated frequently during this period, went back and forth between the two models, but he was open to others as well, and he genuinely wanted to get something done. He recognized the value of returning RWMJS to Rutgers, but he believed that such a step would be politically impossible unless it formed part of a comprehensive solution embracing institutional arrangements in all three parts of the state and unless Rutgers agreed to give up something in return for the medical school—for example, its campus in Newark, its pharmacy school, or its active control over the University's operations outside of central New Jersey. The political imperative of finding a statewide solution and the conviction that Rutgers should relinquish a part of itself in order to obtain something else that it wanted would both figure prominently in developments following release of the Kean report. Lesniak and Caraballo stretched the work of their task force into 2007, but they never managed to create a consensus around any possible model. There were too many competing interests in the mix; only an actively engaged governor deploying all his powers could have compelled agreement on a solution. Rutgers, for its part, was not sorry to see the initiative die. We wanted Robert Wood Johnson Medical School but were not ready to accept corresponding institutional changes in Newark or in South Jersey. Our patience paid off.

The next episode occurred far from the limelight. The leaders of Cooper University Hospital in Camden wanted to establish a medical school there, and they reached out to Phil Furmanski and me to explore the possibility of a partnership with Rutgers. Cooper was already the home of an RWJMS medical program, specifically the site where sizable numbers of third- and fourth-year students received their clinical training. But Cooper's leaders were determined to have a full four-year medical school and to get free from UMDNJ, the parent institution of RWJMS. So they approached us sometime in 2007, and the ensuing discussions went on for a couple of years. Ultimately these talks were inconclusive, primarily because Phil and I worried that taking on a medical school in Camden would not advance, and might even stymie, progress toward our goal of reclaiming RWJMS in New Brunswick. We were also leery of the political influences that likely would have accompanied such an arrangement. In the summer of 2009, Governor Corzine accommodated the Cooper leadership through an executive reorganization plan, creating their four-year medical school and aligning it with Rowan University, whose main campus is in Glassboro, about seventeen miles from Camden.

Across all the years between the Vagelos report and the Kean report, Phil and I seized every appropriate moment to make a persuasive case for bringing Robert Wood Johnson Medical School, the UMDNJ School of Public Health, and possibly other units of UMDNJ into Rutgers. We observed that almost every American medical school was part of a major university; we described the opportunities for collaborative teaching and research that would become available when the health science disciplines were lodged within the same institution as arts and sciences, engineering, and business; and we cited the benefits that such a reorganization would bring to health care and the economy. For the most part, out of respect for the existence of UMDNJ, we made these arguments in private, in confidential conversations with legislators, business leaders, and, very importantly, members of the Rutgers Boards of Governors and Trustees. From time to time, we found public settings in which to express our views. One such occasion came in November 2006, when the Lesniak-Caraballo task force held a legislative hearing. Drawing on my experiences at the universities of North Carolina and Washington, I cited the advantages in education, research, and economic development that would be gained if medicine, dentistry, and public health were moved into the same university as the non-health-science disciplines. "In such a setting," I said, "students have choices that are now denied them in New Jersey; pathbreaking research is undertaken across disciplinary lines; and opportunities abound that we simply do not have in this state." In January 2011, when the Kean task force report thrust the subject of medical education back into the public arena, Rutgers was ready.

Response to the report was largely positive—and predictable. The higher education community lauded it, except for UMDNJ, whose spokespeople said there was no need for the structural changes proposed. Editorials in most of the state's newspapers praised the report, but the *Star-Ledger* in Newark, where UMDNJ was centered, called for "more study" before merging RWJMS and the School of Public Health into Rutgers. Well supported, as always, by my colleagues in the Rutgers administration, I launched a communications blitz on behalf of the report, especially its recommendations concerning the medical school and funding for higher education. I phoned key legislators, issued statements, placed op-ed pieces, and met with newspaper editorial boards.

From Camden, George E. Norcross III, chair of the board of Cooper University Hospital, expressed enthusiasm for a surprising concept that the report had offered up in its Appendix Q, the "University of South Jersey," an entity to be formed by combining Rowan University with Rutgers-Camden. While this concoction received no support, or even a mention, in the body of the Kean report, the appendix presented it "to contribute to the discussion we encourage . . . on this important matter." When a faculty colleague at Camden asked me about Appendix Q, I replied that the report itself "envisions Rutgers-Camden as an integral part of Rutgers," a view I assured him that I shared. Little did either of us know that a proposal to merge Rutgers-Camden into Rowan would later dominate statewide discussion of restructuring the universities.

Releasing the report at a crowded press conference in early January 2011, Governor Christie praised its "insightful recommendations," commended Kean, who was standing beside him, and promised action. The governor agreed with the report's observation that UMDNJ required further study, and he issued an executive order establishing a committee to examine comprehensively whether and how to reorganize the health sciences university. When he met with college and university presidents a few weeks later to discuss the Kean report, Christie again made clear that he was not yet ready to accept the recommendation regarding the schools of medicine and public health; they were parts of a larger whole that his new committee would study. Late in March, I had a rare opportunity to talk with the governor about the medical school. Our chance conversation occurred at the Prudential Center in Newark during an NCAA men's basketball tournament game. Despite the setting, our exchange was surprisingly coherent and uninterrupted. Without saying so directly, the governor let me know that he favored bringing RWJMS into Rutgers–New Brunswick but recognized that it was going to be much more difficult to decide what to do in Newark. Characteristically he expressed confidence that he would find a solution for that problem and said he didn't expect to carry Newark anyway when he ran for reelection. Within a week, the governor promised, he would announce the composition of the committee to study UMDNJ.

And so he did, in early April. The five-member committee would be chaired by Sol J. Barer, the highly respected executive chairman of Celgene, a biotechnology powerhouse. Sol, whom I knew well, had earned his Ph.D. in organic chemistry at Rutgers and now served on the University's Board of Trustees. A second member of the committee,

Robert E. Campbell, with whom I was also well acquainted, had retired as vice chairman of Johnson & Johnson and, during a long and distinguished career, had filled many influential roles in health care and higher education. A third member of the committee was Harold T. Shapiro, former president of Princeton University. It was a distinguished group, from whom the governor said he expected a report in September. Phil Furmanski and I met with the committee in May and communicated frequently with its members, especially Sol Barer and Bob Campbell, throughout the summer. But they were appropriately discreet. We were confident that the committee would affirm the Kean report's recommendation regarding the schools of medicine and public health in New Brunswick, but we did not have any idea what they would propose for the rest of UMDNJ—or, for that matter, the rest of Rutgers.

As the Barer committee was launching its work, another development, far from New Jersey, intensified my passion for getting the medical school into Rutgers. In April 2011, the member presidents of the Association of American Universities (AAU) voted to oust the University of Nebraska from their prestigious organization, on the grounds that Nebraska's research productivity was not up to AAU standards. This was the first time the AAU had ever thrown a university out. As an AAU president, I had voted in favor of keeping Nebraska, but at least two-thirds of my colleagues cast their ballots the other way, and Nebraska was gone. Besides my sympathy for an institution that, as I saw it, had suffered a needless humiliation, I was struck by the structural similarities between Nebraska and Rutgers. Both universities had many faculty and departments in the field of agriculture but lacked a medical school. Because of the way the AAU evaluates research productivity, that was a bad combination. Federal funding for agricultural research is awarded not just on the basis of scientific merit but also, to some extent, because of geographic and even political considerations. From the AAU's standpoint, that kind of research money doesn't count as much as the "purer" funding that is awarded exclusively on the basis of peer review, the kind of support that medical school faculty typically receive. So if your university includes a lot of professors of agriculture whose research productivity is low, by AAU standards, and does not have medical school faculty whose research productivity is high, also by AAU standards, then your institution's overall research quotient is not going to look very good. Fortunately, in spite of Rutgers's structural similarities to Nebraska, our federal research support was considerably better, and Rutgers was never in danger of removal from the AAU. But Nebraska's fate got my attention, and I worried about what might happen to Rutgers. To my mind, the AAU's decision regarding Nebraska provided one more reason why we had to bring back the medical school. The only person with whom I shared my concern was Phil Furmanski, who told me I worried too much.

✻

While we were engaged first with the Kean task force, then with the Barer committee, and then with a myriad of politicians who wanted to help decide the fate of Rutgers and UMDNJ, my administration was also actively pursuing several other major academic objectives. These included enhancing the diversity of both students and faculty; reaching greater numbers of students at new locations and through new technologies; and internationalizing the University, with a special focus on educational relationships in China. Later in this chapter, I will pick up the events of 2011–12 that led to passage of the health sciences education act, but first let me recount these other projects and developments, which were important in their own right and may have helped to set the tone for the restructuring debate. Each of these initiatives had a unique history (in every case beginning before I was president) and trajectory, but all of them reached a peak of activity during the second half of my presidency and especially toward the end. All are still very much alive today.

For decades, diversity has been a signature value for Rutgers and inseparable from its academic character. Countless campus conversations, as well as surveys of faculty, students, and alumni, reveal how highly people of Rutgers prize the racial and ethnic diversity of the University's student body; how much they appreciate their community's acceptance of divergent life styles, sexual orientations, backgrounds, and beliefs; and how strongly they feel that everyone gets a better education in a diverse and welcoming environment. Particularly with respect to the presence of racial and ethnic minorities within the student body, the data support the widespread impression that Rutgers is a diverse university. Among the AAU's thirty-four public institutions, we rank sixth in the percentage of students who are minorities, second in the percentage of students who are African American, and tenth in the percentage of students who are Hispanic/Latino. From 2002 to 2012, Rutgers maintained its already high percentage of African American students (10 percent of the total) and increased the representation of Hispanic/Latinos in the student body from 8 to 12 percent. For many years running, more than half of the University's incoming students have identified themselves as something other than Caucasian.

The ethnic and racial heterogeneity of New Jersey's population helps, of course, to explain the great and growing diversity of Rutgers students. But that diversity is also hard-won. It depends upon major efforts by admissions offices, programs of outreach to middle schools and high schools, and the creation of many specialized occasions for engaging minority students who otherwise would not be bound for college. During my time as president, I encouraged the University's admissions staff to expand these efforts and, led by Vice President Courtney McAnuff, they did. In 2008, we launched the Rutgers Future Scholars Program, which Courtney had devised to provide college opportunities for young men and women from the older industrial cities of Newark, Camden, and New Brunswick where Rutgers campuses are located. To judge from the success of the first several cohorts of Future Scholars, that program is achieving the goals we hoped it would, and a number of universities around the country are emulating it. The intensity of Rutgers's commitment to attaining even greater levels of ethnic and racial diversity within the student body also reflected the intellectual and legal leadership of Jonathan R. Alger, our senior vice president and general counsel. Before coming to Rutgers from the University of Michigan, Jon had played a key role in preparing that institution's legal brief for the United States Supreme Court on behalf of affirmative action; in 2003, that brief supplied the essential arguments that Justice Sandra Day O'Connor set forth in her majority opinion upholding the admissions policy of Michigan's law school. While at Rutgers, Jon maintained his eloquent and well-informed advocacy for ethnic and racial diversity, spoke and published widely on the subject, and did more than any other single individual to confirm the University's reputation as a leader in thought as well as action in support of student diversity. (Jon is now president of James Madison University.)

Two other segments of the student body became more vocal and more numerous while I was president: military veterans and lesbian, gay, bisexual, and transgender (LGBT) students. In 2008, perhaps 250 veterans were enrolled at Rutgers (we didn't really know the number), and they received no special services from the University. That year, two Rutgers-Camden students who had fought in Iraq attended my annual address and in the Q & A took me to task for Rutgers's inadequate efforts to enroll and support student veterans. Inspired by the passion of these young men, the University went swiftly up the learning curve about the challenges faced by veterans who were making the transition to college and about their distinctive needs for academic advising, psychological counseling, and even help with the U.S. Department of Veterans Affairs. By 2012, thanks to an aggressive program of outreach, more than 2,000 veterans were enrolled at Rutgers, and the University's programs on their behalf were receiving national attention and acclaim. Rutgers is now ranked as the top public research university for serving veterans. During these same years, my administration worked quietly with the office of the Secretary of the Navy to establish a Naval Reserve Officer Training Corps (NROTC) unit at Rutgers, to complement our long-standing Army and Air Force ROTC programs. Helped along by Luke Visconti, a member of our Board of Trustees and a naval veteran, that effort was rewarded with success early in 2012.

Gay and lesbian students had been visible and organized at Rutgers since the 1980s, and during my presidency they, too, were asking for more services and support. Following the tragic suicide of first-year student Tyler Clementi in September 2010 (about which I will have more to say in a few pages), I met with about two dozen LGBT students to learn how they felt about their lives at Rutgers and how the University could more fully meet their needs. They offered a number of good ideas, including more housing options and more counseling for students who were coming out—and my administration enacted programs implementing all of their suggestions. But these students were far from angry, and most expressed satisfaction with their lives and studies at the University. Many of them said they had decided to enroll after checking LGBT websites affirming that Rutgers was a gay-friendly place.

So Rutgers has worked hard and successfully for a very long time to enroll and support a diverse student body. The capacity to recruit, welcome, and educate wave after wave of students from different backgrounds, especially students who were not traditionally part of the campus mix, seems to lie deep within the University's DNA. The diversity of the faculty, by contrast, has proved more difficult to achieve. Rutgers ranks near the top among its AAU peers in the percentage of full-time faculty who are female, about 40 percent and rising. But the University does far less well in the representation of racial minorities, where it ranks mostly in the middle of the pack, and, indeed, its rankings fell during my presidency. Across all three Rutgers campuses, African Americans make up a little more than 3 percent of the full-time faculty and Hispanics/Latinos a little more than 2 percent. Regrettably, from 2002 to 2012, the number of black faculty declined from 118 to 108, and the losses were greatest in New Brunswick. (At Rutgers-Newark, the number of full-time black faculty grew from thirty-one to forty-two.) The numbers of Hispanic/Latino faculty increased on all three campuses, but their overall representation remains far too low.

These outcomes do not reflect a lack of effort. We tried through multiple initiatives to improve the racial and ethnic diversity of the faculty, and the numbers cited here would be even worse without those efforts. I'll mention just three. Phil Furmanski's academic affairs office administered a special diversity fund that contributed to the appointment of seventy-six tenured or tenure-track faculty, including thirty-six African Americans and twenty-two Hispanics/Latinos. His office also compiled and distributed a comprehensive manual titled "Increasing Faculty Diversity: A Handbook for Deans, Department Chairs, and Faculty Search Committees," which was loaded with information and best practices designed to aid in the recruitment and retention of faculty. Perhaps most promisingly we launched a cluster hiring initiative that resulted in the appointment of six faculty members in the field of urban entrepreneurship at Newark and three in Caribbean studies at New Brunswick. (The principle here was the same one I had applied long ago as dean of the Faculty of Arts and Sciences: prospective faculty would be more likely to accept positions at Rutgers if they knew they would be coming to the University with like-minded colleagues.) For all this, and more, we barely moved the needle on the dial.

Why is it so difficult to diversify the faculty? I have only partial answers, and they are not particularly original to me. For one, this is a national problem, not just a Rutgers problem: too few minority men and women choose careers in college teaching and research. They practice law or medicine or enter into business. It would take a massive, nationwide endeavor to encourage them to attend graduate school, to support them in obtaining their doctorates, and to assist them in finding satisfying university positions. Many institutions, including Rutgers, have been doing some of this on a local scale for years, but so far it has made too little difference. There are also some distinctive Rutgers aspects of the problem. Many outstanding minority men and women consider Rutgers an appealing place to teach because our student body is so diverse and the community is so genuinely open to divergent beliefs and backgrounds. Unfortunately, however, while they may begin their careers at Rutgers, many minority faculty are lured away to other institutions (often wealthier, private universities elsewhere in the Northeast) by the offer of higher salaries, greater opportunities to mentor graduate students, and other attractions. As I watched some of my minority faculty colleagues depart, I felt sad. Rutgers had helped to launch their careers, but we were not given, or did not grasp, the opportunity to sustain those careers.

For more than forty years, universities like Rutgers have sought to diversify their communities of students and faculty because it is socially just to do so and because education in a diverse environment prepares everyone for life and work in a multicultural, global society. By dint of great effort over the decades, Rutgers has enrolled and educated wonderfully diverse students, and if the University continues to expend that effort, the student body will remain as varied, as interesting, and as deserving as it is today. The challenge for the years ahead is to find the means to achieve the same for the faculty.

Educating nontraditional students has been among Rutgers's core missions for a long time, just as it has been for many public colleges and universities across the country. Men and women who are older than typical undergraduates, who may already be working and raising families, and who need services and support tailored to their circumstances have been getting Rutgers educations in classrooms at Newark, New Brunswick, and Camden for many decades. Within recent years, fast-paced social and economic developments have increased the demand for education among adults of all ages, while at the same time new technologies have greatly expanded the capacity of institutions to provide it. Many of today's students want courses and programs in order to complete degrees they began years ago, to prepare themselves for new careers, to retain their professional certification, or simply to expand their store of skills and knowledge. They need to have learning opportunities available in or near their homes and at times that mesh with the rest of their busy lives. Not just older adults but also traditionally matriculated students increasingly want to do their learning when and where it is most convenient. Fortunately, there are multiple ways of meeting these educational needs, including the establishment of geographically distributed learning centers and, even more important, the provision of online courses and degrees. For various historic reasons, Rutgers had lagged behind its peers in both of these endeavors; now it moved vigorously forward to catch up. Academic leadership came, as always, from Phil Furmanski; from several vice presidents, including Raphael Caprio, David Finegold, and Richard Novak; and, increasingly, from the entrepreneurial deans whom Phil and I appointed.

When I became president in 2002, Rutgers had one regional campus, in partnership with Brookdale Community College in Freehold, New Jersey. The campus offered students an opportunity to receive a Rutgers degree for completing an undergraduate program in liberal studies or nursing. That was it. The University did not have well-developed relationships with most of the other community colleges in the state, and the notion of obtaining a Rutgers degree anywhere besides Newark, New Brunswick, or Camden was quite unfamiliar. Now all that began to change. The University's division of continuing studies responded to the growing demand for a Rutgers education around the state by establishing campuses in partnership with Atlantic Cape Community College (at Mays Landing) in 2006, with Raritan Valley Community College (North Branch) in 2009, and with Mercer County Community College (West Windsor) in 2013. A similar arrangement with the County College of Morris is slated to begin in 2014, and others are in the works. Each regional campus now provides a large and growing array of undergraduate majors, taught on-site by Rutgers faculty from all three of the University's main campuses, as well as essential student services, including academic advising, financial aid, and disabilities services. Beginning in 2009, the regional campuses also began offering several master's degrees, and more are planned. Establishing these new campuses has enabled the University to meet the needs of men and women whose work and family obligations deter them from traveling far from home for their college education. The objective is to enable students to earn Rutgers degrees within classrooms throughout all parts of New Jersey.

Online learning, sometimes in combination with classroom instruction, offers students even greater flexibility and nearly limitless access to courses and programs. At Rutgers, a few graduate and professional programs began online instruction in the mid-1990s, but, compared to many other institutions, the University was slow to take advantage of new technologies for computer-based education. Early in the 2000s an evolution began, both because growing numbers of faculty and deans recognized that online learning offered exciting new educational and revenue-generating opportunities and because the University administration began providing advice and technical support for departments and faculty who wanted to develop such offerings. At first, the results were slow in coming, but beginning around 2007, online education exploded at Rutgers. From that year forward, enrollments in fully online credit courses have grown by 20 percent or more every year.

Now hundreds of courses and several complete degrees are available through Rutgers Online, the University's virtual campus. Many of the online learners are regularly enrolled in undergraduate or graduate programs in Newark, New Brunswick, or Camden, but growing numbers of Rutgers Online students are logging on from across the country and around the world. Building upon the University's reputation for success in educating veterans, Rutgers is vigorously marketing its online offerings to men and women in active military service, wherever they may be stationed.

None of this success has come easily or without controversy. The heavy burden of developing online courses and degrees soon exceeded the capacity of academic departments or even the University's division of continuing studies. In 2010, recognizing the need for substantial technical assistance, as well as the revenue potential of online offerings, my administration launched a lengthy competitive process to identify an experienced private-sector partner, and an agreement with the chosen firm was signed several months after I stepped down as president. Through this partnership, faculty members receive guidance in designing and developing their courses, while the University obtains support in recruiting students and managing enrollment. When an online course is under way, both faculty and students have continuous access to technical help. These arrangements are enabling Rutgers to expand online courses and degrees, especially master's degrees, more rapidly than ever before.

Even with adequate support, questions and challenges remain. Although myriad studies have shown that online education can be every bit as effective as classroom instruction, many faculty members remain skeptical and will choose not to make the leap to computer-based education. Others who are more willing to embrace online teaching nonetheless worry about its potential impacts upon academic freedom and upon the career prospects of future generations of faculty who may, they fear, become redundant once the educational universe is saturated with online offerings. To my mind, the concerns about academic freedom are unfounded: faculty have complete control of the contents of their courses and programs, whether they are offered in a classroom or on the Internet. More difficult to predict are the long-term effects of online education upon the numbers and qualifications of teaching faculty. Every major technological advance in history has had unforeseen consequences for the size and character of the workforce. Men and women will adapt, as they always have. Despite the impossibility of predicting all the impacts of online education, it would have been irresponsible not to have positioned Rutgers to take full advantage of the new technologies.

Similar thinking lay behind my administration's initiatives to advance the internationalization of the University: We do not fully know where it will lead, but the development of relationships with strategically chosen partners around the world is essential to the achievement of Rutgers's goals in education and research. We inhabit a global society whose most fundamental challenges and opportunities have no national boundaries and whose quests for knowledge-based solutions must be similarly universal. Wherever they may reside, our students will spend their lives in that global society, and their Rutgers education should prepare them accordingly. These were not new insights in the early 2000s. Many faculty members were collaborating in research with international scholars, hundreds of students studied abroad, and a number of departments and programs had forged robust partnerships with their counterparts in other countries. As president, I supported and encouraged these activities, but I also wanted to find a way to add value to the ongoing internationalization of Rutgers. I found it relatively late in my presidency, in China.

Only infrequently did I travel internationally; looking back, I should have done much more of that. I made a brief visit to Beijing in 2007, but not until the spring of 2010 did I undertake a multicity, multimission trip to China. In Beijing, Changchun, Shanghai, and also Taipei, I met with university leaders, government officials, businesspeople, and Rutgers alumni. Particularly in Shanghai, walking the crowded Bund—the majestic promenade along the Huangpu River with its breathtaking vistas of dazzling skyscrapers, each an architectural masterpiece—I grasped the energy and power of the Chinese people and became determined to connect Rutgers more fully with them and their institutions. Returning home, I convened a China Strategy Committee composed of thirty-five deans and faculty whom I prodded to develop a comprehensive plan for deepening the University's educational relationships in that country. This they did over the course of about a year. Beginning with a statement of values and a justification for focusing particular attention on this single country, the committee observed that "China can offer Rutgers a range of opportunities . . . to increase its global reach, expand its pool of highly qualified . . . students, cultivate scholarly relationships and collaborations, and contribute in numerous ways to the diversity of the university." In order to realize these broad objectives, the committee recommended, Rutgers should develop comprehensive partnerships with a few carefully chosen universities in China, expand and strengthen its Chinese-area studies programs, recruit outstanding Chinese students, and encourage and enable many more Rutgers students to study in China. Among the committee's particular recommendations was the appointment of a director who would be responsible for implementing the University's China strategy. Following an international search to fill that position, Dr. Jianfeng (Jeff) Wang arrived at Rutgers in early 2012. From within the University's central administration, Dick Edwards, formerly dean of social work and now Phil Furmanski's successor as executive vice president for academic affairs, provided exceptionally committed leadership for Rutgers in China.

New though it is, this initiative is on track for success. Particularly promising is the development of comprehensive relationships with three of China's leading universities: Jilin University in Changchun, the South China University of Technology (SCUT) in Guangzhou, and Renmin University in Beijing (all of which I had visited). In partnership with each other, Rutgers and Jilin, whose relationship dates to the late 1970s, founded the Confucius Institute of Rutgers in 2007 and more recently have established corresponding centers for research and teaching—the Center for American Studies at Jilin and the Center for Chinese Studies at Rutgers. Each university's center will annually host scholars from the other, promote the exchange of students and younger faculty between the two institutions, and sponsor academic conferences to advance knowledge of American studies in China and Chinese studies in the United States. The South China University of Technology and Rutgers have together established the Innovation College on the SCUT campus to encourage scholarly and student exchanges between the two universities, create joint degree programs, and undertake collaborative research. Perhaps most unusually, Rutgers is helping Renmin University establish an international high school of math and science in Princeton, New Jersey. The Chinese students enrolled there will take some of their courses at Rutgers, and when they graduate from high school some will continue their educations at the University. Working with several different universities in China, a number of Rutgers schools, including engineering, business, and environmental and biological sciences, have launched multiyear exchange programs enabling students to divide their undergraduate education between the cooperating institutions and to receive degrees from both. By 2013, nearly two thousand Chinese students were studying at Rutgers, more than double the number just four years earlier.

One more long-sought academic goal was finally realized at the end of my presidency: the acquisition of five acres of land from the New Brunswick Theological Seminary (NBTS) and the development of plans to construct upon that property a major academic facility and an honors college that, until now, we had only dreamed about. Founded in 1784, the NBTS was the first seminary established in North America. Originally located in New Brunswick, it moved to Brooklyn and then back to New Brunswick. In 1856, the seminary acquired and occupied a seven-acre tract of land right in the middle of what would become the University's College Avenue campus. Over the years, Rutgers and the NBTS developed several joint programs and shared library resources, but, from the University's perspective, a more pertinent reality was that the seminary's location awkwardly disrupted the continuity of our main campus. In the early 2000s, as the NBTS fell upon hard times, my administration, led by Phil Furmanski and our vice president for facilities, Tony Calcado, began negotiations with the seminary's leadership to try to obtain an agreement that would benefit both institutions. The University would acquire most of the land belonging to the

NBTS, in return for which the seminary would receive some nearby Rutgers property, assistance with the construction of a new building, and cash. Unfortunately, despite several months of amicable discussions, the University and the NBTS were unable to agree on the value of the land, and the talks broke down.

Sometime thereafter, the New Brunswick Development Corporation's Chris Paladino took an interest in the seminary property and began negotiations of his own with the NBTS leadership. For a while, the situation was messy and conflicted, but the ultimate outcome was a three-way deal in which Rutgers obtained most of the seminary property and, with Devco's help, considerable financial assistance for the construction of several major facilities on the seminary's former land. The largest of these is projected to house the University's language departments, currently scattered in six different buildings on two campuses, as well as many badly needed lecture halls. When it is completed in 2016, this classically designed structure will be the signature academic building that several generations of Rutgers leaders have wanted for the College Avenue campus. The other major facility to be constructed on the seminary tract will be the University's new honors college. Planned for many years, the five-hundred-student honors college will enable Rutgers to enroll top undergraduates from New Jersey and around the world and offer them the best educational opportunities a research university can provide. The seminary deal included other elements as well: a major new student residence hall to be constructed on a nearby surface parking lot (the famous grease trucks lot, where for decades Rutgers students enjoyed megacaloric "fat sandwiches" into the wee hours of the morning), a large public green space (the very thing I originally envisioned for College Avenue), an academic building for the NBTS on the land it retained, and, thankfully, more parking for everyone. In a separate transaction negotiated by Tony Calcado, the University acquired from Rutgers Hillel, the independent Jewish student organization, a valuable piece of land that is contiguous with the five acres obtained from the seminary, in return for which Hillel received an adjacent property on College Avenue on which to construct its new facility.

For all the successes we enjoyed and despite the welcome boost provided by the Kean report, this was a difficult time for Rutgers, especially the 2010–11 academic year. It began with my administration's reluctant imposition of a university-wide salary freeze in response to Governor Christie's 15 percent reduction of our state appropriation. The freeze seriously strained relations between the University and the dozen labor unions representing our faculty and staff and led to seemingly endless arbitration hearings before the state's Public Employment Relations Commission. Then came a series of highly publicized events—some tragic, others only embarrassing—that put Rutgers in a bad light.

In September, Tyler Clementi, an eighteen-year-old freshman, jumped to his death from the George Washington Bridge, just days after his roommate and another student had secretly employed a webcam to view Clementi embracing another man. The circumstances surrounding Clementi's suicide attracted worldwide attention and raised alarm about cyber-bullying. Hundreds of grieving Rutgers students, faculty, staff, and community members held a candlelit silent vigil on a Sunday evening, while thousands of people from all over the world wrote to me in anguish for Tyler and in outrage toward the students who had spied on him. The tragedy also emboldened untrue accusations that the Rutgers campus was a nest of homophobia. In subsequent months, a number of events were held to focus on issues related to Tyler's death, including a conference on cyber-bullying and a special episode of the CNN program *Anderson Cooper 360°* filmed on our campus. Rutgers later teamed with the Clementi family foundation to launch the research-based Tyler Clementi Center at the University. While Rutgers was not held culpable for the tragedy, we have sought to honor Tyler by putting our academic resources to work in promoting social change.

Less than a month later on the football field, a brutal collision gravely damaged the vertebrae and spinal cord of junior defensive tackle Eric LeGrand and paralyzed him from the neck down. The severity of his injuries stunned the University community and prompted an outpouring of concern, affection, and financial support. In the months and years of recovery that followed, Eric displayed an immensity of grace and courage and, though still wheelchair-bound, made more medical progress than his doctors had imagined possible. A hero to thousands, he resumed his studies at the University and gained acclaim as the author of *Believe: My Faith and the Tackle That Changed My Life*, as a motivational speaker, and as a member of the radio broadcast crew for Rutgers's home football games.

In January 2011, the state comptroller's report generated unpleasant headlines about the University's business practices, only to be followed by a remarkable springtime sequence of aggravations. Late in March, Nicole "Snooki" Polizzi, star of the reality TV show *Jersey Shore*, made two paid appearances at the Livingston campus student center before packed crowds of Rutgers students. Her presence and her pay ($32,000) provoked an avalanche of scorn in media reports, Trenton press releases, and personal communications to me, all reflecting the disapproval that many New Jerseyans felt for the hard-partying, bad-behaving young Italian Americans portrayed on *Jersey Shore*, of whom Snooki was the most notorious. "It's really shocking to me that people at the university have paid this drunken, ignorant, and arrogant person to address the study body," wrote one angry woman in an e-mail message to me. "You build a university to have a reputation to help kids get good jobs. Today, it's a laughingstock—it's Snooki U. We should be outraged," declared George Zoffinger, a member of the Rutgers Board of Governors. As usual, the *Star-Ledger* had fun and sold newspapers by making matters worse for Rutgers. Shortly before Snooki came to town, the University had announced that the revered Nobel Prize–winning novelist Toni Morrison would be our commencement speaker later that spring and would receive an honorarium of $30,000. Emulating the old-fashioned "tale of the tape" comparisons that newspapers sometimes published to stir up interest in prizefights, the *Star-Ledger* ran a front-page feature contrasting Snooki and Morrison. The derision was clear: What kind of institution would pay Snooki more than Toni Morrison?

I admitted then, and confess now, that I did not fully understand the outrage. A duly empowered committee of Rutgers students had engaged Snooki, a reality TV personality making a living, to put on two performances—amusing to some, distasteful to others—for which they paid her from student fees, much as they would pay a comedian or musician or author. Students learn from exercising responsibilities like this. They also learn from making up their own minds about what to like and what is distasteful.

And still the spring was young. Since the early 1980s, our students had sponsored a year-end celebration called Rutgersfest, the main feature of which was a free rock concert. This year the show featured several hip-hop bands whose afternoon performances on an outdoor stage at the Busch campus in Piscataway drew an entirely peaceful crowd of around forty thousand, mostly Rutgers students and their friends. (I walked through the crowd pushing my year-old daughter in her baby carriage.) Later that night, however, things got rough across the river in New Brunswick. Summoned via social media, thousands of young people, mainly not our students, converged in the streets, drank freely, and behaved badly. By early morning, the New Brunswick police reported several shootings (none life-threatening), five arrests, and eleven injuries. Easton Avenue and the adjacent streets were awash in litter, glass, and beer cans. Although the scale of the "mayhem," as one newspaper called it, was unprecedented, it was not entirely unexpected. Based on the unruliness that had followed Rutgersfest concerts in previous years, University and city police had been conferring for weeks in anticipation of a difficult evening, and Rutgers had paid to put several dozen additional officers on the streets. Not surprisingly, Rutgers was blamed for the fiasco, and New Brunswick's elected officials let me know how angry they were. Three days later, after consulting with student leaders, I announced there would be no more Rutgersfests. The *Daily Targum* backed me up.

Two weeks after Rutgersfest, nine students occupied Old Queens demanding lower tuition, free transcripts of their college records, and the appointment of three students to the Board of Governors. Newspaper reporters and television camera crews, ever alert to controversy at Rutgers, clogged the driveway outside. Taking our cue from President Mason Gross's legendary courtesy to student protesters in the 1960s, members of my administration did everything they could to make the students comfortable ("What kind of pizza would you like?") while also trying to persuade them to leave the building. After I promised to meet with them the following week to discuss their demands, the students departed quietly to resume studying for their final exams. When commencement day blessedly arrived in mid-May, the University celebrated its thirteen thousand graduates at Rutgers Stadium; it was the first time in decades the ceremony had been held there. Toni Morrison delivered an eloquent, inspiring address. The next day's newspapers reported on the joys of commencement but also recited each and every calamity Rutgers had encountered during the year.

Outside the public eye, one more difficulty afflicted the University at this time, and that was growing tension between my administration and the leadership of the Newark campus. Chancellor Steve Diner and his colleagues took rightful pride in the excellence of the Rutgers-Newark faculty, the extraordinary diversity of the student body, the campus's many contributions to the people of the city, and the innumerable ways in which Newark's academic programs drew strength from the adjacency of New York. The campus boasted faculty luminaries such as Pulitzer Prize–winning scholar Annette Gordon-Reed (now at Harvard), urban renaissance champion and revered public historian Clement A. Price, and neuroscientist and entrepreneur Paula Tallal; it proudly housed the world's foremost jazz archives in the Institute of Jazz Studies; and it offered nationally acclaimed programs in areas such as public management and criminology. Steve himself, over the course of a decade, had made important leadership contributions to Rutgers-Newark and had achieved a national reputation. He and his colleagues chafed, however, at one aspect of the organization of Rutgers: the administration of the entire University was, for all intents and purposes, also the leadership of the New Brunswick campus. This, they believed, put Newark at a disadvantage when resources were allocated among the campuses, a complaint I disputed with detailed quantitative evidence. Sometimes the leaders of the Newark campus seemed to feel that any progress that was made at New Brunswick came, within a zero-sum game, at the direct expense of their own.

These tensions were not new in 2010 and 2011, but they flared afresh because of two issues, student housing and business education. Steve had proudly cut the ribbon on an outstanding new dormitory just a few years earlier, but he now believed that the Newark campus's enrollment growth warranted two more residence halls. One was to be a brand-new building, the other a renovated and reconverted older structure. Based on the best information we could obtain about the demand for on-campus housing at Newark, my administration was reluctant to move as quickly as Steve wanted on these projects. He took his objections directly to members of the Board of Governors, a tactic that created great awkwardness for everyone. The second issue was the growth of business education at New Brunswick. In the 1990s, my predecessor, Fran Lawrence, had combined the New Brunswick and Newark business schools into a single entity called the Rutgers Business School–Newark and New Brunswick, whose dean reported to the Newark chancellor. Now the demand for both undergraduate and graduate business education was growing rapidly on the New Brunswick campus, but the unified business school, reporting to Steve, frustrated that growth, particularly by its unwillingness to establish an MBA program there. (This problem persists to the present day.) Steve and I discussed these issues many times and, for the most part, courteously, but we did not agree. He stepped down as chancellor in the fall of 2011.

By that time, Phil Furmanski was also gone from the University's administration. My best and closest partner in Rutgers leadership, Phil had told me again and again that his days as executive vice president were numbered because he wanted to return to the faculty in the final phase of his career. Although I tried to talk him into remaining with me for one more year, he was adamant. At the end of June 2011, Phil left Old Queens.

Just one year later, I, too, would leave. My decision was probably affected to some extent by the troubled and contentious climate I have described in these pages. The controversies and criticisms were wearying. But other factors contributed far more heavily to my decision. For one, the Board of Governors and I had grown apart. Not a single board member who had appointed me in 2002 was still there in 2011. Some of their replacements, while very smart and energetic, seemed to me to be more business-oriented than Rutgers-oriented. Although they never said so, I suspected they wanted their own president. I had the same feeling about Governor Christie, although he never said so either. Above all, I had personal reasons for wanting to bring my presidency to a close. In 2006, I had married Joan Barry, a wonderful woman who is also a talented and accomplished higher education fund-raiser, and in 2010 we adopted our daughter, Katie. Beginning sometime during that same year, Joan and I began to discuss and plan my departure as president. I wanted to spend more time with Joan and Katie, as well as with my older children, Betsy and Michael. Like Phil, moreover, I wished to finish my career as a Rutgers faculty member and to make the transition while I was still young enough—or believed myself to be young enough—to teach effectively and to write some books. At the end of May 2011, in consultation with the Board of Governors, I announced publicly that I would leave the presidency a year hence. But I would not depart before doing all I could to help Rutgers bring back our medical school.

⁂

In September, the Barer committee issued an interim report calling, as expected, for the merger of Robert Wood Johnson Medical School, the UMDNJ School of Public Health, and the Cancer Institute of New Jersey with Rutgers–New Brunswick. In support of this recommendation, the report cited many of the same reasons that had been given for a decade, above all the opportunities for greater collaboration in research that would be gained when UMDNJ's central New Jersey units became part of Rutgers. Acknowledging the "technical complexity" of carrying out the proposed reorganization, the committee noted such difficult issues as UMDNJ's bonded indebtedness, lease agreements, and union contracts. The report offered no immediate recommendations for UMDNJ's Newark-based entities or its School of Osteopathic Medicine in Camden County. "Additional study," it said, would be required to develop proposals on these subjects, and accordingly the committee thanked Governor Christie for extending its timeline through the end of the year. Ominously, the Barer committee concluded its interim report by noting that going forward it would consider whether "a new combination of public higher education assets in Southern New Jersey" might offer the best way for the state to enhance both medical education and economic vitality in that region. Although little noted at the time, the Christie administration had encouraged the committee to take a comprehensive look at higher education in South Jersey.

Accepting the interim report, Governor Christie endorsed its core recommendation and vowed to move quickly to bring the schools of medicine and public health, as well as the cancer institute, into Rutgers. The University's governing boards and I welcomed Christie's unflinching support of a goal we had long sought to achieve, but everyone knew the road ahead would be difficult. Several of Newark's elected officials objected to dismantling UMDNJ at the expense, as they saw it, of their city. The *Star-Ledger* observed sensibly that the Barer committee had presented only "half a plan" and that it couldn't be implemented "until the other pieces are in place." The UMDNJ board of trustees said coolly that they would "take time to reflect on the recommendations" and formulate a response. Only later would the extent of disarray among UMDNJ's leaders become visible. In November, the president of the health sciences university, William F. Owen Jr., joined with me in issuing a statement of support for merging the New Brunswick elements of UMDNJ with Rutgers. One of Owen's board members immediately challenged the statement and charged that the president had "improperly usurped" the board's authority. The chair of the board backed Owen a week later, but within a month the embattled president announced his resignation, and by January he was out.

Characteristically undeterred by objectors, Governor Christie launched a process for implementing the Barer committee's recommendation. In October, his chief of staff, Rich Bagger, summoned the top leaders of both universities to the statehouse in Trenton, reiterated the governor's support for the plan, and charged us with working together to execute it. A week later, the UMDNJ-Rutgers Steering Committee convened for the first time and approved the establishment of thirteen "integration teams" covering everything from academics to facilities to financials. Chaired by the governor's cabinet secretary, the canny political veteran Lou Goetting, and including a half dozen administrative leaders from each university, the steering committee met every few weeks for many months, alternately at one institution and then the other, and grappled with the staggeringly complex challenge of extracting several large elements of one university and inserting them into another. Our stated goal was to effect the merger by July 1, 2012, although everyone on the committee soon recognized the impossibility of fully transitioning the designated units from UMDNJ to Rutgers that quickly. The star of the steering committee and the architect of its periodic "integration updates" was Christopher J. Molloy, whom I had recently appointed to the new position of interim provost for biomedical and health sciences. Formerly dean of pharmacy, Chris assumed responsibility for overseeing every element of the merger. Ultimately, as we will see, it would not be completed by the original deadline, but rather a year later, and it would involve most of UMDNJ, not just the three New Brunswick units. Throughout it all, Chris Molloy remained the go-to guy for getting it done.

Meanwhile, serious trouble was brewing in South Jersey. Just a week after the issuance of the Barer committee's interim report, George Norcross, the region's political power broker, as well as chair of the board of Cooper University Hospital, began promoting publicly what the (Camden) *Courier-Post* dubbed a "superschool," to be composed of Rutgers-Camden, Rowan University, UMDNJ's School of Osteopathic Medicine, and the recently established Cooper Medical School, which was already affiliated with Rowan. "South Jersey deserves its own research university," said Norcross, ". . . a grand-style research university" to be created by combining all "the resources of higher education facilities in southern New Jersey." Previously buried in Appendix Q of the Kean report, the "University of South Jersey" now burst onto the public agenda. Regional newspapers, including the *Philadelphia Inquirer*, picked up the story, and Rowan's interim president, Ali Houshmand, convened his faculty to describe the academic and economic benefits of a merger with Rutgers. Foreshadowing the furious opposition that would materialize later, students and faculty at Rutgers-Camden objected strongly to losing their Rutgers identity. In October, *The Gleaner*, Camden's student newspaper, declared "WE ARE RUTGERS" and expressed passionate pride in the University. Faculty members from business, law, nursing, and arts and sciences wrote me letters voicing their determination to remain within Rutgers because, as one of them put it, "whatever new university might be created down here . . . would lack the quality and stature of what currently exists" at Rutgers-Camden. Chancellor Wendell Pritchett, showing the leadership he would exhibit throughout the coming turmoil, developed and disseminated an eloquent defense of his campus. "Rutgers-Camden," it began, "is the regional expression of the Rutgers brand in southern New Jersey." Wendell could easily back up his point by citing distinguished faculty achievements in fields as varied as law and philosophy, state constitutional studies, children's development, and computational biology. I used every opportunity to support my Camden colleagues and spoke frequently with Barer committee members, to whom I expressed Rutgers's determination to retain its southern campus.

Alas, our Rutgers voices were no match for the politicians of South Jersey. Not yet anyway. Late in January 2012, Governor Christie released and endorsed the final report of the Barer committee. It reaffirmed that UMDNJ's New Brunswick units should become part of Rutgers and recommended that almost everything else in UMDNJ, including the School of Osteopathic Medicine, should be rebranded as the New Jersey Health Sciences University, headquartered in Newark. The exception was that city's University Hospital, which the report said should be severed from the university and managed by a nonprofit health system under a long-term contract. At Rutgers we had anticipated all these proposals and welcomed them. The blockbusting recommendation was that Rutgers-Camden should be absorbed by Rowan, which would become "a comprehensive public research university that benefits the region and the State." While not entirely unexpected because of the months-long chatter about a "University of South Jersey," the concept of merging our Camden campus into Rowan was still shocking and unwanted. In support of its recommendation, the Barer committee set forth all kinds of laudable goals for South Jersey—expanding educational and research capacity, promoting workforce and economic development, responding to the health care needs of the region—but at no point did it explain how thrusting Rutgers out of South Jersey would advance any of these goals.

Governor Christie adamantly defended the report and declared confidently that its recommendations "will happen." When a questioner reminded him of the previous unsuccessful efforts to rearrange New Jersey's research universities and asked what would be different this time, Christie answered, "It's me." The governor had good reasons to be confident. Then midway through his first term, he had established his mastery of the state's political machinery and already had several major policy achievements to his credit. Lacking Republican majorities in either house of the legislature, Christie depended for his successes upon finding allies among assembly and senate Democrats. His most familiar collaborators from across the legislative aisle came from among South Jersey Democrats who were closely tied to George Norcross and Senate President Stephen Sweeney. They had supplied the critical votes enabling Christie to enact a stringent cap on local property tax increases and to achieve pension and health care reforms in the face of strong opposition from public employee unions and most Democratic legislators. The Barer committee's recommendations provided a perfect fit for the governor's now-proven alliance with South Jersey Democrats: if they worked together again, he would achieve the major reorganization of higher education that had eluded his predecessors for a decade and they would obtain a supposedly grand research university for their region.

For months following release of the report, the governor remained adamant that Rowan would absorb Rutgers-Camden. Whenever he was asked about it, Christie repeated some version of his earlier declaration that the takeover "will happen" and brushed off suggested compromises such as a consortium or partnership between the two schools. At a town hall meeting, the governor made headlines by getting into a shouting match with a Rutgers-Camden student who spoke out in defense of his campus. Several years earlier, this same student, a former Navy SEAL named William Brown, had been among those who publicly urged me to step up the University's support for student veterans. Irritated by his remarks, Christie called the young man an "idiot." Behind the scenes, too, the governor and his aides exhibited an unswerving commitment to the Barer plan. Late in February, Christie's new chief of staff phoned me with a direct warning that it was time for me to speak out in favor of the report. Its recommendations would be enacted, he said, and the governor did not want to have to criticize me or Rutgers for failing to support them. The governor did not want to have to talk about why a leadership change was needed at the University. I should get on board immediately. A couple of weeks later, another member of Christie's staff came to New Brunswick to meet with me and the top members of my administration. He spoke every bit as clearly as had the chief of staff: if Rutgers and its boards didn't get behind the Barer recommendations, we would end up in a big fight with the governor that would be hurtful to Rutgers.

While Christie remained firm, the ground was shifting beneath the feet of his South Jersey allies. Beginning just days after the report and continuing throughout the winter and spring, Rutgers-Camden faculty, staff, students, and alumni forged a massive movement protesting against the loss of their campus. Skillfully and passionately, they deployed every conceivable means, both old and new, of winning the public to their side—bumper magnets, supermarket conversations, mass meetings, online petitions, electronic messaging, letters to the editor, and blunt confrontations with elected officials. Every element of the campus community became engaged in the struggle. Members of the faculty, unanimously valuing their affiliation with a major research university, decried the proposed merger as a threat to academic excellence. Drawing upon their particular fields of expertise, faculty in the schools of law and business compellingly challenged both the legality and the financial soundness of the proposal. Students spoke out saying how much they cherished their *Rutgers* education and declaring they had no intention of enrolling at Rowan. Above all, the campus's forty thousand alumni, most of them living in South Jersey, rose up in behalf of their alma mater. They made saving Rutgers-Camden into the most celebrated cause the region had seen in years, and their fervor reverberated throughout the state. Public opinion polls soon showed overwhelming popular support for keeping Rutgers in Camden, a position echoed by editorials in practically every New Jersey newspaper.

South Jersey politicians heard the message. Senator Sweeney, for one, was booed loudly when he rose to speak at a Board of Governors meeting on the Camden campus in mid-February. In response, they began reacting in two ways: by retreating a bit from the concept of Rowan's total absorption of Rutgers-Camden and by placing greater emphasis on getting more money for South Jersey's universities. Hedging now on whether the Rutgers campus should become part of Rowan, South Jersey leaders affirmed that, under any circumstances, the history and traditions of both institutions should be respected; soon they began acknowledging the value of the name of Rutgers and saying that it should remain in Camden; increasingly they used the word "partnership" to describe the future relationship between Rowan and Rutgers. Whatever the exact organizational arrangements might be, the colleges and universities of South Jersey deserved greater financial resources. Compared to its population, these politicians said, their region had far too few seats in higher education classrooms and many fewer dollars than it deserved. Students at Rutgers-Camden, they charged, were actually subsidizing the rest of the University with their tuition. There was nothing new in the conviction that South Jersey was being shortchanged. It was a familiar theme in the region's politics, but in the spring of 2012 it became a central motif in the debate over restructuring the universities. Besides George Norcross and Steve Sweeney, Assembly Majority Leader Louis D. Greenwald and Senator Donald Norcross (George's brother) voiced determination to get a fair share of the state's resources for their region. To illustrate the point, Senator Norcross, in particular, was fond of saying that South Jersey's money went "up the Turnpike."

It is curious that Governor Christie obtained from his Barer committee, and then resolutely defended, a more radical plan for reorganizing higher education in South Jersey than almost anyone else wanted.

Why would he care about the details of the precise relationship between Rowan and Rutgers? My own guess was that he didn't really care but supported a proposal he knew would stir up a lot of local trouble for his Democratic "allies." As long as an eventual compromise remained attainable, which it did, the governor could have both the honor of succeeding in a policy arena where his predecessors had all failed and the fun of destabilizing his friends in the other party.

I was in a difficult spot during the winter and spring of 2012. In my last months as president and with ebbing influence, I was also between a proverbial rock and a hard place. The governor's office was pushing the Rutgers boards and me to say it was fine for our Camden campus to become part of Rowan. My Camden colleagues and, as we will soon see, the University's Board of Trustees wanted me to join them in unequivocally opposing the loss of Camden, even if that meant forgoing the medical school in New Brunswick. I wasn't going to do either of those things because, although there were dark hours when I despaired of both keeping Camden and securing the medical school, I persisted in the belief that a way could be found enabling Rutgers substantially to retain its southern campus while allowing the rest of the Barer committee's recommendations to be enacted. Succumbing either to the governor or to those within the University who placed the Camden campus above everything else would, I believed, have worsened the chances for achieving both goals. The situation was further complicated because, although the issues raised by the Barer report were of the utmost important to Rutgers, they were not our only political objectives in the spring of 2012. As always there was our annual state budget to defend and, for the first time since 1988, a real likelihood of placing a higher education facilities bond issue on the November ballot. Senator Sweeney was the chief legislative advocate for the bond issue, and he and I—along with other legislators and other university presidents, especially Montclair State's Susan Cole—were working well together on that. Governor Christie would, of course, have the major say on both the budget and the bond issue. I didn't have a lot of maneuvering room amongst these forceful players and critical objectives, but I did my best to use the room I had.

Beginning in late February and continuing well into the spring, an ad hoc group of about a dozen came together outside the public eye to try to devise an agreeable compromise plan for higher education in South Jersey. From the political arena were George Norcross, Senators Steve Sweeney and Donald Norcross, and several of their South Jersey allies. Senator Joe Vitale of Middlesex County also attended most of the meetings. The Rutgers participants included three members of the Board of Governors, Chair Ralph Izzo, Gordon MacInnes, and Joe Roberts (the latter two former legislators); and three members of the administration, Camden Chancellor Wendell Pritchett, Vice President for Public Affairs Pete McDonough, and me. Wendell launched the group's work with a draft document providing significant autonomy for Rutgers-Camden and envisioning major academic partnerships between his campus and Rowan University, including its Cooper Medical School. Soon the South Jersey team offered up its own proposal setting forth full-blown governance mechanisms for Rutgers-Camden, for Rowan, and for enterprises to be shared between them. It was an exceedingly complicated scheme, with separate boards for Rutgers-Camden and for Rowan, as well as a joint Rowan-Rutgers partnership governing board. Together these three boards would have full operational and financial authority over the two institutions, acting both separately and collaboratively, but the proposal also stated that (somehow) the Rutgers Board of Governors would maintain control of academic standards at Rutgers-Camden. Ungainly though it was, the compromise scheme was preferable to letting Rowan swallow the campus whole, and it kept us in a constructive conversation with the South Jersey players at a critical time. In revised form, some of its proposed governance devices made their way into the final legislation.

Well-intentioned as we compromisers may have been, it was becoming clear that no plan surrendering significant authority over the Camden campus was going to be acceptable to the Rutgers Board of Trustees. On February 23, some twenty Camden faculty members passionately and eloquently addressed the trustees at their public meeting, and from that time forward the great majority of the fifty-nine-member board fiercely defended that campus, even if it meant losing the medical school. Their arguments and questions were legion. No solid reasons, they said, only political expediencies, had been advanced for excluding Rutgers from South Jersey or for linking the proposed transfer of central New Jersey assets with the Camden-Rowan caper. How much would it cost? Who would pay? If Rutgers accepted this cynical deal, how would the University ever regain its independence from the politicians? For more than half a century, the small, beloved Camden campus had been part of Rutgers. Would a mother abandon her child? No medical school was worth it. Across the phone lines and through the electronic ether flew harsh language, draft resolutions, threatened ultimatums. Those of us who had been secretly negotiating with the enemy fell under suspicion for not protecting Rutgers's best interests, particularly Ralph Izzo, Pete McDonough, and me. On May 3, the trustees overwhelmingly adopted a resolution expressing their commitment to Rutgers-Camden and opposing its severance from the University. Any proposed merger in New Brunswick, they said, should be considered separately, on its own merits. The trustees' resolution mattered because, although lawyers for Governor Christie and some of the southern politicians argued otherwise, the transactions proposed by the Barer committee could not be enacted without approval by both Rutgers boards. Twice earlier in my presidency the trustees had contributed to shaping major outcomes for the University: they helped kill the Vagelos plan in 2003, and they provided crucial, timely support for the reorganization of undergraduate education in 2005. In the spring of 2012, they played their most important role in memory.

For many long months, the fate and future of higher education in South Jersey had commanded the state's attention. The Barer committee's proposals for New Brunswick aroused little controversy, and from Newark, whose political forces were far less unified than those to the south, not much had yet been heard. At last, late in May, Essex County legislators and Newark's Mayor Cory Booker entered the conversation. Having watched for months the developments and demands in South Jersey, they now wanted significantly greater autonomy for Rutgers-Newark and a lot more money for all of higher education in that city, specifically including relief for UMDNJ from the enormous burden of its accumulated debts. For University Hospital, Newark's most essential health care provider, the Essex leaders demanded debt relief, infrastructure improvements, and a big piece of the anticipated higher education bond issue for new construction at the hospital. Perhaps most crucially, they expressed a willingness to see all of UMDNJ's Newark assets merged into Rutgers, so long as their requirements for autonomy and resources were met. This was a game-changing idea coming, as it now did, from the political leadership of Essex, but it was not entirely new. The ongoing deliberations of the UMDNJ-Rutgers Steering Committee had laid bare the monumental complexity of moving several large elements of one university into another; transferring the whole thing would be a lot easier. Such a concept, moreover, was not necessarily anathema to the faculty and staff of UMDNJ. Little noticed at the time, the university's interim president, Denise Rodgers, had revealed months earlier that "there is a substantial portion of our employees . . . who want to go to Rutgers University."

By early June, Senators Steve Sweeney, Donald Norcross, and Joe Vitale believed they had enough pieces in place to introduce legislation vastly restructuring higher education in New Jersey. An identical companion bill was introduced a few days later in the assembly. The proposed legislation would merge all of UMDNJ's assets and debts into Rutgers, except for University Hospital in Newark and the School of Osteopathic Medicine in Stratford. Rutgers-Newark would have a new board that was primarily advisory to the Board of Governors. The Camden campus, by contrast, would be granted far greater autonomy from the rest of Rutgers; it would have its own line item in the state budget and a governing board with operational and financial control over the campus. The legislation also bound Rutgers-Camden securely to Rowan through a new joint board with authority over both institutions.

The Rutgers boards and I found the legislation unsatisfactory, primarily because it stripped from the University control of the Camden campus and effectively merged it with Rowan. Camden would have the Rutgers brand name but be governed elsewhere. On June 6, convening

in a rare joint meeting, the Rutgers Boards of Governors and Trustees adopted a set of principles affirming the University's traditional
governance of its three campuses but promising somewhat greater
autonomy for Newark and Camden. The boards expressed openness
to collaboration between Rutgers-Camden and Rowan, providing
such collaboration was "duly authorized" by Rutgers. The boards also
appointed a joint committee of governors and trustees to represent
Rutgers in negotiations with the legislature. Therein lay a dilemma—
and a barely concealed division between the two boards. As Bob
Braun, the ever-present *Star-Ledger* columnist, observed after speaking
with several trustees, "principles are non-negotiable" and yet the joint
committee seemed to be authorized to compromise with legislators
over the final form of the bill. As the media reported in the days ahead,
most of the trustees would refuse to deviate from the principles; some
of the governors, and I, were open to compromise. Because Governor
Christie had decreed, and key legislative leaders had accepted, a July
1 deadline for passing the bill, only three weeks remained in which to
achieve the seemingly impossible—a negotiated agreement consistent
with the boards' principles.

Astonishingly, that is exactly what emerged as the month of June,
and my presidency, came to a close. Some of the most important developments occurred in public, others in private. Some concerned governance, others money—the very same issues on which the Vagelos plan
had foundered nine years earlier. First were the public developments.
On June 14, board members Gerald Harvey and Lora Fong, a governor
and a trustee respectively, told the Senate Higher Education Committee that Rutgers would not accept the governance model for Camden
that was envisioned in the legislation. "The Joint Rutgers-Rowan Board
as proposed in the current bill . . . is unacceptable," said Gerry. "It is a
non-starter." Later in the month, two more board members, Dudley H.
Rivers and Candace L. Straight, one a trustee and the other a governor,
testified the same way. "Simply put," said Candace, "Rutgers must control its own destiny and preserve its autonomy." In their public utter-
ances, Rutgers board members stuck resolutely to the joint principles
and stated flatly that the bodies they represented would not approve

any legislation that took from the University its control over Rutgers-Camden. When the Office of Legislative Services authoritatively confirmed that the proposed legislation "would require the consent of both [Rutgers] boards," the University was in the driver's seat.

Behind the scenes, there was some give and take, but not much giving by Rutgers. Board of Governors Chair Ralph Izzo and Vice Chair Gerry Harvey played their covert roles exceptionally well—Ralph in private conversations with Governor Christie and George Norcross, Gerry in discussions with South Jersey legislators. Vice President for Public Affairs Pete McDonough, well trusted by both the governor and key lawmakers, also played a critical role in discussions outside the public eye. From these conversations came agreement on a joint board for Rutgers and Rowan that was significantly weaker than originally proposed; the new board would have authority only over such collaborative health science programs as the two institutions mutually agreed to establish. After all the tumult, Rutgers-Camden would remain fully a part of Rutgers. Dozens of other amendments were also added to the legislation, most but not all of which improved the bill from our vantage point. Besides governance, the subject of money also played a part in the private conversations, although, with one exception, it is impossible to reconstruct exactly what commitments were made or implied. The final statute as adopted provides that Rutgers and Rowan shall each annually allocate $2.5 million to the Rowan-Rutgers joint board. Maybe that's all there was, but some of the participants in the private meetings later claimed that South Jersey had been promised more money than that. Senator Donald Norcross was certainly optimistic on the eve of the final legislative vote: "It's a win for South Jersey," he said, "which will receive substantially more education-related funds from Trenton and for Camden." I assume he knew what he was talking about.

For all their seeming harmony on behalf of the joint principles, the governors and trustees remained in tension. The amendments to the bill had by no means addressed all of the trustees' concerns, and everyone knew that major uncertainties remained about the extent of the financial liabilities that would fall to Rutgers with its acquisition of UMDNJ, now slated in the revised legislation to take effect a year hence. With the July 1 deadline just days away, Ralph Izzo, having satisfied himself and most of the other governors that the bill was good enough and, in any event, as good as it was going to get, masterminded a brilliant bit of brinksmanship. On June 28, led by Ralph, the Board of Governors adopted by a vote of ten to one a resolution supporting the merger legislation "in general" and noting that both Rutgers boards would have plenty of time to conduct "thorough and comprehensive due diligence" and to make informed final decisions before the takeover became effective. With a nod of approval in hand from Rutgers's preeminent governing board, both houses of the legislature overwhelmingly adopted the amended legislation that evening. They also voted to place a $750 million bond issue for higher education facilities on the general election ballot. On my very last day in the president's office, I had the pleasure of reporting these achievements to the Rutgers community. Our medical school (and much more) was coming home. Governor Christie signed both pieces of legislation later in the summer, and the bond issue passed easily in November.

Only a remarkable constellation of men and women and circumstances made possible such an outcome. By 2012, thanks to a stream of advocates stretching from Roy Vagelos to Tom Kean, a statewide consensus had formed in favor of restoring Robert Wood Johnson Medical School to Rutgers. But that could not be accomplished without corresponding decisions concerning the rest of UMDNJ and, in the minds of some people, the rest of Rutgers. For reasons that lie deep in South Jersey—and in our state's culture of "want something, gotta give something"—a plan was hatched to make Rutgers relinquish its Camden campus to Rowan in return for getting the medical school from UMDNJ. Through a breathtaking sequence of developments that could not have been foreseen, that plan was thwarted. First, the Rutgers-Camden community, led by Chancellor Wendell Pritchett, rose up to declare that it would not be cast out of the University; it would do whatever it had to do to preserve itself as part of Rutgers— and it did. Next, the Board of Trustees changed the calculus of decision making within the University by vehemently rejecting what they saw as a political scheme to change the nature and character of Rutgers. Not a medical school or anything else, they said, justified the loss of the Camden campus and the University's historic autonomy. The trustees' principled stand proved to be the decisive episode in the saga. Next, in true New Jersey fashion, a handful of individuals, led by Chris Christie and Ralph Izzo and with George Norcross in the mix, gathered in private to try to craft a legislative package they could all live with, and they succeeded. Fortunately, as it turned out, Governor Christie seemed not really to care very much about the details of how higher education was organized in South Jersey. But fortunately, too, he *did* care about reuniting medical education with the rest of the state university, and he deployed his formidable political skills to get it done.

Do I wish that I had joined the trustees in proclaiming that Rutgers would never give up its Camden campus? Well, sure, with perfect hindsight about the outcome, I can say that I wish I had been on those barricades, too. But back in the moment, when each of us was making our decisions, neither they nor I knew whether saving Camden would cost Rutgers its medical school. Not fundamentally caring whether it did or not, the trustees defiantly rolled the dice—and won. I did care, and, thanks to all the brave and talented souls named above, I and Rutgers also won.

REFLECTIONS ON
LEADING RUTGERS

So this is my story of Rutgers as I have known it since child-hood. I learned about Rutgers first from my father and mother and then from my own early forays onto campus—tagging along with my dad, selling lemonade on the golf course (briefly), and rooting for the foot-ball team. As a young man, I discerned my parents' keen commitment to the many obligations of a state university and their concern for Rut-gers's future. Later still, as a faculty member and then a dean, I observed and modestly assisted in the University's growth toward distinction in research—and relished the recognition that Rutgers was receiving as a fast-rising institution. As its president during the early 2000s, I led a university that was still growing in stature, still aspiring to improve in its core missions of education and discovery, and still learning to fulfill its responsibilities to the people and communities it served. Although I might wish that I had had none of the shortcomings acknowledged in these pages, during my presidency Rutgers embarked on some very ambitious objectives, worked hard amid challenging circumstances to attain them—and mostly succeeded. These accomplishments are worth totting up, and I will do a bit of that here, but more consequen-tial are lessons learned along the way and goals still to be realized.

To place in perspective the progress we made and the ambitions that remain, it is important to remember that Rutgers is both a very good state university, typical in many ways of such institutions, and also highly unusual in its history and organization. During my presidency, Rutgers continued its decades-long journey to join the ranks of the nation's very best public research universities, and, indeed, by the time I departed the office, the University had become much more similar to those institutions than it was when I arrived. In 2012 compared to 2002, Rutgers had many more dollars in research support from the federal government and many more programs applying academic know-how to real-world problems, in New Jersey and beyond. The University had obtained authoritative approval to acquire a full array of health science schools and was on the verge of admission to an association comprising a dozen of the nation's most highly regarded state universities, the Big Ten. My administration did not invent the goal of making Rutgers more like the best of its peers, but we advanced it.

Even as it grew in similarity to the most well regarded institutions of its kind, Rutgers retained distinctive features derived from its early history as a private college and from its experience of cobbling together disparate elements that had originated elsewhere or had never become well integrated. These Rutgers characteristics shaped both the goals we pursued and the obstacles we faced in achieving them. Improving undergraduate education on the University's largest campus in New Brunswick required melding four historically and culturally separate liberal arts colleges into the single School of Arts and Sciences. Obtaining the health science schools that were formerly part of UMDNJ meant committing Rutgers to a vast, multiyear project of assimilating organizations that were far different from our own (a project my successor is now ably carrying on). Both of these endeavors were significantly helped along by the Board of Trustees, a vestige of the University's private heritage. The trustees, about whom I will have more to say shortly, gave the New Brunswick plan of undergraduate reorganization an essential boost at a critical moment in 2005 and, with respect to the health sciences, raised compelling objections both to the Vagelos-McGreevey plan of 2003 and the Barer-Christie plan of

2012. The trustees' objections contributed to a final outcome that was far better than it otherwise would have been.

٭

Stepping down as president of Rutgers in 2012, I found satisfaction in the achievements of the previous decade. In reorganizing the New Brunswick campus for the benefit of undergraduates, we confronted a locally revered but highly anomalous collection of colleges, rallied the community to undertake far-reaching changes, and followed through to secure a wider range of goals than anyone had originally envisioned. Acutely conscious of belonging to a nationwide movement for improving undergraduate education within research universities, we also knew we were working in a distinctive Rutgers environment. Only through a deliberative and consultative process involving faculty, students, and board members could the university community reach the difficult decision to abolish the old colleges; my background as a Rutgers faculty member, and as my father's son, fit me well to lead that conversation. When it was done, we had established the School of Arts and Sciences, restored the faculty's authority over undergraduate education, and assured every student access to the full array of academic programs. First-year seminars, expanded opportunities for research, and our students' success in competing for prestigious scholarships all followed. More unexpectedly, so did the transformation of our formerly neglected Livingston campus and the creation of a unified association of our four hundred thousand alumni.

Those were the signature academic achievements of my presidency, for which my administration has been generously credited, but they were not alone. Rutgers's progress in research occurred far less visibly or controversially but was just as pronounced. The single best indicator of research productivity is the amount of financial support that a university's faculty obtains competitively from agencies of the U.S. government. By that measure Rutgers did extremely well: we increased our federal research support by a larger percentage than any other public member of the AAU and all but one of the private members. That achievement sprang both from farsighted decisions made under previous administrations and from the deliberate steps we took to assist and encourage faculty in their pursuit of research grants from the federal government. In 2013, the acquisition of UMDNJ's health science schools propelled Rutgers even further up the rankings. Not just undergraduate education and research, but also the economic and racial diversity of our student body, the extent of online learning, and the University's international reach all saw genuine progress. Despite the continuing decline of support from the state of New Jersey, the University's overall revenue, on which these academic endeavors depended, grew from $1.3 billion annually to $2.1 billion during my presidency.

In intercollegiate athletics, the University's most conspicuous activity, Rutgers entered a new era of competitive success and elevated esteem. The catalyst for these advancements was the football program, which now won many more games than it lost, played regularly in post-season bowls, excited fans around the country, and made a convincing case for enlarging Rutgers Stadium. The women's basketball program, whose competitive accomplishments were of long standing, also contributed to raising the reputation of Rutgers athletics, especially when its young stars responded to Don Imus's vulgarity with such grace and courage. Amid these triumphs, the University suffered embarrassment when media investigations of athletics and then an independent committee disclosed managerial missteps, undue insularity, and a lack of transparency, especially in regard to the football program. The committee report criticized me for failing to establish sufficient presidential control over athletics, and it recommended a myriad of policy changes, all of which we accepted. Under new leadership, the department of athletics adopted administrative practices that were appropriate to a far larger and more successful sports enterprise than Rutgers had ever known before. Behind the scenes, while these improvements were under way, the University quietly began seeking admission to the Big Ten Conference. Our invitation to join, which came a few months after I stepped down as president, corroborated the newfound success and stability of Rutgers athletics.

Some observant critics may argue that basketball coach Mike Rice's repugnant abuse of his players, followed by the University's imperfect response to that calamity, refutes my claim of a bright new era in Rutgers sports. Their point may prove well-founded, but I believe that the passage of time will confirm the durability of the auspicious developments I have portrayed. More worrisome are two other perils arising from participation at the highest levels of intercollegiate athletics, neither of them unique to Rutgers: the dangers of presidential inattention (of which I was guilty) and of competitive pressures to spend ever more money. As I and many presidents around the country learned the hard way, when something goes wrong in athletics, critics in the media will dwell upon and dramatize the problem and cause the whole university to pay a reputational price. A president who fails to devote adequate time and attention to athletics will regret it, take my word. The other worry concerns the continuously escalating expenditures, especially for coaches' salaries and for facilities. The costs of Rutgers athletics went up on my watch and will continue to grow. So, too, of course, will athletic revenues, especially after Rutgers begins to receive the full financial benefits of Big Ten membership. But discipline and hard work will be necessary to keep the growing expenditures within the bounds of the available revenue.

The last accomplishment I'll mention is returning Robert Wood Johnson Medical School to Rutgers and bringing in, as well, most of the rest of UMDNJ. I have told my version of that story in the foregoing chapters and will not repeat it here. For almost a decade, leading New Jerseyans, from Jim McGreevey and Roy Vagelos to Tom Kean and Chris Christie, sought some variant of the reorganization that finally gained approval in 2012. They rightly argued that unifying the health sciences with all the other academic disciplines would improve education, research, health care, and the economy. Phil Furmanski and I had a part in that conversation, too—Phil on the basis of his teaching and research in biology and his experience at NYU, and I on the basis of my observations at the universities of North Carolina and Washington. The decision for unification that finally came in 2012 was owed in part to the high-minded reasons that Phil and I and the others had been citing all along, but, even more, to a remarkable display of political machination and gubernatorial determination. However achieved, the outcome was long overdue and highly welcome. Now Rutgers and New Jersey have a chance to obtain the advantages that can come when medicine, dentistry, and public health are located in the same institution as arts and sciences, business, law, and the rest. This is a great and historic opportunity, but Rutgers will have to make a significant effort if all of its benefits are to be realized in the years ahead.

Several features of the 2012 restructuring act may actually hamper integration of the health science schools with the rest of Rutgers. The legislation provides that all of the elements of UMDNJ that have now become part of Rutgers, together with several academic units, including pharmacy, that were part of Rutgers all along, shall constitute the "School of Biomedical and Health Sciences." That school shall have its own chancellor reporting to the university president, a chancellor who must be a physician and must be based in Newark. Even leaving aside the excessive prescriptiveness regarding the position of chancellor (as well as a number of other academic leadership positions specified in the law), it is troubling that by legislative fiat the units formerly within UMDNJ will constitute their own separate pod within Rutgers, instead of having the Newark components become fully part of the Rutgers-Newark campus and the New Brunswick components become fully part of the Rutgers–New Brunswick campus. For deans and faculty within Rutgers Biomedical and Health Sciences (its new name), the path of least resistance may be to keep the pod intact and aloof, rather than to explore and realize the now limitless opportunities for collaboration with Rutgers's non-health-science schools.

The legislation also provides that state support shall be appropriated separately for each of the University's three campuses and for Rutgers Biomedical and Health Sciences. This means, at best, that the fundamental decisions about the institution's budget will be made in Trenton rather than at Rutgers and, at worst, that the different components of the University may now end up competing against each other for scarce state dollars. That, too, would seem inimical to attaining the long-sought goal of integrating the health science disciplines with the rest of Rutgers. I do not know what political interests and considerations lay behind these unfortunate features of the 2012 legislation, but it is not difficult to speculate what they may have been.

Across all the years, whenever discussion arose about various possible plans for restructuring higher education, many people believed, and often it seemed, that Rutgers would have to give up something—perhaps pharmacy, perhaps Newark, perhaps Camden—in order to get Robert Wood Johnson Medical School. In the end, that belief proved unfounded: Rutgers got practically all of UMDNJ and gave up nothing. More precisely, it gave up no part of itself: no campus, no school, no faculty. Slowly appearing, however, is the reality that Rutgers may indeed have lost something of great value, namely a considerable part its autonomy from the state government and from the politics surrounding state government. The intrusive features of the 2012 legislation are a case in point. Senator Stephen Sweeney's avowal in 2013 to pass legislation abolishing the Rutgers Board of Trustees is another straw in the wind. For a third, there are the newspaper reports that political pressures may have shaped the University's response to the Mike Rice fiasco.

The restructuring act of 2012 achieved for Rutgers and for New Jersey the long-sought goal of unifying the health sciences with the rest of the state university. But along with the law came two great challenges upon which the future excellence of Rutgers will depend: first, to attain the full benefits of collaboration between and among all the academic units that are now, at last, lodged within the same university; and second, to stave off what appear to be newly aggressive forms of political interference in Rutgers. That will be a tall order for any president.

Reflecting a bit more, and for the last time, on the relationship between Rutgers and New Jersey, it is hardly surprising, or even necessarily troubling, that elected state officials should have a role in governing the University. Rutgers is, after all, the *state* university; it receives approximately one-fifth of its annual budget from the government of New Jersey; and the state governor appoints a majority of the members of its preeminent governing body, the Board of Governors. Among my goals as president was to strengthen the relationship between the University and the state by bringing the institution's research expertise more fully to bear upon the problems and challenges facing the people of New Jersey. Indeed, I *wanted* the state's elected representatives to ask more from Rutgers. Fortunately, there were only a handful of instances in which state officials interfered with the workings of the University in ways that my Rutgers colleagues and I judged to be inappropriate; for the years ahead, I hope that such instances will remain infrequent (although, as noted above, I have my concerns on that score). More disturbing than outright interference was the rhetorical practice of denigrating the University or casting doubt upon its integrity, something that occurred typically in legislative press releases, during senate and assembly budget hearings, or in governmental investigations of Rutgers. The chairman of the State Commission of Investigation captured the spirit of that rhetorical style and perfectly exemplified it when he told me, "This is how we work, Dick. We cherry-pick the facts to make you look as bad as possible to support our recommendations." I can (reluctantly) understand why newspapers trying to boost circulation would resort to the sport of ridiculing Rutgers and to "gotcha" journalism, but it ought to be unacceptable for state officials to behave that way. In fairness to the politicians, they, too, are enmeshed in—but did not create—the less lovely features of New Jersey's political culture. And cultures are hard to change.

If the tempo of outright political interference with Rutgers should rise, the Board of Trustees can be counted upon to push back, just as it did most notably in 2012, when the governor and the legislature seemed poised to mandate Rowan's absorption of Rutgers-Camden. Although the governor of the state appoints a small minority of the trustees, the members of that board mainly appoint themselves and thus are largely independent of the state government. The same is not true of the Board of Governors, which is lawfully and justly constituted to be more responsive to the governor and the legislature; it must weigh the goal of autonomy for Rutgers against other worthy objectives. So, too, must the university president who, while not appointed by government officials, is inevitably reliant upon them for the institution's annual budget and for many routine forms of cooperation and support. It is reasonable to conclude that Rutgers's governing structure is ideally balanced. In the Board of Governors and the president, it has leaders whose predominant responsibility is to the University but who are also obliged to take seriously into account the wishes of New Jersey's elected officials. In the Board of Trustees, it has a body with considerably less authority than the Board of Governors, but with more freedom to stand up for Rutgers on the (one hopes) rare occasions when political pressure menaces the University's core goals and values.

For the years ahead and looking long into the future, Rutgers and New Jersey must become better partners than ever before. Prosperity and opportunity depend critically upon the quality of the education received by tens of thousands of the state's men and women who attend Rutgers every year, upon the new knowledge created by its faculty, and upon the application of that knowledge to solve real human problems. As state appropriations for higher education have declined, not just in New Jersey but everywhere, tuition has risen (I bear some of the responsibility for that), and the dream of a college education has been put at risk for the economically disadvantaged and even for the middle class. In New Jersey, that risk has been mitigated, so far, by steadfast state support for need-based financial aid and by Rutgers's use of its own resources for that same purpose. But if these trends continue, someday New Jersey and its state university may find themselves accelerating, rather than alleviating, the rise of economic inequality within our society. What a tragic fate that would be for our state's people—and for Rutgers, a place where the sons and daughters of immigrants, of the poor, and of those with little education themselves, have come to learn, to grow, and to rise.

What will it take to avert so heartbreaking an outcome and ensure that public higher education remains capable of meeting the needs of future generations? It will take many things, among them college and university leaders who can tell a story that compellingly explains the wider purposes of their enterprise.

SOURCES

As with any memoir, this book draws heavily upon the author's memories of the events described herein, but I could scarcely have written it from that source alone. My colleagues and friends who are named in the acknowledgments generously shared with me recollections of their own and provided vital facts and figures when I needed them. I also relied heavily upon many files of documents, mostly concerning my presidency of Rutgers but some stretching back to my earlier days as a faculty member in the history department and as dean of the Faculty of Arts and Sciences. These files include correspondence, memoranda, committee reports, minutes of meetings, notes on conversations, newspaper clippings, and much else. All of these materials are now publicly available in the Rutgers University Archives (hereinafter the Archives). I am indebted to University Archivist Thomas J. Frusciano for accepting these papers and seeing to their proper organization and accessibility.

Although I have chosen not to burden this book with footnotes or endnotes—a decision that did not come easily to a historian—the reader who wants to find the written sources upon which I relied will have little difficulty doing so. In most cases, the relevant documents are named in the text and can be located in the Archives or elsewhere in the Rutgers University Libraries. My website, http://richardlmccormick .rutgers.edu, includes my presidential speeches, annual addresses, and messages to the Rutgers community. The University's two governing boards, the Board of Governors and the Board of Trustees, figure prominently in this book; minutes of the open sessions of the boards' meetings may be obtained from the Office of the University Secretary.

The paragraphs below indicate some of the particular writings I used in each chapter, as well as publications to which readers may turn for additional information about subjects I have touched upon.

PREFACE AND ACKNOWLEDGMENTS

The definitive study of Rutgers's rich and unusual history during its first two centuries is Richard P. McCormick, *Rutgers: A Bicentennial History* (New Brunswick: Rutgers University Press, 1966). I have relied upon it at appropriate points throughout this book. I am indebted to my friend and colleague Jorge Reina Schement, currently the University's vice president for institutional diversity and inclusion, for suggesting to me the "neighborhood" analogy employed in the third paragraph of the preface.

1. SIX SCENES FROM A UNIVERSITY PRESIDENCY

Comprehensive longitudinal data on decades of "disinvestment in higher education" by all fifty American states may be found in *Postsecondary Education Opportunity*, a research newsletter published monthly in Oskaloosa, Iowa. For consistent and reliable reporting on all the national trends in higher education that are mentioned in this chapter and throughout the book, see the *Chronicle of Higher Education*, published weekly in Washington, D.C. The founding and early years of Douglass College are recounted in George P. Schmidt, *Douglass College: A History* (New Brunswick: Rutgers University Press, 1968). In this and other chapters, I refer often to the (Newark) *Star-Ledger*, the daily newspaper that provides the most comprehensive coverage of New Jersey and Rutgers. Bob Braun's insightful column appeared in the *Star-Ledger* on December 22, 2008. The *Daily Targum*, the independent student newspaper at Rutgers–New Brunswick, reports consistently and well on events at the University; virtually every subject treated in this book found reflection in its pages. Richard P. McCormick, *The Black Student Protest Movement at Rutgers* (New Brunswick: Rutgers University Press, 1990), tells the story of the dramatic events that led

Rutgers to become a more racially diverse institution beginning in the late 1960s. Data on the first class of Rutgers Future Scholars may be found in "Rutgers Future Scholars Program Update, September 2013" (filed in the Archives). On the career of the most higher-education-friendly governor in New Jersey's history, see Alvin S. Felzenberg, *Governor Tom Kean: From the New Jersey Statehouse to the 9/11 Commission* (New Brunswick: Rutgers University Press, 2006).

2. COMING OF AGE AT RUTGERS

On Richard P. McCormick's professional career see Michael J. Birkner, *McCormick of Rutgers: Scholar, Teacher, Public Historian* (Westport, CT: Greenwood Press, 2001). For a perceptive analysis of American studies in the 1960s, with particular attention to the work of Leo Marx, see Bruce Kuklick, "Myth and Symbol in American Studies," *American Quarterly* 24 (October 1972): 435–450. Many of Warren I. Susman's most influential essays were published in his *Culture As History: The Transformation of American Society in the Twentieth Century* (New York: Pantheon, 1984). Paul G. E. Clemens's forthcoming history of Rutgers from 1945 to the present covers the University's transformation in the 1980s both amply and excellently. The words of Amiri Baraka quoted here may be found in "An Open Letter to the Community from Amiri Baraka," *Rutgers Review*, March 13, 1990. All of the various committee reports noted in this chapter may be found in the Archives.

3. A DIFFICULT FIRST YEAR AS RUTGERS PRESIDENT

The documents and files that I accumulated on the Sonja Haynes Stone Black Cultural Center (now called the Sonja Haynes Stone Center for Black Culture and History) are located in the University Archives of the University of North Carolina at Chapel Hill. A brief account of my presidency of the University of Washington may be found in Norman J. Johnson, *The Fountain and the Mountain: The University of*

Washington Campus in Seattle (Seattle: Documentary Media LLC and the University of Washington, 2003), 69–75. This same volume illustrates a truly beautiful university campus, from which I drew some of my ideas about how Rutgers ought to look. For an authoritative analysis of the University of Washington's response to the passage of Initiative 200, see Richard D. Kahlenberg, *A Better Affirmative Action: State Universities that Created Alternatives to Racial Preferences* (New York: Century Foundation, 2012), 40–44. Ron Morris, M.D., "How Rutgers Medical School Became CMDNJ," tells the sorry story of Rutgers's loss of its medical school in 1970; this unpublished manuscript, written in 2009, may be found in the Archives. This chapter mentions many of my messages to the Rutgers community during 2003; all of them are on my website and also filed in the Archives. There are extensive archival files on each of the major developments recounted here, including Rutgers's presidential search in 2002, the Vagelos report, and the *Seattle Times* story published on November 2, 2003. Bob Braun's column expressing doubts about whether I was strong enough to stand up for Rutgers appeared in the *Star-Ledger* on November 5, 2003.

4. THE ACADEMIC HEART OF THE MATTER

The description of New Brunswick's undergraduate colleges given in this chapter employs words that are drawn directly from my September 16, 2005, annual address. Richard P. McCormick's concerns about the 1981 campus reorganization, concerns that became relevant again when the Task Force on Undergraduate Education convened in 2004, may be found in the Archives in an unpublished essay entitled "Thoughts on Academic Reorganization." Related archival files chronicle the dissemination of the Qualls report, the extensive campus-wide debate it inspired, my March 2006 recommendations to the Board of Governors, and the improvements in undergraduate education that followed. Two key reports document the reorganization of Rutgers alumni: "Rutgers University Alumni Relations: The Imperative for Change" (2007) and "Advancing the Imperative for Change: The Rutgers University Alumni Association" (2008). The University's Office of

Institutional Research and Academic Planning provided data obtained from the National Science Foundation documenting the growth of federal research support both before and during my presidency. All of that information may now be found in the Archives. I am grateful to Robert J. Heffernan, the director of the Office of Institutional Research and Academic Planning, and to his staff colleagues for supplying the data and answering my questions about it.

5. INTERCOLLEGIATE ATHLETICS

Richard P. McCormick, "Going Big Time: The Rutgers Experience" (filed in the Archives and probably written in 2002), traces the University's bumpy pathway toward big-time sports. C. Vivian Stringer's *Standing Tall: A Memoir of Tragedy and Triumph* (New York: Crown Publishers, 2008) includes a richly moving account of her team's 2006–07 season and of its encounter with Don Imus. The Rutgers Office of University Relations compiled a massive record of the Imus incident, including transcripts of the offensive radio broadcast and the press conference at which Stringer and her players responded, newspaper clippings, and the thousands of e-mail messages I received; those materials are all located in the Archives. Senator Raymond J. Lesniak's quoted words concerning fund raising for the expansion of Rutgers Stadium may be found in the (Bridgewater) *Courier-News*, December 6, 2007 ("Jon Corzine's Rolodex"), and in the *Star-Ledger*, July 27, 2008 ("really didn't get off the ground"). The findings of the Athletics Review Committee and the record of the University's response to the ARC report may be found in the Archives. On December 17, 2008, the (East Brunswick) *Home News Tribune* reported and quoted Speaker Joseph J. Roberts's letter to me concerning the dismissal of Bob Mulcahy.

6. RUTGERS AND NEW JERSEY

The Rutgers Office of Public Affairs prepares and regularly updates its listings of the University's activities in each of the state's forty legislative districts; the latest version of these documents may be found on that office's website, and the May 2013 version is in the Archives. The Archives also include files on virtually all of the subjects covered in this chapter, including the Constituency Research Project, meetings with legislators, preparations for legislative budget hearings, relations with the governors, and the 2010 medical marijuana debacle. The quotation by an assemblyman expressing sharp criticism of New Jersey's college and university presidents may be found in "News from the Assembly Democrats," April 25, 2008. The comparative information on funding for higher education in all fifty states during the years just prior to the severe recession beginning in 2008 was published as Appendix M of "The Report of the Governor's Task Force on Higher Education" (the Kean Report), dated December 2010. The reports of the State Commission of Investigation (2007) and the Office of the State Comptroller (2011) may be found on the websites of those bodies as well as in the Archives.

7. GETTING A MEDICAL SCHOOL, CONCLUDING A PRESIDENCY

The report of the Kean task force is cited under chapter 6. Governor Chris Christie's Executive Order No. 51, January 4, 2011, established the University of Medicine and Dentistry of New Jersey Advisory Committee (the Barer committee); three months later the governor appointed the committee's five members. The Advisory Committee's "Final Report," January 25, 2012, also includes that same body's "Interim Report," September 20, 2011. Materials filed in the Archives massively document the developments that followed the issuance of both Barer committee reports; these materials include, among other items, internal Rutgers correspondence, notes on meetings and telephone calls, and comprehensive files of newspaper stories. The minutes of the Boards of Governors and Trustees, citied earlier, provide important perspectives on the controversies that played out during the winter and spring of 2012. Drawing upon both their scholarship and their firsthand observations, three faculty members at the Rutgers School of Law–Camden have written a highly perceptive and detailed account of the Camden developments covered in this chapter: Perry Dane, Allan R. Stein, and Robert F. Williams, "Saving Rutgers Camden," *Rutgers Law Journal* 44 (forthcoming 2014). George Norcross's advocacy for a research university in South Jersey was reported and quoted in *NJBIZ*, September 30, 2011, and in the (Camden) *Courier-Post*, October 1, 2011. Senator Donald Norcross's quoted expression of confidence that more state money would be coming to South Jersey may be found in a June 28, 2012, press release from the New Jersey Senate Democrats, "Norcross and Vitale Help Forge Agreement on Higher-Education Initiative." All of the academic issues covered in this chapter, as well as the trying events of 2010–11, are documented in the Archives. On September 5, 2013, the *Daily Targum* published a long story on the growing numbers of international students at Rutgers, with special attention to several countries, including China.

8. REFLECTIONS ON LEADING RUTGERS

The restructuring act is Chapter 45 of the 2012 Laws of New Jersey, "New Jersey Medical and Health Sciences Education Restructuring Act." The final sentence of this chapter paraphrases a point made in Jeffrey Selingo, "As Colleges Evolve, So Must Their Presidents," *Chronicle of Higher Education*, March 8, 2013.

INDEX